Praise for the First Publication of
House of the Hidden Places:
A Clue to the Creed of Early Egypt

Daily Chronicle

The purpose of Mr. Adams' work is to show that a very intimate correspondence exists between the passage-chambers of the Great Pyramid, and the various stages, upward and downward, traversed, according to the Egyptian Ritual, by the holy dead in passing from the light of earth to the light of eternal day. The Pyramid thus has, as the prime object of its erection, the symbolising of the cardinal features of the old national religion.

Morning Post

Mr. Marsham Adams, already known as a devoted labourer in certain fields of Egyptology, describes and supports as a solution of the fascinating problem, the intimate correspondence, as he regards it, between the design of the Pyramid and the writings which are commonly entitled "The Book of the Dead."

The Freemason

To our readers therefore we most strongly commend a work which will be interesting to them from the exposition it contains of the mysterious Egyptian creed of bygone ages.

The House of the Hidden Places
and
The Book of the Master

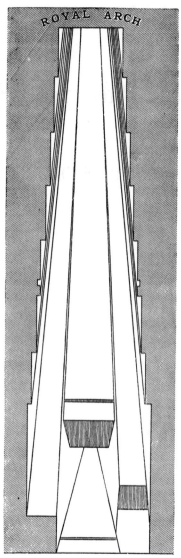

THE "STONE OF GOD."

Throne in the Luminous Hall of Truth.

The House of the Hidden Places

A Clue to the Creed of Early Egypt

and

The Book of the Master

or The Egyptian Doctrine of
The Light Born of the Virgin Mother

W. Marsham Adams

Ibis Press
An Imprint of Nicolas-Hays, Inc.
Berwick, Maine

First published in 2004 by
Ibis Press, and imprint of
Nicolas-Hays, Inc.
P. O. Box 1126
Berwick, ME 03901-1126
www.nicolashays.com

Distributed to the trade by
Red Wheel/Weiser, LLC
P. O. Box 612
York Beach, ME 03910-0612
www.redwheelweiser.com

Library of Congress Cataloging-in-Publication Data available
on request

BJ
Cover design by Kathryn Sky-Peck.
Printed in the United States of America

10	09	08	07	06	05	04
7	6	5	4	3	2	1

The paper used in this publication meets the minimum require-
ments of the American National Standard for Information
Sciences—Permanence of Paper for Printed Library Materials
Z39.48–1992 (R1997).

CONTENTS.

---◆◇◆---

FOREWORD.

——◦•◦——

Among myths about the pyramids of Egypt that were prevalent in medieval Europe, one of the most persistent was that they were once the granaries filled by the patriarch Joseph. It was by no means the most wild myth, and it has been noted that even in our own day,

> . . . much stranger theories continue to be concocted concerning the nature of pyramids, and the pragmatic accounts of generations of archaeologists have done little to dispel the popular belief that they are embodiments of some lost mystic knowledge and/or the key to the understanding of the universe.[1]

A similar opinion was expressed more than a hundred years ago by William

Wynn Westcott, who, in the course of a
review of *The House of the Hidden Places,*
stated that, "The Great Pyramid has fas-
cinated many great students of Egyptology
and has led to the formulation of most
surprising theories, and to the suspicion
that its study is a fertile cause of mental derangement."[2] He felt, however, that
Adams had managed to keep "fairly within
the boundaries of a sweet reasonableness"
although he could see flaws in Adams's
argument. Westcott also neatly summa-
rized his theory: "according to our author
the Great Pyramid is petrified religion."

Other reviewers of the time were less
succinct, but could still encompass the
essence of the book in a single sentence.
Thus Bertram Keightley described its "leading idea" as "the correlation of the Ritual
in the Book of the Dead with the structure
of the Pyramid, and the viewing of both
together as expressing the mystic pilgrim-

age of the Soul."[3] This description, which is accurate enough, was expressed in less prosaic terms by A. E. Waite, who noted that Adams "claims to have discovered a perfect and unbroken correspondence between the winding passages in the Great Pyramid and the passage of the soul from death to immortality as figured in the Book of the Dead."[4]

But had Adams succeeded? Most of his contemporaries thought not, but more recent opinions about the purpose of the pyramids are not wholly at odds with Adams. In his authoritative study, *The Pyramids of Egypt* (revised edition, 1972), Iorwerth Edwards suggested that pyramids represented

> . . . the primeval mound which emerged from the waters of chaos, as patches of high ground emerged annually from the Nile when the waters of the inundation receded. On this mound Atum, the god of creation, was believed to have first manifested him-

self and to have created the universe. It was thus the symbol of existence, as opposed to non-existence, and consequently, when placed above the grave or embodied in the tomb, it was imagined that it could serve as a potent source of magic from which the dead might hope to receive a renewal of existence (p. 219).

Further, another purpose of the pyramids is given in the "pyramid texts," the magical spells painted within the step pyramids of the earliest dynasties. According to these, the pyramid provides a "staircase to heaven" for the spiritualized body of the dead pharaoh to "mount up to heaven thereby." And not necessarily a purely physical staircase.

The true, smooth-sided pyramid was thought by the Egyptologist J. H. Breasted to have been a copy of the solar symbol found in the temple of Heliopolis. But it may, like the earlier step pyramids, have also provided a stairway to heaven. The pyramid texts include descriptions of the pharaoh climbing to heaven on the rays of the sun, and as it is clear that he was ascending to the stars—specifically to the circumpolar stars—it was essential that the pyramids be correctly aligned astronomically.

None of this conflicts substantively with Adams's theories, and while his critics were right to point out specific flaws in his arguments, they were less than just in rejecting his ideas outright. He did not help his case, however, either by his tetchy responses to criticism or by his fondness for flowery language.

Adams first presented his ideas about the Great Pyramid in a paper printed in the *New Review*, a London literary monthly, in December 1893. They were immediately reported fully in the "Psychical, Occult and Mystical" journal, *Light*. The editor quoted Adams as stating

that the "Ritual of Ancient Egypt" is full
of "allusions which become vocal only when
applied to the Grand Pyramid. Such are
the festivals of the 'Northern Passage,' of
the 'Southern Passage,' that of the 'Hidden
Lintel,'" and so on. He noted also that,

> Mr. Marsham Adams states that the allu-
> sions are astronomical as to their basis,
> and maintains that the Egyptians took a
> determinate horizon for their fundamental
> conceptions, the "horizon of the point in
> the sky which is occupied by the sun at
> the vernal equinox."[5]

He goes on to quote Adams's somewhat grandiloquent concluding paragraph,
in which "the sacred procession of the
Egyptian dead moves silently along"
until they enter "the Hidden Places, and
penetrate the secret of the House of
Light." Finally they tread the "Path of
Illumination,"

> And a glory which is not of earth reveals
> in its divine unity the full mystery of the

Hidden Places, the House of New Birth, the Well of Life, the Lintel of Justice, the Hall of Truth, the Orbit of Illumination, the Throne of Judgment, and the Orient Chamber of the Open Tomb.

This florid prose did not sit well with all who read it. In the next issue of *Light*, 6 January 1894, a detailed critique by F. W. Read—who would later review *The House of the Hidden Places*—identified "the fundamental fallacy of [Adams's] position." Read pointed out that the copy of the *Book of the Dead* used by Adams was the "Papyrus of Turin": well preserved, clearly written, and the longest copy known—it has 165 chapters—but dating from the 7th century B.C. at the earliest. Such a late copy, differing in many respects from earlier versions, should not be used, argued Read, to draw parallels with the structure of the Great Pyramid which had been built some 3,000 years earlier. It may have been the standard version for the first Egyptologists, but it was certainly not so for the Egyptians.

Adams chose not to reply to this criticism and devoted himself to converting his paper into the first of two books on his theory. *The House of the Hidden Places: A Clue to the Creed of Early Egypt from Egyptian Sources* was published by the highly respected firm of John Murray early in 1895. It was not well received. The most eminent Egyptologists, such as E. A. Wallis Budge and W. F. Petrie, ignored it, although Adams did receive, privately, apparent commendations from both Gaston Maspero and A. H. Sayce. Esoteric journals were scarcely more positive—neither in 1895 nor in 1933 when E.J.L. Garstin's edition appeared.

Bertram Keightley, writing in *Lucifer*, found that "On the whole this is a disappointing book," while A. E. Waite referred to it as "fantastically entitled"

in his brief note in *The Unknown World*.[6]
Only in *Light* was the book considered at
length, but to be brutally dissected and
found wanting. Reviewing it anonymously,
F. W. Read returned to his attack. He
again pointed out Adams's "grave and
fundamental error," but this time he discussed the various versions of the *Book
of the Dead* in some detail. He rejected
the parallel between the Great Pyramid
and the ritual text, and stated that, "In
any case, the 'Hidden Places' must be the
underworld, not the Great Pyramid." Read
concluded with a rhetorical question: "Was
there ever so flimsy a foundation for so
gigantic a theory?"[7]

Adams responded with a long, ram-
bling but lively letter in which he denied
that he had claimed the Turin papyrus,
or any other, as containing the "canon
of the Egyptian faith." This, he stated,
was found in "the secret symbolism of

the Grand Pyramid," which is the subject
matter of his book. He also lamented that
"a journal which claims to be the representative of occult research" should not "have
recognised the PATH in the House of the
Hidden Places, so jealously concealed from
all but the Initiate and the Illuminate six
thousand years ago."[8]

The battle between author and reviewer
continued in a response by Read printed
immediately under Adams's letter, in
which he denied that any of his criticisms
had been answered and cast doubt on the
support he had supposedly received from
Maspero and Sayce. To this affront Adams
responded by quoting the exact words to
which he had referred. Professor Sayce had
agreed that "The parallelism [between the
Book of the Dead and the construction of
the Great Pyramid] is certainly very striking," while Maspero had indeed supported
his theory:

The Pyramids and The Book of the Dead reproduce, the one in stone, the other in words, the
same original, the alleged tomb of Osiris. I
would add that my researches into this subject
are still unpublished, and that no Egyptologist
has attempted anything on the subject with
which you have concerned yourself.[9]

But Read had scored a more telling point
by challenging Adams to supply references
for his quotations from the *Book of the
Dead*. This was a far more serious criticism, and a just one. It was to be repeated
by G.R.S. Mead in his *Thrice Greatest
Hermes* (1906). "Mr. Adams," wrote Mead,
"has severely handicapped his work; indeed,
he has destroyed nine-tenths of its value
for scholars, by neglecting to append the
necessary references to the texts which he
cites. Such an omission is suicidal." Mead,
however, recognized something in Adams's
work that Read and his fellow critics did
not, and he continued his comment with
these words: "Our Trismegistic literature

permits us—we might almost say compels us—to take his view of the spiritual nature of the inner tradition.[10] It is a weakness of Adams's text that it fails to make explicit his real insight into Egyptian spirituality, but it is there for the perceptive reader to find, within the language of masonic symbolism and practice in which it is presented.

Adams explained that his thesis involved "collating the masonic secret of the monument with the doctrinal secret contained In the mysterious books of Thoth" (p. 6), and his early critics stressed the masonic component of his work, even if they did not fully understand it. Thus Bertram Keightley noted that Adams ". . . hints at an esoteric doctrine in Masonry, and speaks often enough of the progress of the soul on the Path of Light towards ultimate union with the Divine."[11]

For Westcott, "the Great Pyramid is said to be a masonified copy of the religion

of ancient Egypt," and he felt also that
Adams was "within bounds" in comparing
the "stages of existence" defined in the
Book of the Dead with "grades of initiation
into an occult Society, and specifying such
as Postulant, Catechumen, Initiate, Adept,
Illuminate and Grand Master."[12]

But Westcott felt obliged to add the
caveat that the *Book of the Dead* does
not refer "to the departed soul in terms
which suggest shades of development such
as these names imply." He could scarcely
say anything else when he was actively
promoting just such a progress among
living initiates within the Hermetic Order
of the Golden Dawn—an order that was
steeped in the symbolism of ancient Egypt,
and that utilized the *Book of the Dead* in
its rituals.

Adams himself, in replying to his critics, emphasized the masonic element in his
text, referring to "the mysterious symbols

in the very heart of the Masonic Light,
which correspond to the 'five-fold dominion
of the regenerate senses, and the seven-fold
elevation of the illuminated intellect.'"[13]
The importance of the masonic parallel
was also recognized by an anonymous
reviewer of Garstin's edition, who suggested that "those who want to understand
the intentional or unintentional meaning of
the ritual of initiation of some Masonic
degrees, should have this book."[14]

All of this suggests that Adams had
some unique insight into masonic symbolism and masonic spirituality, but
although the review of his second book
in *The Freemason* refers to him as
"Bro[ther]. Marsham Adams"[15] there is
no evidence of his ever having been a
freemason. Indeed, there is little evidence
of *any* aspect of Adams's life. By his own
account Walter Marsham Adams had been
a Fellow of New College, Oxford, and it

may be inferred that he had read classics and mathematics, for he published an English translation of the first book of the *Iliad* (1873), and was the author of two manuals on geometry and trigonometry. The first of these, *Outlines of Geometry,* was published in Melbourne in 1866, so it is possible that, as a young man, Adams held teaching posts in Australia.

His six other books give no real clue as to his occupation. In addition to the two on ancient Egypt, he wrote two historical works, a history of fisheries, and a play: *Zenobia: or, the Fall of Palmyra: a Tragedy, in Three Acts* (London, 1870).[16] But whatever his other interests, it was Egypt which had captivated him. He had visited Egypt before writing *The House of the Hidden Places,* and soon after it was published he traveled there again to study Egyptian astronomy. His research enabled him to deliver a public lecture, at New College, Oxford, on the "Scientific Precision of the Astronomy of Early Egypt." This was well received, and he felt encouraged to begin work on his second study of Egyptian religious beliefs and practices. *The Book of the Master, or the Egyptian Doctrine of the Light Born of the Virgin Mother* appeared in 1898, published as before by John Murray.

It excited less controversy than its predecessor and went un-remarked by the esoteric press, but it did receive praise from *The Freemason*, which commended Adams for ". . . the thoroughness of [his] investigations, and the scrupulous care with which he has conducted them, . . . the ability with which he has arrayed his arguments, and . . . the justice of the contention for which he has been striving so earnestly throughout his book.[17]

Despite this encouragement, the book languished and its author faded from

view. When Mead heaped praise on his
"illuminative study" in 1906, Adams was
already dead, and twenty-seven years were
to pass before his work and his memory
were revived.[18]

A condensed edition of both works was
published in 1933, one of the few works
to issue from The Search Publishing
Company, the ill-fated successor to the publishing ventures of Mead's Quest Society.
Perhaps because of Mead's endorsement
of Adams's work, E.J. Langford Garstin
became an enthusiast for his ideas and supplied this reissue with a "Foreword, Notes
and an Appendix." They throw little extra
light on the two books, and in some ways
Garstin completely misunderstood Adams,
but it did introduce him to a new generation of readers. Garstin's edition does have
its value and it has been reprinted more
than once, but the full text reprinted here
is of much greater benefit to all who feel

drawn to Egyptian spirituality.

And that spirituality can lead one in surprising directions. Adams himself quoted "a Roman Catholic professor of theology," who wrote to him expressing surprise at "the profound doctrines of the Catholic faith, and the numerous illustrations of our own Scriptures which seem to me, in reading your book, to have been foreshadowed beneath the symbols of that most mysterious religion." Adams also stated clearly that the Light, to which he constantly refers, "is the very term by which the mystical Evangelist designates the Second Person [of the Trinity; i.e. Jesus Christ)," while the Egyptian Mysteries equally clearly foreshadowed Christianity. In his eyes the Great Pyramid was ". . . not a closed, but an open tomb. It is the tomb not of a man, but a god: not of the dead, but of the risen. It is the tomb of the divine Osiris whom Adams perceived as a type or symbol of Christ."

Whether or not we agree with the theories and the faith of Walter Marsham Adams, his books leave us, as Mead so astutely perceived, on the horns of a dilemma. Critics, he wrote,

> . . . must either declare that our author has invented it all and pay homage to what in that case would be his sublime genius, or admit that the ancient texts themselves have inspired Mr. Adams with these ideas. And if this be a foretaste of what Egypt has preserved, what may not the future reveal to continued study and sympathetic interpretation.[19]

Forty years after Mead wrote those prophetic words, the Nag Hammadi papyri were discovered in the sands of Upper Egypt.

—R. A. GILBERT
BRISTOL, MAY 2004

Notes

1. Ian Shaw and Paul Nicholson, *British Museum Dictionary of Ancient Egypt* (London: British Museum Publications, 1995), p. 235.

2. W. W. Westcott, "The House of the Hidden Places," review in *Ars Quatuor Coronatortum* viii, (London, 1895): 17.

3. Review in *Lucifer* xvi, no. 96 (August 1895): 525.

4. Review note in *The Unknown World* 2, no. 3 (April 15, 1895): 99.

5. "Notes by the Way," *Light* xiii, no. 677 (December 30, 1893): 617. The editor was Edmund Dawson Rogers.

6. *Lucifer* xvi, no. 96, p. 525; *The Unknown World* 2, no. 3, p. 99.

7. *Light* xv, no. 741 (March 23, 1895): 135.

8. "The Creed of Early Egypt," in *Light* xv, no. 744 (April 13, 1895): 178–179.

9. *Light* xv, no. 746, (April 27, 1895): 200. Maspero's words are quoted in French. In his edition of 1933 Garstin gave only a translation of the first sentence.

10. G.R.S. Mead, *Thrice Greatest Hermes,* vol. 1 (London, 1906), p. 45 [of the reset edition of 1964].

11. *Lucifer* xvi, no. 96, p. 525

12. Westcott, "The House of the Hidden Places," pp. 171–172.

13. "The Creed of Early Egypt," p. 179.

14. Review of *The Book of the Master of the Hidden Places,* by L.B., in *The London Forum* 58 [i.e. *The Occult Review*], no. 4 (October, 1933): 273.

15. *The Freemason,* April 1, 1899, p. 162.

16. The historical works were: *The Drama of Empire,* London, 1891 and *The Carving of Turkey,* London, 1894. In 1883 Adams wrote *A Popular History of Fisheries and Fishermen of all Countries from the Earliest Times* for the International Fisheries Exhibition in London.

17. *The Freemason,* April 1, 1899, p. 162.

18. The exact date of his death is unknown, but Mead refers to his "recent death" so it probably occurred in 1905.

19. Mead, *Thrice Greatest Hermes,* p. 56.

PREFACE.

THE singular correspondence which may be traced between the passage-chambers of the Grand Pyramid—called by the Egyptians of old The "Khut," or "Lights"—and the various stages traversed, according to the creed of that ancient nation, by the holy dead in passing from the light of earth to the light of eternal day, was first pointed out by me last year in the pages of the *New Review*. Previously to publication the article was submitted in substance to M. Maspéro and Professor Sayce; and I desire to express my sincere thanks to those eminent authorities for the recognition and encouragement which they afforded me, as well as to Mr. Mengedoht, the hieroglyphic scholar, for

his revision of my work. In the present
book the same analogy is worked out in much
fuller detail—not completely indeed, for that
may well need the labour of years ; but sufficiently, I would hope, to present a clear basis
for further investigation in either direction.
In the case of the Ritual, we obtain what
appears to me to be a consistent and intelligible analysis of that hitherto impenetrable
creed, through the gradual transformation of
the faculties in successive stages of illumination. With regard to the Pyramid, we are
led to suggest a spiritual and most far-sighted
purpose for its construction. For in that
marvellous edifice, the very stones of which
in their silent harmony seem to rebuke the
idle charges of folly and pride heaped by
ignorance upon the architect, we have nothing
less than an indestructible and immutable
symbol of the national religion.

The value of the general theory here pro-
posed depends therefore, it is evident, upon

the accuracy of the correspondence established, or sought to be established, between the path so jealously concealed within the interior of the Pyramid of Light and the path described textually in the well-known collection of sacred Egyptian writings, which is called by us the "Book of the Dead," but which claims for its own title the "Book of the Master of the Hidden Places." But those points of correspondence are so numerous in themselves, and form so severe a system of checks upon each other, as to reduce almost to nothing the chance of their arising from mere coincidence ; while no amount of ingenuity—the deadliest perhaps of all opponents to truth—could suffice to satisfy the innumerable conditions connected with the worship, the kalendar, and the civil constitution of the country which such a correspondence must fulfil.

Nor let it be supposed that an inquiry of this kind is merely of archæological interest,

or that a determination of that early creed
can have no greater value than to satisfy an
idle curiosity. Very far from it. If there be
a fact in the general development of nations
which historical research has clearly demon-
strated, it is the extreme tenacity of antique
belief, and its enduring influence on the
organization of society; since religion, far
more than convention, appears to have been
the basis of ancient law. Each generation,
as it passes, modifies no doubt, but only to
a very slight extent, the form of the social
bond; and that not for itself, but for the
generation which succeeds. If therefore we
would trace more clearly the relation of man
in his complex individuality to the yet more
complex organism of human society, wherein
each individual has his particular function,
we cannot do better than examine thoroughly
the creed of the earliest civilization on record.
And the side-lights which such an investigation will be found to throw on the political

and social constitution of that remarkable nation, illustrating, in point after point, peculiarities which hitherto have appeared to be anomalies, appear to me to be strong confirmation of the principle I have set forth. More striking still, the religions of other nations of the ancient world become suddenly luminous when held up to the Light of Egypt. And as chord after chord is struck, the full diapason of the creeds responds.

A singular circumstance, which may illustrate this remark, arises from the necessity of expressing the secret analogies between the references to the Light, which abound in the Ritual, and the Hidden Places of the Grand Pyramid, the "Light" of the Egyptian world. For in dealing with the ideas thus masonified, so to speak, in that mysterious structure, I have been led, or rather compelled, to employ phrases and symbols current among the Masonic brotherhood of the present day, such as Grand Arch, Purple Arch, Royal Arch,

the Star, the Open Angle (the princes of which
as well as the princes of the Circle, are mentioned in the Papyrus of Sinahit, of very high
antiquity), and other insignia of the craft.
Whenever therefore such expressions occur—
and they run necessarily through the entire
work—it should be remembered that they are
here designed to refer to the actual masonry of
the Grand Pyramid, and the analogous features
in the Ritual of ancient Egypt. At the same
time, whether any vestige of this secret doctrine of the Light may survive in the esoteric
doctrine of which those subject to Masonic
rules are not permitted to speak, is an interesting question which naturally suggests itself,
though it evidently cannot be established by
open discussion.

The consideration however, which to my
own mind tends most strongly to confirm
the evidence of a connection between Pyramid
and Ritual is, I confess, of a somewhat personal
character. For in order to detect such an

analogy, if it be real, the chief qualification requisite is a certain patience in collating and analyzing the results which others have obtained in their respective departments of knowledge. But to call it into existence if not already latent; to construct in imagination the path of the just, and to express it in terms of the motions of light; to portray the mystery of the depths unseen by the mystery of the visible heavens, to shadow forth the features of light in the passages of profoundest darkness, and its motions in a building which for ages has remained immutable, that were an intellectual masterpiece which surely demands nothing less than a creative genius of the very loftiest order. So majestic is the outline of the conception as it rises solemnly on the view, so sublime is every feature of the prospect, now defining, now transcending, the utmost limits of space and time ; with such graduated measure, yet such overwhelming splendour, does it illuminate mystery after mystery of the invisible world, that I cannot for a moment believe it to be the offspring of my own imagination. Far more probable does it seem that, though much of the moral and spiritual imagery still remain obscure, yet we have here a genuine clue to the most profound and fascinating enigma of the ancient world; and that the more closely we study the Path of Light in its Masonic form, the more deeply shall we penetrate the earliest wisdom of which man has left record, and understand the Egyptian belief concerning the dark passage of death and the Entrance on Eternal Day.

THE HOUSE

HIDDEN PLACES.

CHAPTER I.

THE PYRAMID OF LIGHT.

CLOSE to the verge of the immense desert
which stretches its arid wastes across the
whole breadth of the continent to the shore
of the Western Ocean, just at the apex of the
famous delta which marks the meeting point
of Upper and Lower Egypt, at the very spot
where the busy life of the earliest civilization
on record was bordered by the vast and barren
solitude, stands the most majestic and most
mysterious monument ever erected by the

hand of man. Of all the other structures which made the marvels of the ancient world, scarcely a vestige is left. Where are the hanging gardens, the boast of the monarch of Babylon? Where is the far-famed Pharos of Alexandria? Centuries have passed since earthquake laid low the Colossus which bestrode the harbour of Rhodes; and a madman's hand reduced to ashes the temple of Artemis, the pride of Ephesus. But the Grand Pyramid of Ghizeh still remains undestroyed and indestructible, ages after the lesser marvels have passed away, as it stood ages before ever they came into being. Certainly more than fifty, it may be more than sixty, centuries have gone by since that building, which never since has needed the care of man, first concealed from view its hidden places, those secret chambers of which no other building on the globe contains the like. Upwards of two million times has the sun risen and set upon its mighty walls, since first the pure and unbroken surface of polished casing-stones flashed back the rays like a veil of dazzling lustre, and vindicated its ancient title of The Light.

What the concealed significance may be of that secret masonry ; by whom, and for what purpose, the complex plan was designed ; at what epoch the huge structure was erected, are questions which have perplexed many minds in many lands, and have resulted in a discord more akin to Babel, than to the grandeur of its silent majesty. It was built by the Jews in the days of their captivity, says, or rather said, one school of theorists. It was built by Chemmis, but attributed by Egyptians in hatred of him to the Shepherd Philition, is the account given by Herodotus. It was built by Ibn Salluk, say the Arabs, just before the Flood, to preserve the royal treasures from the predicted inundation. It was built by Melchisedec—or somebody—vehemently asserts the Scottish professor of astronomy, who seems always to write in a whirlwind of miscellaneous indignation. It was indisputably intended by the founder for his tomb, one party stoutly maintains,—a tomb in which he left especial instructions that he should not be buried, and in which nobody could possibly have been buried, replies another. It was an observatory, maintains a third,—where every place for observation was carefully closed up, retorts a fourth. It is the " prophetic floor-roll of human history," screams Professor Smyth,—with all the dates gone wrong, softly sneers Mr. Flinders Petrie.

Side by side with that masonic mystery, well nigh as impenetrable at the present moment as when the Hir Sheshta, or " Master of the Secret," was an officer of Pharaoh's household, has come down to us another enigma, the strange collections of sacred writings, or Ritual * of Ancient Egypt, which

* This title, which was conferred by Champollion, is vehemently repudiated by Mr. Budge, though without

modern writers have called the "Book of the Dead," but which claims for itself the title of the "Book of the Master of the Hidden Places." Vivid as is the interest now awakened in those writings, little progress has been made in elucidating their meaning. The doctrines inculcated by their religion, the relations of the worshipper to the object or objects worshipped, the signification of the particular symbol under which those relations were at once veiled and expressed, are but little better understood at the present time, notwithstand-

any particular reason assigned. But it appears to me to be as good a word as any which can be used as a popular expression ; though doubtless the Catholic term, "Office of the Dead," would be preferable if it were sufficiently familiar to our ears. The title "Book of the Dead," devised by Lepsius, appears to me, I own, singularly unfortunate. For in the first place the Papyrus is not a book, but a collection of sacred writings ; and in the second, that title appears to refer to the practice of bury-ing copies or parts of the copy with the mummy ; so that it gives the idea of regarding the holy departed as dead ; whereas the whole conception of the doctrine was the entrance of the departed on life and light.

ing our greatly increased knowledge of the sacred writings, than when the hieroglyphs themselves were undeciphered. Yet, strange to say, prominently as these mysteries stand out in every matter that relates to ancient Egypt, no one has hitherto thought of collating the masonic secret of the monument with the doctrinal secret contained in the mysterious books of Thoth, to whom the origin of Egyptian wisdom is attributed.* Such an omission is the more singular, because indications are not wanting on either side to hint at the connection. That Khufu (miscalled by the Greeks, Cheops) should have adopted the pyramidal form in the hieroglyph of his name is not surprising, as he was the monarch under whom the building was erected. But it is not perhaps unworthy of notice, that the form of the Pyramid enters into the hieroglyph of the

* M. Maspéro courteously informs me that the same idea has occupied himself, but that he has not published.

star Sothis, or Sirius.*   For the Grand Orient,
or position of that star when its rising forms
the immediate harbinger of dawn on midsummer morning, was, as is well known, the
great starting-point for the age-long cycles
of the Egyptian reckoning.   And whereas the
figure usually employed to denote the Pyramid
embraces both the edifice and the rocky platform on which it is built ⌐△⌐ , the form used
in the hieroglyph of Sothis consists of the
masonic portion alone △ , that is to say, the
structure which represented to the Egyptian
mind the Eternal Light, apart from its earthly
support ; while a Papyrus dating from the
time of Khufu, the founder of the building,

---

* When a star rises, not simultaneously with the sun (in
which case the star would be invisible), but just so long
before dawn as to appear for a few moments on the
horizon before it is swallowed up in the growing light, it
is said to rise "heliacally," and "the heliacal rising of
Sothis" on the day of the summer solstice, or midsummer—an event which occurs every 1461 years (viz.
four times $365\frac{1}{4}$)—was the epoch of the Egyptian secular
cycle.

speaks of Isis as the ruler of the Pyramid;
and a later inscription, that of Syene, calls
her also the "Mother of God," and identifies
her with "The Divine Sothis, the Star, the
Queen of the Heaven."

On the other hand, the sacred writings, or
Ritual of ancient Egypt, are full of allusions
which become vocal only when applied to the
Pyramid of Light.   Such are the festivals of
the "Northern Passage" and of the "Southern
Passage," that of the "Hidden Lintel," that
of "Osiris, who dwells in the roofed house"
and in the "Pool of the Great House."   So in
the Kalendar of Esne, we read of the "Festival
of the Sockets," and again of the "Opening of
the Doors," which is closely connected in the
Ritual with the "Chapter of the Orientation,"
and the raising of Osiris from the Open Tomb.
The whole progress of the Departed seems, in
fact, to take place in some kind of building.
The Ritual is full of references to his "Going
in" and "Coming out," to "Going in after

coming out," to passing gates and gateways,
and doors and staircases. Nay, the very titles
employed, whether in the written or the
masonic record, point directly, though secretly,
to each other. Where else, if not in these
chambers, so jealously concealed, the like of
which not even the later pyramids contain,
shall we look for the Hidden Places, the
master of which is claimed for its own master
by the "Book of the Dead"? Again, hundreds of years before the date of the principal papyrus containing those writings, as
early as the twelfth dynasty, the inscription
on the coffin of Amamu, buried in the sacred
city of Abydos, makes a similar allusion, and
shows that the secret places determine the
order of the Ritual. "Thou hast not gone
dying, thou hast gone living to Osiris.*   Now

---

* More correctly written Ausar ; but in this and other
sacred names I have kept the older spelling, not as being
in any way preferable in itself (which it certainly is not),
but in order to avoid introducing a fresh and not absolutely necessary element of unfamiliarity.

thou hast found the *words of order, the mystery of the secret places.*"

What a sudden significance, then, attaches to the title " Ta Khut," " The Light," whereby the Grand Pyramid, that monument of flame, was known to the Pharaohs, when, turning to the sacred papyri, we find the title of the opening chapter to be the Pir M Hru, or Entrance on Light—that is, not the light of common day, which the deceased was quitting, but, as is shown by the image of the setting sun, wherewith the descent of the tomb was always associated, of the invisible Light of the Unseen World, renewed for ever in the splendour of Osiris. For the doctrine contained in those mystic writings was nothing else than an account of the path pursued by the just, when the bonds of the flesh being loosed, he passed through stage after stage of spiritual growth, until initiated in the new birth and illumined in the hidden life, he became indissolubly united with him whose

name, says the Egyptian Ritual, "is Light,
Great Creator." And that path which the
Ritual gives in writing, the grand Pyramid
of Light materializes in the masonry.

In the double symbolism of Pyramid and
Ritual lie both the chief difficulties of de-
cipherment and the strongest evidence of their
correspondence. For as the departed in his
progress was to become united in the fulness
of intimacy with his Creator, so it was necessary that he should progress in the knowledge
of the mysteries which envelop alike the
spiritual and the material creation. To know
Osiris in his forms of manifestation was the
secret of power, to "understand Osiris in
all his names, Osiris in all his places," conferred the crown of illumination. But in
the attainment of that infinite knowledge
there were many stages which must be
traversed by the finite mortal, many grades
which must be achieved by the holy departed, when the mouth of the tomb, the

portal of Eternal Day, had been opened for
him, and the Catechumen of the Divine
Wisdom had been admitted as the Postulant
of Immortality. The "inner man" or "person" of the deceased, the "Ka" (or postulant
with the upraised arms, ⎩⎧) must be re-created
in incorruption, the soul must be born anew,
before that postulant could be initiated into
things divine ; the Initiate must pass the
fiery ordeal, and become approved as Adept ;
the Adept must be justified in the Tribunal of
Truth, before he could emerge from the shadow
of the Halls of Death into the immediate presence of the Source of Light. The Justified
must become the Illuminate, the Illuminate
must be consummated as Master, before he
could attain the innermost mansion in the
divine house of Osiris. For each of such
grades, according to the creed of Egypt, the
Creator has assigned a distinct locality in the
great exterior manifestation of Himself, the
universe of space ; and each of these localities

is described symbolically in the books of the mystical Ritual, and inscribed masonically in the features and the dimensions of the Hidden Places of the Pyramid.

Not to every one therefore did that house lie open, nor could there be a more unpardonable offence than the profanation of its secrets. " This Book," says the final chapter of the Ritual, " is the greatest of mysteries. Do not let the eye of any one see it ; that were abomination." So, too, the secrecy enjoined by the Ritual was enforced by the structure of the building ; nor was it ever violated so long as Egypt remained Egyptian. And as it was the characteristic of that religion to be concealed, and as the manifestation of the Creator is deeper and more secret yet than the knowledge of His works, so it was essential that the symbols relating to Him, and to the connection of man with Him, should not betray their deepest mysteries even to the Initiate ; but should reserve their more secret meaning for the Illuminate after full probation. Here, then, was the problem which lay before the first Hir Shesta, the "Master of the Secret," the originator of the "wisdom of the Egyptians;" to express, but in expressing to conceal, to veil, but with a veil of light, the mysteries of the Deity; to choose such symbols as would without betraying their nature convey their living energy, their illuminative power, and, above all, their illimitable endurance. No ordinary image, it is clear, no mineral, no animal, no plant, no man, could suffice for an expression such as this. Only the orbs of heaven, obeying in their lustrous course the laws that know no change, could fulfil the required conditions. Alike in the pictured and the masonic record the path of the just is traced amid the shining worlds, and his progress measured in the terms of celestial motion.

A remarkable instance is that of the orbit of the earth, involving a knowledge of the

rotation of the earth on its axis, and its
revolution around the sun, on which rested
the ancient kalendar of Egypt. The "Lord
of the Orbit" (Neb Sennen) was a title of the
Egyptian monarch. And in the Pyramid we
find the orbit, together with many other
phenomena masonically expressed on the walls
of the magnificent and unique upper Chamber
of Ascent. Similarly, another great astronomical conception, viz. the horizon, runs not
only through the "Book of the Dead," but
through all the funereal imagery of the
country, as in the "Sai-an-Sinsin," or "Book of
the Migration of the Soul;" and in that of
Queen Anchnes-ra-neferab and other papyri.
What horizon then is the "horizon of heaven,"
to which such mystery attaches, and what is
its apex, the Grand Zenith of the celestial
dome? We have no such general conception, and consequently our ideas of the celestial
mechanism lack something of simplicity. But
suppose that on the day of Equinox, the equal

division of light and darkness, we are standing
on the Equator, the equal divider of the earth
into the hemispheres of North and South, and
that we take up our position, say at the point
where it is cut by the meridian of Memphis,
close to the lake from whence flow the waters
of the life-giving river. At our feet is spread
the great plane, passing through the celestial
poles, and bounded by the Purple Arch which
encircles the floor of the starry dome. From
the midst of our Horizon on that day rises
the sun right upwards,* and at the summit of
his course, where day by day he equally divides
the heaven East and West, on that day alone
he equally divides also the Grand Arch, or
Grand Meridian, which rises transverse from
the same horizon, and stretches from pole
to pole of the azure depths. Then we shall

* The conception here described, though not explicitly
defined by our astronomers, is implicitly contained in the
terms Right (or direct) Ascension, the mounting straight
upwards of the stars ; and Declination, or the falling off
on either side from the equinoctial plane.

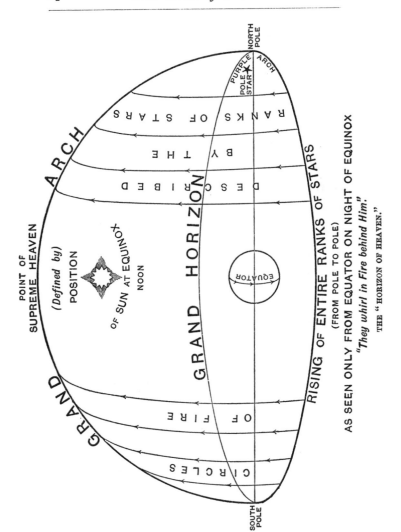

POINT OF SUPREME HEAVEN

ARCH

GRAND

GRAND HORIZON

POSITION *(Defined by)* OF SUN AT EQUINOX NOON

RANKS OF STARS BY THE DESCRIBED

PURPLE POLE STAR NORTH POLE ARCH

EQUATOR

CIRCLES OF FIRE

SOUTH POLE

RISING OF ENTIRE RANKS OF STARS

(FROM POLE TO POLE)

AS SEEN ONLY FROM EQUATOR ON NIGHT OF EQUINOX

"They whirl in Fire behind Him."

THE "HORIZON OF HEAVEN."

have marked out the four Cardinal Points of
the universal sphere—the four points whereby
the sides of the Pyramid of Light were defined ; the fiery seats, according to the Egyptian theosophy, of the four "Sons of Light,"
whereof the most famous was Hapi, the presiding Spirit of the Nile. Into that Grand
Horizon too, when the equal day is done,
the sun passes beneath the Western waters.
And out of it, the whole host of stars, from
pole to pole, in serried array, each preserving
his appointed distance from the solar path,
follow him through the silent night — the
"night of reckoning the spirits;" one-half
springing into light as their leader disappears,
the rest completing their numbers, just in
time to herald his return from the Eastern
point of the same Grand Horizon. "The
road is of fire," says the Ritual; "they whirl
in fire behind him."

Now this horizon seems strikingly indicated
by the entrance passage of the Grand Pyramid,

which, as is well known, may be defined by
reference to the position of the pole-star. For,
taking as the date of the IVth dynasty that
given by Dr. Brugsch (about B.C. 3700),* we
find that about two hundred and sixty years
later (B.C. 3440), the pole-star of the period
(Alpha-Draconis) occupied, as Professor Smyth
has pointed out, just that position ; so that
it would shine right down the passage. And
thus the disciples of the Master of the
Secret, who in successive generations must
have watched for more than two centuries
the approach of the star, would receive in
its final co-ordination the most convincing

---

* In deference to the very high authority of Dr.
Brugsch, on all matters connected with Egyptian history,
I have adopted, and still adhere to the date which he
estimated for the Grand Pyramid.   The recent discoveries
of Mr. F. Petrie may perhaps point to an earlier date ;
and the question cannot be considered as settled ; but
on such a point the general harmony with other historical
records is the supreme test : and of that knowledge
none was more skilled than the great master whom we
have recently lost.

proof of the truth of those astronomical
relations, wherein their mystical religion was
embodied.   Hence when we read in the
Ritual, of the "Good Paddle of the North the
Opener of the Disc," we recall at once the
narrow paddle-shaped passage widened at the
entrance towards the North, which opens the
sacred interior to the outer universe; the
pointer of the dial which sweeps through
space, indicating perennially the position occupied by each successive star, which for a
brief period of centuries keeps watch before
the pole.

Taking in our hands now, the sacred writings of the Pir M Hru, let us approach the
masonic Light; and opening the book at the
first chapter, where Thoth the Eternal Wisdom
commences to instruct the catechumen freed
from the corruption of the body, let us with
him penetrate the interior of the building,
and take such a preliminary view of its secret
places and their analogues in the Ritual, as

may enable us to study more deeply the twofold expression of that masonic mystery. Reciting chapter by chapter as we mount, grade
by grade along with the Catechumen of Light,
we approach at the fifteenth step a gateway
two courses yet above us, just as the catechumen in the fifteenth chapter approaches
the "double gate of the horizon," the double-
arched gate which points towards the pole-star;
when he invokes " Haroeris the great guide of
the world, the guide of the souls in their
secret places, the light dwelling in the horizon."
From this point the first veil of secrecy begins.
For so effectually was the opening concealed
from the uninstructed eyes by a revolving
stone, that the position, once lost, was impossible to recover; and for two hundred years
after passing under the barbarous Omar, the
building remained impenetrable, until Caliph
Al Mamoon, in the ninth century of our era,
forced an opening at random through the
solid masonry, and hit accidentally upon the

entrance passage.   Entering by the low gateway, thus built in the Northern side, at a
considerable height above the ground, we have
before us the passage of the horizon of the
point of Equinox, which, while descending
Southwards into the depths of darkness, points
Northwards towards the star of the Purple
Arch.   As we cross the gate on the seventeenth

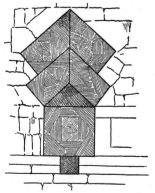

Gate of the Ascent.   Northern Face: Course xvii.

course we recognize the point where, in the
seventeenth chapter, the catechumen is admitted as a postulant, and exclaims, "I go
from the Gate of Taser (the Ascent).   What

is the gate of Taser? It is the gate where
the god Shu (the Light) lifts the disc of
heaven. The Gate of the North is the Gate
of the Great God:" he continues, speaking
evidently of the same gate; exactly as in the
Pyramid the only entrance is the Gate of the
Ascent in the seventeenth course of Northern
face. Bidding now with him farewell to
the light of earthly day, and treading the
descending passage, we pass, some little way
down, a very fine and beautifully ruled
double line,* scored perpendicularly on the

---

* The detection of this line is connected with a circumstance of a highly singular character, which seemed
at one time to lend some appearance of support to the historic theories of Professor Smyth. It was due not to any
measurer or observer of the Pyramid, but to a student
who had never seen the building, but believed that if the
professor's theories were correct, some such special mark
would point out that particular spot. Examination being
made—for the professor had never noticed it—the prediction proved to be true; an act of divination which
would have been remarkable enough if those theories had
been true, but which seems strange indeed when one
considers their palpable error.

slanting wall so as to point downwards to
the foundation, and separating the upper
section of the passage where the Departed in
the Ritual is bereft of every faculty except
that of motion, from the more advanced portion where his mental faculties are gradually
restored to him.   Continuing the long descent,
we arrive at an aperture in the western
wall, and passing through the opening thus
disclosed mount gently into a kind of grotto
at the bottom of the Well, a square perpendicular shaft, with footholds cut in the
precipitous sides.   Into that chamber of the
Deep Waters the postulant descends on
the Western side, as the sun at the close of
day goes down into the Western waters, and
bursts forth in splendour on the hidden world.
From the top of the shaft a level passage runs
to the place of the divine birth mentioned in
the Ritual, the Chamber of the Moon, where,
according to Egyptian teaching, Osiris each
month renewed his birth.   In that chamber,

once rigidly blocked up, the liberated soul was
born anew; and thence it came forth to
descend the ladder of the shaft, as we see in
the papyrus of Ani,* and to become re-united
with the postulant awaiting it in the Well of
Life. Then, when the soul is restored, initiation takes place and strength is given to
endure the ordeal.

Returning from the bottom of the well to
the Passage of the Horizon, and pursuing our
course still further downwards, we come, after
a short level continuation, to the subterranean
chamber or the Place of the Central Fire,
where the initiate undergoes his ordeal; a
chamber hewn out of the solid rock, and having
an inaccessible floor covered with huge blocks
of varying height resembling a pool of petrified
flame, or the masses of the mountain chains
formed by the action of the earth's central

* I am indebted for this illustration to Mr. F. Compton
Price, the well-known expert in ancient characters, who
has just completed the splendid facsimile of that papyrus
for the Trustees of the British Museum.

fire ; while beyond that terrible chamber a small passage leads to nothingness. Resuming our exploration of the edifice, and coming forth from the place of ordeal, as the Initiate, now become the Adept, turns back and avoids the place of annihilation ; we remount the Passage of the Horizon until, at a little distance below the scored line, we come to a granite gate, or portcullis, built in the roof. This great gate, which originally was totally hidden by masonry and was only discovered by the falling of a stone when Al Mamoon was forcing his entrance into the pyramid, stands at the threshold of the Secret Places. Not only was the whole gate carefully hidden, but the lower portion of the passage within was blocked with enormous stones, still unremoved, and perhaps irremovable. So even now the Lintel is still hidden, and admission is only effected through a hole forced by violence in the wall of the passage above the blocks ; while a precisely similar difficulty is experienced by the adept

in passing the Lintel of Justice before entering
the Double Hall of Truth. Creeping with
difficulty through the hole, we find ourselves
in a small low corridor about one hundred and
twenty-nine feet long, inclined upwards at an
elevation slightly less than that of the depression of the Entrance Passage, and corresponding to the lower portion of the Hall of Truth
where the adept justifies himself before the
forty-two judges of the unseen world, "The
Gods of the Horizon, and the Gods of the
Orbit." Then, stooping beneath the low gateway, by which it is terminated (but not
obstructed) at the top, "The Gateway of the
Festival," we stand upon a kind of landing-
place, from which the whole system of the
interior passages opens out. On every side, is
"the crossing of the pure roads of life" of
which the coffin of Amamu speaks. On the
Western side, is the mouth of the well, "The
gate of Anruhf" leading down to the "roads
of darkness." Before us lie the fields of

Aahlu, the blessed country where the justified executes the works, which he is privileged to perform for Osiris. " I have digged in Anruhf," he says later on, " I have drilled the holes," the holes, that is, for the good seed, the corn which grew seven cubits high, the holes which are drilled in the ramps of the Southern Ascending Passage, but to which no significa-tion has yet been attached.

Beyond the fields, the road leads direct to the Queen's Chamber, the Place of the New Birth, where the soul received her second life ; and here on the Eastern wall, within a staircase of five ascents, is a kind of niche or image, the " type," to use the expression of the Ritual, into which the soul is new born with the fivefold dominion of the regenerate senses. From the same point also, at the head of the well, diverge the interior ladders on the coffin already spoken of. Sheer down, " the ladder which has been made for Osiris," descends into the well. Northwards, " the

ladder of Earth," slopes downward to the
Hidden Lintel, the entrance of the upward
path.   Upwards to the South, but with a very
slightly different inclination, runs the ascending passage, called by some writers " the
Grand Gallery," forming the upper portion of
the Hall of Truth, the Grand Lodge, or
Luminous Chamber of the Orbit.   This
remarkable structure, consists of a corridor,
about one hundred and fifty-seven feet long,
and twenty feet high, built entirely on a slope,
floor, walls, and roof, except a small portion at
the Southern or upper end.   On either side of
the sloping floor, are twenty-eight ramps, each
with a hole in it, a reference to which in the
Ritual has been already noticed.   And at the
upper end the slope of the floor-line is closed
abruptly, just above the Queen's Chamber by
a block three feet high, forming a dais, or
throne of judgment.   From hence along the
top of the block, or seat of the throne, the
passage runs level for about sixty-one inches,

the wall at the side being not quite vertical,
but impending very slightly towards the slope.
At the back of the throne the gallery is
brought to a termination, by the Southern
wall closing down in seven over-lappings
within forty-two inches of the seat and leaving
as an exit further South, a narrow and grave-
like tunnel.   In the sloping roof of the
gallery, running downwards from South to
North at a somewhat greater inclination than
the floor, are thirty-six overlappings, like
the waves of a river of light, and corresponding to the number of decades in the orbit
of the Egyptian year.   And on the side wall
of the dais at the upper end of the gallery
are also seven overlappings, one above another,
arching over to the summit; while in the
position corresponding to that occupied by
our own globe among the planets, runs a deep
groove or orbit along its entire length.   Thus
we are confronted with a vivid connection
between the Orbit and " the Passage of the

Sun" in the Double Hall of Truth, the Lower
Hall of Truth in Darkness, and the Upper
Hall of Truth in Splendour, with the Throne
of Radiance at the higher end. And above
that throne rises the habitation of the seven
great spirits in the service of their Lord, the
Creator, who, the Sacred Books tell us, "protect the coffin of Osiris."

Now comes the most mysterious portion of
the building. Stripped of its noble proportions, and reduced to an altitude so low, that
a man must creep on hand and knee to pass,
the passage pierces the southern wall of the
Grand Gallery, and runs straight on, first into
the Ante-chamber, or "Place of Preparation,"
and then into the splendid hall called the
King's Chamber, in the most secluded portion of the building. In each of these halls
is one and only one object. In the ante-
chamber is a kind of masonic veil, which no
one can pass without bowing the head. In
the King's Chamber is a sarkophagus, not

closed, but open; while the air channels wherewith this deeply buried room is amply ventilated proclaim that it is not a chamber of the dead, but of the living, the place of "the Orient," where, in the Ritual, Osiris is awakened from his slumbers. In this portion of the building the structure changes its material for granite, forming, as it were, a house by itself within the Pyramid, an inner House yet within the House of Osiris, entered by the low and grave-like passage leading from behind the throne. This is the House of Glory described on the coffin of Amamu already quoted, the house to which the Illuminate approaches after passing the tribunal of Osiris. Here is the " Gate of the pure spirits," which they alone can enter who are washed in the waters of Life and radiant with the splendours of the Orbit. And here, too, it would seem, takes place the solemn address described in the Sai-an-Sinsin, " of the Gods in the House of Osiris," followed by the response

of the "Gods in the House of Glory;" the
joyous song of the holy departed who stand
victorious before the judgment seat, echoed
triumphantly by the inner chorus of their
beloved who have gone before them into the
fulness of light. Above is the "Empyrean
Gate" ("the opening of Athor," as the Ritual
calls it), which leads to the "Secret Places
of Heaven;" the ascending spaces above the
King's chamber, once completely closed, and
constituting the innermost, the loftiest, and
the most secret of the Hidden Places. And
the whole is dominated and crowned by a
gigantic triangle of granite, masonically expressing the divine Trinity of Egypt.

Such is the complex and hitherto unexplained system of gateways and passages,
shafts, channels, and chambers; some leading
upwards, some downwards, some level; some
rough in the last degree, others exquisitely
polished; some magnificent in their proportions, some so low that a man must creep,

so narrow that he can with difficulty pass,
to be found within the Pyramid of Light.
It is absolutely unique; no other building,
it may be safely averred (not even the later
Pyramids), having contained any structure
bearing the least resemblance to the higher
chambers. Striking as it is in every feature,
the most remarkable circumstance of all is the
evident intention of the architect to preserve
that secrecy which lends a majesty to the
strange theosophy of Egypt. What then was
the design, the secret and jealously guarded
design, with which this wondrous edifice was
constructed? That its various features are
meaningless, or the mere result of caprice, is
a suggestion to which the forethought and
lavishness of calculation displayed in every
detail unmistakably give the lie. Nor again
can we maintain that they are necessary for
the purposes of an ordinary tomb. For, in
the first place, they are not to be found in the
other Pyramids, which were used for that

purpose ; and, secondly, if there be any intention which the architect has openly manifested,
it is to create such a series of obstructions,
that no human body could be buried therein.

In truth, the Grand Pyramid is the House
of a Tomb ; but it is not a closed, but an
open tomb.   It is the tomb not of a man, but
a god ; not of the dead, but of the risen.   It
is the tomb of the divine Osiris, whose birth
on earth, descent into the under-world, victory
over the serpent Apep, resurrection and judgment of the dead, were the most prominent
features in the creed of Egypt, and in union
with whom the holy departed achieved the
path of illumination, and passed in safety
the divine tribunal.

Viewed in this light, the practical value of
the structure begins to become clear.   On
that doctrine rested the whole organization
of social life amongst the ancient Egyptians.
The kalendar, the festivals, the duties of the
monarch, the rights of the priesthood, the

relations of the provinces to their paramount temples, all were illustrated in the Path of Light.   Endless confusion therefore in the State would result, no less than injury to the religion, from any misconstruction, or misrepresentation of doctrine (such as seems to have taken place under Khu en Aten); a circumstance all the more likely to occur, on account of the obscurity of the symbols employed.

Now the masonic symbolism of the Grand Pyramid affords a simple and practically indestructible means for perpetuating without betraying the doctrine of Egyptian wisdom. That expression, once formulated, was never repeated; the other tombs and Pyramids of Egypt claiming kinship only by subordinate and particular features with the work of the Grand Master.   While then the written records of the Ritual, none of which now extant probably possess a higher date than that of Khufu, were liable to change and error, no lapse of time could impair, no variation could affect in the secret places, the masonry of the Pyramid of Light. This embodiment, at once secret and unalterable, forming literally a Masonic Ritual of the whole doctrine of Light, accounts for the singularly piecemeal fashion in which the sacred words were committed to writing. During the first three dynasties one chapter alone has a dim traditional claim to have been written, while one other is said to have been revealed to Men Kau Ra, the grandson of the builder of the Grand Pyramid. And though on the later Pyramids sacred inscriptions begin to appear, it is not until the XIth dynasty that they become at all common. Of the various chapters so published (that is, used as inscriptions or written on papyri) at different times, there have been, as Mr. Budge mentions in his " Treatise on the Mummy," four principal recensions. The first is that of the Ancient Empire, written in hieroglyphics, to which the important inscription on the coffin of Amamu

belongs. Then comes the Theban recension,
also in hieroglyphics, of which the papyri have
been with great labour collated and published
by M. Naville; followed during the succeeding
dynasty (XXth) by another written in the
Hieratic (or priestly) characters. And last of
all, we have the recension of the XXVIth or
Saite dynasty, to which is due the great
papyrus * now preserved at Turin, of which

* An English translation has been published by Mr.
Birch, in Bunsen's " Place of Egypt ; " and one in French
has been produced by M. Pierret. While speaking on
this subject, it is impossible to refrain from a regret at
the almost incredible carelessness with which the papyri,
relating to every kind of topic, have been scattered
loose-cast over half the museums of Europe, without the
preservation of any general account of their contents, or
even of their existence. Some are to be found at the
Bodleian; others at the Louvre; others, again, in the
museums of Bologna, of Naples, of Turin, of Leipsic,
of Berlin, of Copenhagen, of Stockholm, and of Rome ;
while our insatiable sarkophagus, the British Museum,
entombs them by the thousand. If France, the country
to which belongs so distinguished a record in these
matters, could be induced to join with us in urging the
Government of Egypt to issue a Commission for the

Lepsius published a facsimile in 1846, consisting of upwards of one hundred and sixty original, with three supplementary chapters. Now it was during that recension that the order of the chapters is said to have been fixed for the first time. What canon then, or standard of order, did the revisers employ? It certainly was not the relative antiquity of the chapters, for the only one which claims to remount to the Ist dynasty stands one hundred and thirtieth in the papyrus, while that which is attributed in it to the IVth dynasty—and which is entitled

purpose of requesting from the various European Governments the fullest possible information with regard to the papyri and other relics of ancient Egypt, which they may happen respectively to possess, a favourable answer would doubtless be returned ; so that a mass of invaluable evidence would be opened up, wherein we might not unreasonably hope to trace the action and inter-action of the religious, political, and economical factors in that complex constitution. And thus material might be collected for commencing a general Encyclopædia of Archaic Sociology ; and possibly for founding a science of organic society in its concrete development.

"The Entrance on Light in one Chapter," as though it had once been the single chapter in use—comes sixty-fourth. But the answer to the question appears to be contained in the last of the supplementary chapters; for the papyrus proclaims the key to be within the reach of all who understand in full the masonic secrets. "This Book," it says, "is the Book of the Master of the Hidden Places." And in those Hidden Places therefore the Secret of the Master of the Hidden Places, the "Mystery of the words of order," as the coffin of Amamu says, is to be found. This is the version, therefore, which we shall compare with the Ritual in stone, its predecessor by more than three thousand years; the very magnitude of the intervening period serving to exhibit in a more striking light the closeness of the correspondence. Nobly indeed does that stupendous monument respond to the mystic title which it bore. Surrounded by darkness as profound as that which the Almighty has made His secret place ; in the midst of scenery invisible to the eye, but faithfully pourtraying the glories of the celestial expanse, the Grand Architect has set up the throne which the lapse of ages has had no power to impair, and has immutably inscribed in its secret places the immutable path of the just in characters of light, embodied in the immutable motions of the heavenly orbs.

CHAPTER II.

THE HOUSE OF OSIRIS.

AMONG the innumerable transformations witnessed by the present century of revolution,
none has a more startling character than that
of the resurrection of primæval Egypt. For
more than a thousand years from the day
when the barbarous Omar celebrated the funeral
rites of the ancient learning in the flames of
the great Library at Alexandria, to the day
when Champollion, like another Sothis,
heralded the dawn of a new era of Egyptian
brilliance, an ever-growing obscurity buried
the entire land. Less than a century has
elapsed since the most appalling penalties, in

this world and the next, were fulminated by the Sultan against the official who should dare to allow a Christian " to approach the sacred port of Suez, the starting-point of the holy Haj." To-day that port is the crowded entrance of the most cosmopolitan highway of the globe. For centuries Egypt, as it was the earliest, so it was the most jealously guarded seat of Moslem law. To-day its courts recognize a multiplex jurisdiction of alien nations, for which no precedent exists in the history of any other state.* Within living memory its hieroglyphs were an enigma hopelessly abandoned ; its temples hidden beneath the accumulated filth of generations of Arabs ; the very age of its ruins unguessed within thousands of years. To-day the mighty

* The case of the Holy Roman Empire may perhaps suggest itself as a precedent ; for foreign princes undoubtedly sat in the Diet. But those princes had jurisdiction not by virtue of treaties or in right of their foreign kingdoms, but of the Imperial principalities of which they happened to be possessed.

buildings stand clearly forth to attest their pristine majesty; the canons of the kings may be consulted in their original records; and the errors made by careless scribes, who thought no mortal eye would ever look upon the papyri concealed within the breast of the mummy, stand detected by the hieroglyphic scholarship of Europe.

A peculiar fascination surrounds every detail of life in early Egypt. For all other empires can be assigned with more or less certainty some point of historic origin. For China, for Assyria, for even Babylonia, we can dimly discern the traces of rude beginnings. The days of Romulus or of Kekrops are but the Middle Ages of history when compared with the days of Khufu or of Mena. India does not claim for her earliest Vedas an antiquity exceeding four thousand years. The sacred writings of China count less than a thousand more; the beginning of Babylonia about a thousand still beyond. On the banks of the

Nile alone do we find, centuries before the date
of the Accadian Sargon, a settled monarchy
and a constituted state, an elaborate Ritual
and organic hierarchy, a specific architecture
and a copious alphabet. Hence it is that the
principal anomaly which usually blurs our
conception of antiquity, namely, the interference of an element alien to the environment
in the formation of the customs of a race, more
particularly when that race has been transplanted from some wholly diverse soil, is
absent from the horizon of Egypt; and the
picture which we may draw of Egyptian civilization has its source, its development, and its
consummation in the conditions of Egypt
alone. No feature of attraction is wanting in
that remarkable scene. The stately river, the
source of perennial life and freshness to the
entire land, the long line of majestic temples
crowning the banks, the laughing population
crowding its waters, the dances, the games,
the songs, the wrestlings, the perpetual feasts,

the boats of pleasure jostling with the sacred
boats of the dead, all these things make up a
picture, which set in the dazzling clearness of
the cloudless sky leaves a charm that can
neither be rivalled nor forgotten.

That picture, too, demands no painful effort
of the imagination to fill up for ourselves from
broken and disjointed details.   We are not
called upon to piece out, into such consistency
as we may, the fragmentary hints of social
life laboriously gathered from chance allusions
hidden in a score of different writers.   Nor
need we content ourselves with descriptions
of events written centuries after their occurrence.   We can go straight to the fountain-
head, and consult the original records.   On
the huge propylæa of the temples, on the walls,
on the enormous sarkophagi, on the architraves,
on the pillars of the immense buildings, we
find the deeds of the princes set out in the
sacred hieroglyphs.   For the battle of Lake
Regillus we must trust to the traditions

preserved by Livy; for that first great battle
of Megiddo, which took place hundreds of
years before Josiah lost his life upon the
same plain, long before ever Regillus was
fought, we have the cotemporaneous account
of the conqueror Thothmes, and the lists of the
spoils drawn up by royal officers. Nay more,
the monuments of Egypt give us not descriptions alone, but actual representations of the
scenes. Of the triumphs celebrated by the
renowned Julius, what trace is left for posterity
to gaze upon? But the triumphs of Rameses,
and of Seti, which took place well-nigh as long
before the time of Cæsar as Cæsar's day was
before our own, live yet in every detail. The
garments, the ornaments, the countenances,
even the colour of the hair of the different races
which took part in those processions, all may
be seen to-day upon the walls of the palaces
which witnessed them. Of Moses and of
Solomon, of the founder of Rome, nay, of the
great apostle of the Gentiles, we possess not

even a traditional likeness. But the features
of Pharaoh may be as familiar to us as they
were to his adoring subjects. A triple enclosure formed by massive columns, of infinite
pathos in their lonely grandeur, is all that is
left to tell us how the earth-shaking Poseidon
was worshipped in his home at Pæstum. But
every feature of the procession which trod the
long aisles of Karnak, the vessel of purification,
the wings on the sacred scribe, the company
of the singers, the quadruple ranks of priests,
the sacred ark borne upon their shoulders,
the cherubim with outstretched wings shadowing the Deity enthroned between, have all
been preserved for our inspection, no less
than the words of the solemn litany which
the worshippers addressed to Ra, the unseen
Light.

Two marked peculiarities characterize the
records of the earliest times. Nothing is more
striking than the knowledge of science which
the priests of Egypt are more and more

generally admitted to have possessed, in proportion as the facts are more carefully investigated.   What architect of the present day
would undertake to erect a building, more than
four hundred feet high, full of chambers of the
most elaborate description, which should never
need repair for five thousand years ?   What
other nation not only discovered the transcen-
dental relation between radius and circumference — the foundation of all curvilinear
measurement—but utilized it as a principle
of architectural construction ?   What other
building is oriented with such perfect accuracy
that, if Mr. Flinders Petrie be correct, the
minute displacement wrought in the course
of ages represents (and consequently measures)
the secular variation due to a recondite cosmical force ?   Where else shall we find
expressed in masonic form the different proportions of the surface of the earth, given
according to the various methods of calculation, as, according to the same authority, the

architect of the Grand Pyramid has expressed
them in the area of its pavement at the
different levels ?   Where else shall we find
an antique kalendar based on the periodic
motion of the earth ?   What other people
knew, as Dr. Brugsch and M. Maspéro aver,
the proper motion of the sun in space ; or
who possessed the lovely Sothiac cycle, the
Cycle of Grand Orient, which measured whole
ages by the herald star, as it dawned for a
moment on the eastern horizon.

Equally striking, and even more distinct
perhaps, is the perpetual presence of the life-
giving river.   From end to end of its territory,
from age to age of its history, in the religion,
in the commerce, in the honours of the dead,
wherever we may turn, and on whatsoever
object we may fix our eyes, we never for a
moment lose sight of the blue waters of the
Nile.   That beautiful stream, flowing tranquilly for hundreds of miles beneath the
serene sky, alone gave verdure and plenty

to the long and narrow strip of fertile soil
which lines its borders, cut off by deserts on
either hand, and alone permits the very existence of an Egyptian people.

According to ancient tradition, and agreeably
also to the records, the ancestors of the race
in very remote times were not of Northern
but of Southern * extraction, being originally
natives of Poont, situated near the Equatorial
sources of the Nile.   In harmony with this
tradition, we find that the central point of

---

* As a contrary opinion is still held by some Egyptologists, and was sanctioned by Dr. Brugsch himself, I may
be permitted to quote the opinion of a very distinguished
authority in support.   M. Maspéro, when I put the
question to him, most courteously informed me that
though years ago he had held the opinion then prevalent
of a Northern origin, he had changed his views on further
research, and now believes the Egyptians to have come
from the South.   If this view be correct—and many facts
seem to support it—endless difficulties are resolved, or
rather do not arise to require solution, which have
resulted from a belief in the famous " prehistoric Asiatic
family ; " that is to say, in a family of the existence of
which no record can be produced.

the Egyptian universe, the horizon of which traces out, as we saw, the sacred Horizon of the Ritual, determined by the pole-star and defined by the Pyramid, was the Aptu, or Southern " Apex of the Earth," mentioned by Dr. Brugsch in " The Holy Land of Khent," situated in that immediate neighbourhood. For our point of reference was demarcated by the intersection of the Equator with the grand meridian of Memphis; and that inter-section takes place just by the Western shore of the great Equatorial lake from which the famous river derives its life-giving streams : hence on the day of Equinox, an observer standing at the fount of the river in the patriarchal land of Egyptian tradition, would witness that grand " Passage of the Sun," and march of the universal hosts of space, which solemnizes the day of the " Reckoning of the Spirits." From that point of origin, we marked out the four Cardinal Points of the universal sphere the thrones of the four

Egyptian spirits of the Light, with Hapi in
their midst, protecting the Southern fountains
of the Nile. These four bright spirits, the
guardians of the heavenly dome, were imaged
to the Egyptians under the form of the cynocephalous ape, the creature which bears the
closest resemblance to humanity; and from
them, as the four living creatures before the
throne of Ra, assistance was invoked by the
Justified in the Ritual at the moment when
the full splendour of the Orbit was bursting
upon his illumined sight. Thus the whole
system of Egyptian astronomy, in its scientific delineation no less than its mystical
significance, would seem to have been devised
originally, not with any reference to the later
settlement of the race upon the lower streams
of the Nile, but to their original dwelling-
place among the sunny fountains of the South;
while the Grand Meridian appears to have been
defined, not by its local relation to Memphis,
but from its passing through the apex of the

earth, beneath the Grand Arch of the universe
and the apex of the celestial dome over the
point of origination.

Yet, remarkable as is this primæval locality
when viewed in the light of Egyptian tradition,
its interest is increased tenfold when we regard
it in combination with the other features of
the great watershed of which it forms an
essential part, and which reminds us irresistibly of the famous watershed described in
our own Scriptures as forming the primæval
dwelling-place of man. There are—not the
full streams but—as in Genesis, the "heads"
of the four rivers, which go "forth to water
the whole country." There, beyond the Zam-
besi, lies the land of gold, with its mines of
unknown antiquity : while the odorous herb
of which the hieroglyphic name is Betru (or
Bedru, the L being in Egyptian identical
with R) suggests the original of the Hebrew
Betelu, converted by the Greeks into Bdellium.
There is the fountain of the Niger, which

encompasses in its windings the whole land
of the Blacks.   There is the source of the
inundating Nei-los, in Egyptian "the Boundary Burster;" of which the Hebrew word
Hiddekel, signifying "Violent," is but a pale
reflection.   And there is the Congo, the river
of "Life," corresponding precisely with the
Hebrew Perith (fruitful), transformed by the
Greeks into the Euphrates.   More striking
still, in the eastward portion of the great
basin lies the wonderful garden, or Paradise,
three thousand square miles in extent, so
glowingly described by Stanley, and full of
animal life, the sceptre of which was one
of the insignia (the "Tad") borne by the
great deity Amen; while from that garden
flows the single river, the Shari, exactly
as in our scriptural account the single river
flowed in the midst to water the garden which
was placed in the eastward * part of the

* In the innumerable attempts at the identification
of the birthplace of man, as recorded in Scripture—

immense watershed of Eden. And as, according to the same account, the first traces of the
never-ceasing current of human wandering
commenced on the Eastward of the garden,
so does the stream of the infant Nile, which
takes its rise near this point, tend Eastward
of the grand meridian before bending Southward towards the lake which still bears the
patriarchal name of the Egyptian Nou ; * and

attempts which may be counted literally by the hundred,
and which have gone far towards rendering any true
exposition of human development an almost hopeless
achievement—the garden is constantly confused with the
watershed, and the "heads" of the rivers with their full
courses, while the single river is omitted altogether.

* From the same source a good deal of light may, I
think, be thrown upon the scriptural account of the
Deluge, regarded as a phenomenal inundation of the
Nile valley, the dwelling-place of the primæval family,
as I have endeavoured to show elsewhere ; and this,
again, will be found to react upon various questions
connected with the early settlement of Egypt ; the
worship of Nou, the deity of the water ; the sacred ark
of Amen, the prototype of the ark of Moses ; the especial
reverence paid to the Nilometer, or "Tat," the symbol
of the divine Nou, with its threefold measure of the inundation ; the sudden immergence of that lonely yet majestic

below it, to the ruins of Assur, discovered by
Caillaud on the banks of hoary Meroe.

From that country their course appears to

civilization ; the dim tradition of bygone generations ; the
intense reverence paid to the patriarchal monarchs ; the
universal jurisdiction claimed by the divine royalty of
Egypt ; and, above all, the serene contemplation of death
as the luminous entrance to the fields of light. The
Babylonian tradition also given in the Deluge tablet,

The sacred Tat or Measure of the Inundation.

translated in "Records of the Past," is in agreement of the
same view ; for, according to that tradition, the theatre of
the cataclysm was certainly not Babylonia, since the hero
declares positively that he crossed the sea. In fact, so far
as I have been able to trace, there is no nation, from India
and China in the East, to Mexico and Peru in the furthest
West, whose native traditions and archæological relics
are in discord either with the Egyptian tradition of the
primæval land of Poont, or with the scriptural description
of the primæval watershed, if we are content to read, by
the light of Egyptian tradition, the account handed down
to us by Moses, whom those Scriptures expressly characterize as pre-eminent in Egyptian knowledge.

have been effected by a twofold route.   In part,
according to a very ancient tradition, mentioned
by Dr. Brugsch, they proceeded along the banks
of the river, sojourning for a while, it would
seem, in the island of Meroe, where the hoary
temple of Amen and the ruins of Assur, mentioned above, mark their ancient presence ;
while others appear to have come down by the
Red Sea, as Mr. Petrie's discoveries indicate,
and thence to have crossed the desert to Coptos.
From this most important circumstance, it
is essential to bear in mind that to the
Egyptian the South was the " Great Quarter,"
to which especial reverence was due.   Hence
it was that every year the sacred images were
carried into the ancestral country ; an echo
of which tradition is found in the visits of
the gods of Homer to the " blameless
Ethiopians."   Hence, in the ancient inscription
on the coffin of Amamu, we are told how the
holy dead, " after flying over the whole face
of heaven," is " established among the blessed

company in the south." And in that same
archaic papyrus we read of the celestial land
of Khent, or Khent-Amenti, the habitation
of the Hidden God, imaged on earth by the
"Holy Land of Khent" at the Apatu or
Southern apex of the earth. Hence also the
most sacred portion of the temple was placed
towards the same quarter; and the Grand
Pyramid, from the entrance to the innermost
chamber, was oriented North and South.

In truth, to the mind of the Egyptian, the
whole bed of the immense river was but the
sacred image of the unseen land watered by
the "celestial Nile" of which the Ritual
speaks; "The Nuter Khart," or Holy Land
of the Dead, with its triple division into
Rusta, the territory of Initiation; Aahlu, the
district of Illumination; and Amenti, the
secret home of the hidden God.

Far towards the South, beyond the alternate
reaches of stream and desert, lay the patriarchal
land of Poont, like Amenti, the distant home

of the unseen Father. At the tropical extremity
of Egypt, immediately below the celestial or
tropical arch traversed by the sun at the
summer solstice (at that epoch about 24° N.
the inclination of the earth's axis to the plane
of its orbit, being at that time about half a
degree greater than at present), was the cataract or " Gate of the Nile," through which
the ancestors of the race entered the country.
That cataract or throne of the life-giving
waters, situated beneath the Royal Arch of
the solstitial throne, marks the point attained
by the Illuminate in the Ritual, when he has
achieved, in Aahlu, the " passage of the sun,"
and " opens the gate of the Nile," the cataract
of heavenly light.

As the deceased, in making that ascent,
entered into the presence of the forty-two
judges of the dead (the Gods of the Horizon
and the Gods of the Orbit), each judge supreme
in his particular province ; so also was all the
land of Egypt parcelled out into forty-two

nomes or districts, twenty nomes in the Lower,
and twenty-two nomes of the Upper country.
To each nome was assigned a great temple as
capital, with a specific function and priesthood.
And as the temple formed the vast enclosure
of the shrine, so also did the district become
the vast enclosure of the temple. Nor were
the temples alone dedicated to sacred things,
but the structures of daily life shared the
divine significance. And for every division of
the country, as De Rougé has shown, the
palace and the canal, no less than the temple
and the district, bore a name of mystery and
reflected the region of the holy dead.

All along the valley of the river, as it
descends Northwards; at Thebes, at Abydos,
at Tentera, were the great shrines sanctified by
manifestations of the Deity. At the Northern
extremity, where the ocean formed the boundary
of the country, was the mouth of Rosetta, or
Rusta, imaging, as we learn from the Papyrus
of Khufu, the mouth of the tomb, and looking

towards the pole-star, the never-failing light
of the depths, that pointed for the Egyptians
the path to the hidden life.   In the midst of
the land where the Nile branched out into the
great angle of the delta, the dominating angle
in the conformation of the valley, stood
Memphis (or Mennofer), the "Holy Place;" the
seat of the double government of Egypt, with
its palace dedicated to the Creator-spirit Ptah,
its cemetery bearing the title of "Blessed
Immortality," like our own "God's Acre," and
its canal called after the Voyage of the Unseen
Waters.   There, too, was the territory of
"Sochet Ra," the Fields of the Sun.   And
close to the sacred city, on the western bank
of the river, rose the "Pyramid of Light,"
built upon a lonely rock, which faces the great
quarter of the South, the house of Osiris, to
which, says the papyrus of Amen Hotep,
"Thoth," the Eternal Wisdom, "conducts the
Illuminate."

A degree of sanctity, peculiar even in that

land of reverence, enveloped the mysterious
building. " A sense of enchantment," we read
in another papyrus, pervaded the whole territory surrounding the Great House ; and even
the hurried traveller to-day can with difficulty
resist the spell, as he gazes on the solemn
walls.   But for the initiated of old, the
supreme end of their existence, the order of
their festivals, the purity of their religion, the
stability of their monarchy were concentrated
in the awful masonry.   As the territorial
constitution of the country, with its forty-two
provinces of the Lower and Upper kingdoms,
corresponded interiorly with the forty-two provinces of the Judges of the Dead, the Upper
Gods of the Orbit and the Lower Gods of the
Horizon, the political framework being the
envelope of the spiritual theosophy ; so was
it with the exterior and interior of the Great
House.   For from the point where the adept
appears before the forty-two judges in the
Double Hall of Truth, on surmounting the

blocks at the lower end of the Chamber of the
Shadow, to the throne at the upper end of the
Chamber of the Splendour, where he received
the crown of illumination, there are exteriorly
forty-two courses; so that they form the envelope of that Double Hall of inner Truth.
And as the lucid river itself imaged the
stream of the "celestial Nile," so also was the
course of that river imaged masonically in the
hidden places in the House of Osiris. Upon
the walls of the Chamber of the Splendour was
sculptured the orbit of our planet among the
sevenfold company around the solar throne,
the orbit which measures the rise and fall of
the life-giving waters of the Nile. Along the
roof descends the stream of sculptured rays,
thirty-six in number, corresponding to the
thirty-six decades of days in the orbit of the
Egyptian year. At the upper or Southern end
of the chamber, as at the upper or Southern
end of the kingdom, beneath the Royal Arch of
the Sevenfold Ascent, or "Burning Crown," as

the Ritual calls it, is the Throne of the Cataract.
Behind it, the low gate leads through the
narrow channels to the chambers of the South
with the hidden chambers in the height,
crowned by the Grand Arch which dominates
the whole interior of the building ; as the
gate of the Nile leads beyond the cataract
to the Southern land of Poont and the long-
hidden source of the river, where the land of
Khent, beneath the Southern apex, imaged
the celestial land of Khent, or Khent-Amenti,
mentioned in the Papyrus of Amamu, the
Interior Habitation of God in the supreme
heaven.   At the junction of the upper and
lower chambers is the upper mouth of the
Well, forming a key to the secret interior,
just as the city of Memphis with the house
of Osiris itself was the secret key to the
constitution of the double kingdom.   There
too the lesser passage from the secret Chamber of Divine Birth, the "Chamber of Isis,"
"the Light of the Hidden Nile," unites with

the main current of the masonic river ; just as
in the vignette of the celestial Nile, a branch
of the stream pours into the main current,
from "Annu (or On) the secret birthplace of
the gods." From that point the masonic stream,
like the Nile at the same point, forks out into
a delta, one branch leading down to the
Hidden Lintel, the other forming the Well of
Life, in the territory of Rusta, wherein, as we
learn from another papyrus, was the tree of
immortality. And in the rock which bounds
the Chamber of the Horizon, and upon which
the house of Osiris is built, we recognize the
"Rock of the Horizon of Heaven," of which
the Ritual speaks.

Again, the very form of some of the hieroglyphs betrays a pyramidal origin. Thus if we
outline the junction of the upper and lower
chamber, by tracing the roof-line of the Well,
below the roof-line of the gallery, with the
three rampstones in front, and the projections
of the upper and lower galleries at the place,

we shall have the hieroglyph pronounced "Taui," $\overline{\circ\circ\circ}$ which is well known to mean Upper and Lower Egypt, though no explanation of the form has hitherto been suggested. Similarly, suppose that we delineate the Double Hall of Truth (from the Hidden Lintel to the Empyrean Gate at the southern end of the

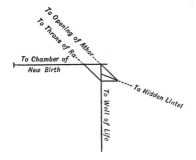

Pyramidal region of Thoth.

roof above the throne), together with the Chamber of New Birth and the Head of the Well, we shall have the portion of the structure more particularly subject to the dominion of Thoth: the divine person, by whom the initiation is effected. Then if we form a

cypher of that region, by tracing a line-plan
indicating only the direction of those parts
in relation to the Head of the Well, where,
as we shall presently see, the rite of initiation
is accomplished, we shall have the sacred
symbol reserved to that deity alone.   And

Sacred hieroglyphic symbol peculiar to Thoth.

as by the power of Thoth the adept, after
passing his ordeal, is introduced into the
presence of the forty-two judges in the Double
Hall, corresponding to the forty-two nomes or
provinces of Egypt, so also does that symbol
of Thoth enter into the hieroglyphic names
of every one of the nomes with but a single
exception.

Upon the same harmony between the
celestial and the terrestrial country embodied
in the masonry of the Pyramid of Light,

depended also the order of the princes of
Egypt. For as the Great House itself, the
Place of Osiris, the universal God, was
represented in its totality in the person of
the supreme Monarch ; so also the two great
divisions of that House, the territory of
initiation with its directing angle at the
Hidden Lintel, and the territory of illumination
with its Sculptured Orbit in the Grand Gallery,
the places respectively of the Gods of the
Horizon and the Gods of the Orbit, were
represented in the two great divisions of the
Egyptian Court, the princes of the Angle and
the princes of the Circle. And so also was
that seven-fold celestial company, the ranks
of which were sculptured above the throne in
the Chamber of the Splendour, represented in
the seven-fold ranks of the " Companions of
the King," which immediately surrounded the
person of Pharaoh. Thus the Great House
with the Double Hall of Truth within, formed
a masonic organization not only of the

religious but of the political constitution of
the kingdom ; with ascending grades from the
Purple Arch of the Star defining the Sacred
Horizon of Rusta (or Rosetta) to the Royal
Arch of the solstice or limit of the solar seat
above the water throne of the cataract, and
beyond again along the Grand Arch of the
Celestial Meridian to the culminating point of
the sun at Equinox above the source of the
river, in the primæval land of Poont.

As we stand before the portal of that
" Great House," the " Pir Aa," while we recall
the familiar title which the Pharaohs thence
derived, and as we contemplate the heaven
reflected in the blue waters of the river as it
flows without, and its image masonically expressed in the path within, " the disc " seems
lifted " from the tomb," and we gaze upon the
unseen world. Egypt, for so many centuries
the land of the buried, has suddenly become
the land of the risen dead. And the message
which the long-silenced voice proclaims as

with a tongue of fire, is the primitive belief in
the divine origin and end of man. It is not
the Ritual nor the Pyramid of Light alone,
which speak to us of the eternal day. Everywhere and always throughout ancient Egypt
the same doctrine is proclaimed. From the
orbit of the earth, from the pole-star of the
heavens, from the dawning of Sothis, from the
radiance of the sun, from the waters of the
river, from the palaces, from the temples, from
the tombs, from the very bowels of the rifled
dead, comes forth a voice which for ages has
been hushed in the grave; and that voice
with startling clearness bears testimony to a
judgment beyond the tomb, and the fatherhood of the unseen God.

NOTE ON THE SACRED ANGLE.

AMONG the jewels placed as the last ornaments upon the
sacred mummy, was sometimes included the Golden
Angle; one of the most obscure, but at the same time

most interesting symbols employed by the Egyptians.
The Angle is found, not held in the hand, but borne
aloft upon the arm of the great Deity, " Amen, the Eternal
Father," and is also one of the sceptres carried by Ptah,
the Creator-Spirit.   What is more singular, the well-
known image called the Pataikos which was carried by
the ships of Phœnicia, has been identified very clearly by
Champollion with the same god Ptah ; and the meaning
of Pat-Aik in Egyptian is the Dedication of the Angle.

Great Angle, borne aloft by Amen, Source of Life, in Trinity of Egypt.

The same figure is also found among the rock-sculptures
on the coast of Asia Minor.

While the sacred symbol of the Angle was thus widely
diffused, the name itself (disguised to us in various
languages) seems to have been borne by several races of
the Levant.   About the central or narrower part of the
Mediterranean, just where the Italian peninsula juts out
towards the projecting promontory of Africa, we meet
the name of Angle in the important island of Sikelia or
Sicily, a country which from its position has caught the

current of many migrations and supplied the arena of
many collisions. That island took its appellation not
from the Romans—for they, as Ovid tells us, called it
Trinacris, from its three-cornered shape—but from the
Sikeli, a tribe who, according to Thucydides, immi-
grated into it from the Southern part of Italy, with
which territory the island was for centuries intimately
associated. Now the Sikeli bear a name which
is meaningless in Greek or Latin, but in Egyptian
signifies, without change or modification of any kind,
" Sons of the Angle ; " while the similar but more
suggestive title of " Pirates of the Angle " is found in
the Greek name Laestrygones, another race who dwelt
there, of such high antiquity that Thucydides confesses
his ignorance of their origin. From hence, too, we
may not improbably derive our own word "sickle," or
"sikel," as it used to be spelt.   For the sickle-sword (of
which an Angle was a symbol in the priestly alphabet of
Egypt) was, as may still be seen upon the monuments,
the sacred weapon with which the Egyptian monarch slew
the captives ; and as Captain Burton has shown in his
well-known treatise on the sword, it is the instrument
from which both the Eastern scimitar and the cutlass of
our own sailors take shape.

Again, at the Eastern extremity of the Levant, the
name of Angle once more appears in a double form, and
a still more marked and suggestive connection. Right
opposite the mouths of the Nile, just in the locality
where sea-immigrants from Egypt would probably land
after passing the almost harbourless coasts of Palestine,
lie the countries of Kilikia and Phœnicia, each expressing

that idea of Angle (in Egyptian Kilik, in Hebrew Phœne) ; while the two together form the Angle of the bight through which runs the great dividing line of East and West.

Yet once more in Egypt itself, according to the account contained in Genesis—and Moses, it must be remembered, was at least an expert in Egyptian tradition —we find among the descendants of Ham the tribe of the Patroosim, which in that language means the Frontiers of the Angle (Pat-Rois), and connects them with those princes of the Angle who formed, as we have seen, an integral portion of the court of Pharaoh.

What angle then is this of such supreme importance that it should be the symbol of the great Deity, and should give a name to the princely races of the earth ? Of the highly important part played by the relation

Great Angle of the Nile Delta, Source of Life, in Triangle of Egypt.

between Angle and Circle in the structure of the Grand Pyramid we have already spoken ; but there is another Angle which still remains for consideration, namely, that between the two branches of the Delta into which the river forks at Memphis below the Great House. Now this Angle supplies a simple key to a very curious problem in cosmography. Upon examining the well-known triple division of the ancient world, it is

somewhat difficult to perceive upon what principle it was
effected. Russia can even now be scarcely considered as
forming, either by race or by conformation, a portion of
Europe proper; while, as Scythia, it seems to have been
regarded as entirely separate. Asia Minor, on the other
hand, possesses a shore line almost continuous with that
of Greece; and her population, at least upon the coasts,
seem to have been derived in great measure from kindred
sources. Nor is it easy to find the central point from
which the three dividing lines branch out. It cannot,
for instance, be situated in Babylonia, where some might
be inclined to place it, because Syria lies to the west;
neither again can it be in Armenia, where others might
look for it, since a considerable space divides that
country from Africa. If, however, we take up our stand
in front of the Great House at Memphis, the masonic
record of primæval science, the entrance to which indicates the principal division of the universal sphere,
and look abroad upon the great river which we have
seen represented within, we shall find that the form
which that river assumes at the spot suggests three divisions of the entire hemisphere. Behind us, towards the
South, stretches the long valley leading up to the hidden
sources of the far-distant primæval land; indicating the
huge peninsula of Africa enclosed between the seas, and
constituting also the southern boundary of the vast
Mediterranean basin. And right along that valley, above
the Great House, through the whole kingdom of Upper
Egypt, stretches the Grand Meridian, tracing out upon
the earth the Grand Arch of the Universe, and traversing
their ancient home beneath the supreme dome of highest

heaven.   Next, if the lines of the northern fork be prolonged indefinitely, then Eastward of the most Eastern
branch lies the continent of Asia ; Westward of the most
Western is Europe proper.   Finally, between the legs
of that earth-dominating Angle, lies the famous kingdom
of Lower Egypt, with the princes of the Angle ; while
on the coast beyond is Kilikia, the land of the Angle ;
and further again, but still within the legs of the same
Angle, stretches the immense plain of Scythia, separating
and yet uniting East and West.   Upon the Southern
borders of that plain, on the coast of the Black Sea,
according to the ancient traditions of our Sagas, the
ancestors of Odin and of the sea-going race, which still
bears the proud name of Angles, had their pirate home.
And it is not a little remarkable that the same Saga
refers more than once to the boundary line of East and
West as passing close by their ancient city upon the
Black Sea, and mentions as their neighbours the tribe of
the Vans, whose name appears frequently upon the
ancient monuments, and is still preserved in the Armenian
lake which lies by that boundary line.

It is strange too, to observe that no sooner are the
records of our ancestors permitted to speak as to their
own history, records incidentally confirmed both by classic
historians, such as Florus, and by the ancient monuments,
than a glimpse of still higher antiquity opens out through
the title of our nation, connecting itself with the wide-
spread symbol of the Egyptian Angle ; and a flood of light
is poured upon our words and customs by reference to
Egyptian sources.   Thus the familiar name of Viking, for
which no meaning has been assigned, signifies in Egyptian

an Angle-dweller, that is, an Englishman ; and the two
words composing it are still preserved in English as
" wick," a place, and " kink," an indentation.   Berserk
again, another well-known but unintelligible appellation,
means in that ancient tongue " foam-plough ; " a striking
and most natural image for those ploughers of the ocean
to employ, and one which harmonizes exactly with the
numerous poetic titles given by the Vikings to their true
home, the ship.   Odin himself, though the descendant of
ancestors who had been settled for generations upon the
Euxine, bore an Egyptian name—the significant name of
Destroyer ; and his standard, the raven, was the Egyptian
symbol of destruction.   Nor was it only in his character
of pirate * (itself an Egyptian word), but as teacher also,
that his associations connect themselves with the same
source.   According to tradition, he was acquainted in
some measure with the process of embalmment, and he
claimed to know the secret of the sacred writing, while
his followers were distinguished by the winged head-
dress which was borne by the sacred scribe of Egypt, as
representing the dominion of east and west bestowed
by Ra upon Thoth, the Lord of Wisdom.   So with the
funeral feasts, the elaborate ceremonies and the inter-
course with the dead which had so rooted a hold in the
hearts of our Scandinavian forefathers.   The Asars, or
holy ancestors whom they worshipped, were the very
counterpart both in name and in attributes with the
holy souls of Egypt who had become united with Osiris
(more properly Uasar), and were themselves described

* Some etymologists strangely derive this word from the Greek
πειράω, " to attempt ; " as though a pirate, of all people in the world,
were a man to leave his work half finished.

by his name. The title of Hersir, or Leader of the Host, which, as Du Chaillu has pointed out in his valuable work, was older than that of the king, bears in the hieroglyphic (Her-ser) the identical signification of Chief Organizer. The land of Kent (Khent) * was a territory of the holy dead, and its hieroglyph was a sail. Nay, there is scarcely a feature in the strange mythology of Scandinavia which does not reflect an image more or less distorted of some portion of the Egyptian Ritual. Or, to give but one more illustration of a different but equally curious character, our national shout, "Hip, Hip, Hurra!" which rises spontaneously though unmeaningly to our lips, and which is said to be the shout also of the Cossack dwellers by our ancient home upon the Black Sea, conveys in the hieroglyphic (Hep, Hep, Hura), "On, on, to plunder," the significant cry of our pirate ancestors at the moment of accomplishment. Strangest of all it is to think that the last of the Hidden Places of the earth to be opened to civilized man should have been the traditional scene of his earliest dwelling-place ; that the source of the historic river which, by its mighty Angle, traces out the lines of the first settlement of the globe, should to-day be the centre of its latest division by the world-dividing nation of Angles ; and that while the vast lake which marks the ancient "apex of the earth" bears the name of the monarch of that race, the Egyptian kingdom itself should be ruled at the dictation of her ministers.

* Pierret, in his Hieroglyphic Lexicon, states that Khent means always to ascend the Nile towards the south, and that the sail is always deployed ; thus answering, in the Path of Light, to the ascent of the Orbit by the illuminate beneath the open sail of the firmament.

It is true that these traditions, like those of other nations also, are entirely at variance with the remarkable adventures of the famous "Aryan race," that marvellous creature of modern myth-making which flits with all the brilliance of a will of the wisp over the most impossible morasses of Imaginative History. Happily however, its illustrious creator, Professor Max Müller, has himself given what we may hope will prove the death-blow to his scarcely less celebrated offspring, by utterly denying before the British Association any reality to its existence ; by laughing to scorn the idea of any such thing as an Aryan skull, and by stating plainly that the Aryan race is nothing more or less than a figment of philological convenience. For not until the last glimmer of that alluring but most misleading meteor has disappeared, will the ancient records of nations be permitted to throw their true light upon the past. Nor until then shall we understand our own laws and language, our customs and constitution, or trace the history of that Imperial nation of the waters which perpetuates the name of the sacred Angle. And surely no kingdom ever yet possessed a more romantic story in the past, or attained a position of more absorbing interest or more perilous pre-eminence than that occupied by England to-day, as she stands in the central land of highest antiquity, with hands stretching to every quarter of the globe—a solitary figure of commanding majesty, but uncertain in policy, unguarded in frontier, and almost unarmed in defence ; while surrounded by the seething nations which count their hosts by the million, and listening with a careless ear to the muttered breathings of universal war.

CHAPTER III.

THE HIDDEN GOD.

DEEPLY embedded in the heart of some ancient forest, we find here and there a massive and hoary boulder, its antiquity far exceeding that of the venerable trees, and its whole appearance telling of a distant soil and a by-gone day. As we sit upon the granite block, with the branches waving high above our heads, our wonder at its presence is deepened by the quiet scene. For countless ages that great stone has lain motionless, lifeless, changeless, amid all the infinite movement of changing life around it. No human power brought that huge mass where it lies; no eye can trace the path along which it was driven by the forces

of nature. And not until we have traced the
mighty variations and convulsions which in
the recesses of time our whole globe has
undergone, not until we have looked back far
beyond the earliest seed-time of the forest, to
the days when the surrounding country for
hundreds of miles formed the bottom of an
immense ocean, through which the icebergs
bore the huge rocks torn from its frozen
shores, can we understand the position of that
primeval stone.

Something of a similar character may not
unfrequently be discerned in regard to the
religious belief and worship of a nation, when
a tradition or custom survives the convulsions
and changes of the centuries, and remains
firmly embedded in the national life, though
every trace of significance is long buried in
the past. Most superstitions, it is probable,
had once an intelligible meaning, even if that
meaning were founded on a mistaken belief;
but such survivals are by no means due to

superstition alone. Who, for instance, can explain the Latin titles used for the psalms in the Prayer-book of the Church of England, without going back more than three hundred and fifty years to the time when England used the same language in her public worship as the rest of Christendom? So in the Latin Mass the Kyrie Eleison betrays its connection with the Greek; and the word Hosanna in the office for Palm Sunday carries us back to the Hebrew.

But there is one word in particular which is employed not on any special occasion but in every service, not once or twice but after every petition, not as a portion of the prayer but as its summary and its seal. If a stranger stand outside the closed doors of a church while service is going on, there is one word, and probably but one which he would hear distinctly repeated again and again. " Amen," " Amen," " Amen," that is the aspiration which time after time comes rolling forth with the

full strength of choir and congregation. That
is the word by which the apostle denotes the
absolute nature of the Deity as compared with
created matter. "In Him all things are
Amen." That is the title with which the seer
of the apocalypse invokes the advent of his
Divine Master at the conclusion of the vision :
"Amen, Veni Domine Jesu." That is the
title which the Master assumed to Himself,
"Amen, I say to you." And that is the title
by which the Egyptian priests of old addressed
the secret Deity—Amen, that is to say, in
Egyptian, "The Hidden One."

That the existence of the one God was widely
known by some classes of men at least among
the nations of antiquity there can be little
doubt. Among the Chinese, according to the
most eminent authority, Dr. Legge, the word Ti
represented the same idea as we express by the
word God ; and its assumption as a title by the
earliest dynasty of the Emperors of China would
be quite in accordance with the ancient belief

that the monarch ruled as the divine representative. When the disciples of Manu approached that sage to beg for instruction in the wisdom which afterwards formed the foundation of Indian law, they addressed him as follows: " For thou, O lord, alone knowest the purport (or rites) and the knowledge taught in the whole ordinance of the Self-Existent (Svayam bhu), which is unknowable and unfathomable." And their master, in his reply, laid down the principle of the One Uncreated God, the Giver of Light. " The Divine Self-Existent," he said, " indiscernible, making the elements and the rest discernible, appeared with creative force, dispelling the darkness."

Again, in the Mahabharata, the earliest production of post-Vedic literature, a translation of which, as well as of the laws of Manu, is given in the magnificent series of the Sacred Books of the East, the most enduring monument to its illustrious editor, a similar doctrine is ascribed to Vyasa. " In the commencement was Brahman, without beginning or end, unborn, luminous, free from decay, immutable, eternal, unfathomable, not to be fully known."

Equally explicit are the utterances of some of the Greek poets.

" One Self-begotten, from whom all things sprang ; " is one of the lines attributed to the famous Orpheus.

" To God all things are easy, nought impossible ; " so sang Linus, a brother of the same bright band. A fuller but not less accurate description is given by Xenophanes—

> " One God there is, greatest 'mongst gods and men ;
> Not like to mortals, or in form or thought.
> In full he sees, he hears, in full he knows,
> And without labour doth his mind move all."

Another poet, Cleanthes, whom St. Paul quotes in his famous speech to the Athenians, strikes at the root of the exclusiveness arising from the characteristic principle of ancient idolatry, that a deity listens to no prayers except from his own descendants, by proclaiming that all men are the offspring of God, and that consequently the right of prayer to Him is universal—

> " O thou most glorious and immortal One,
> O many-titled, O Omnipotent,
> Zeus, Lord of Nature, ruling all by Law,
> Hail ! whom to worship is the right of all ;
> Since all of us are of Thee."

Even the Roman mind, dim-eyed as it was for the invisible world, was not altogether without a glimpse of this truth, to which Horace has given expression when speaking of the supreme deity—

> " From whom none greater than himself is born ;
> Nor doth his equal, or his second, live."

But the truths which sparkle here and there in the teachings of India, China, or of Greece, fade and vanish before the blaze of Egyptian theosophy. Take, for example, the following extract given by Mr. Budge from the hymn to Amen-Ra, the hidden deity, the Self-Existent Light : " Hail to thee, Ra, Lord of

Law, whose shrine is hidden; Master of the gods, the god Chepera (Self-Existent Light) in his boat; by the sending forth of (his) Word the gods sprang into existence. Hail, god Atmu (Light), Maker of mortals. However many are their forms, he causes them to live, he makes different the colour of one man from another. He *hears the prayers* of him that is oppressed; he is kind of heart to him that calls unto him; he delivers him that is afraid from him that is strong of heart; he judges between the mighty and the weak.

"O Form, One, Creator of all things. O One, Only Maker of existences. Men came forth from his two eyes, the gods sprang into existence at the utterance of his mouth. He maketh the green herb to make the cattle live, and the staff of life for the (use of) man. He maketh the fish to live in the rivers, the winged fowl in the sky; he giveth the breath of life to the germ in the egg, he maketh birds of all kinds to live, and likewise the reptiles that creep and fly, he causeth the rats to live in their holes, and the birds that are on every green twig.   Hail to thee, O maker of all these things, thou Only One."

Nor was the unity the only truth concerning the Godhead known to the priesthood of Egypt.   Throughout the extent of the kingdom, at Thebes, at Ombos, at Tentera, at Memphis, at Annu (or On) a Triune God—of whom some knowledge seems to have been attained by Greece—invoked by many names, but everywhere consisting of three persons, consubstantial and co-eternal, was worshipped as supreme.   "I am Tmu in the morning," says the Creator, in a well-known passage, "Ra at noon, and Harmachi in the evening;" that is to say, as the dawn, the noon, and the sunset (which these names denote) are three several forms co-existing perpetually and co-equally in the substance of the sun, so also did the three divine persons co-exist perpetually and co-equally in the substance of the

Uncreated Light.   Thus, after declaring the
sacred Unity in the most emphatic and explicit
terms, the hymn already quoted proceeds to
invoke the three persons by name, using,
nevertheless, the singular pronoun for the
collective Three.   "He is of many forms;"
so the hymn proceeds, "O Amen, establisher
of all things, Atmu and Harmachi, all people
adore thee, saying, Praise to thee because of
thy resting among us, homage to thee because
thou hast created us.   All creatures say Hail
to thee, and all lands praise thee.   From the
height of the sky, to the breadth of the
earth, and to the depths of the sea art thou
praised."

If the Divine Trinity however were the
only secret of the Ritual, there would not be
so great a difficulty in following its symbols.
But there is a depth of mystery beyond, a
mystery the greater because manifested in a
visible form.   We read in the Ritual of an
incarnate, and not only of an incarnate, but of

a suffering and a dying God. We are confronted with the tears of Isis, and with the agony of Osiris—an agony so overwhelming that gods and men and the very devils, says the Ritual, are aghast. Moreover, not only is the twofold action of the same sacred person as man and as God recognized, but it is embodied in an animal symbolism ; just as, amongst Christians, the symbol of the Lamb is used for the Divine Person, the calf and the eagle for the Evangelists. Take, for example, the vignette of the Ritual representing the resurrection of Osiris as taking place in the presence of the Egyptian Trinity. The human form, being the highest available, is required by the supreme Three ; and in order to represent the lower nature, or divine humanity, it is necessary to take a lower creature whose characteristic should indicate that of the Divine Person represented. Of such a form was the cat, whose eyes, varying in form like the sun with the period of the

day, imaged to the Egyptian the splendour of
the light.   And thus we have the cat cutting
off the head of the serpent of darkness in the
presence of the sacred Three.   And that symbolism, when its original meaning was lost,
that is, when the knowledge of God was no
longer retained in their science, would naturally
give rise to the foolishness of animal worship.

No less profound was the relation between
the Creator and His works, as intimated in
their well-known symbol for created life, called
the Ank * or Sacred Mirror, wherein every great
deity contemplates perpetually his own image ;
but which is rarely grasped in the hand of any
except Amen.   But how should the universe
be represented by a mirror, and, if it be, why
should the heavenly powers behold themselves

---

* Another signification, that of a fisherman's knot, has
of late been adopted by some authorities ; but the shape
of the knot differs essentially from that of the Ank, the
head of the latter being upright upon the stem.   And
again, how should a fisherman's knot stand upright on
the knees of the gods ? and, if it could, why should it ?

reflected in it? Since Egypt gives only the symbol, but betrays no clue to the secret, the great Master of mediæval philosophy shall declare to us that profound relation, which alters not with the passing of ages. According to the teaching of Aquinas, the universe exists in a twofold manner, first ideally in the mind of God, and secondly materially externally to him, so that in creation the Almighty contemplates His own mind as in a mirror. As a dramatist before he gives living expression to his characters conceives in his own mind their forms, their countenances, their actions, passions, and conditions of life, with all the details of their environment; and as his work reflects the image of the author's mind, so in the theosophy of Egypt did the entire cosmos, embracing all space, all time, and all orders of created being, reflect a single thought in the mind of the Creator.

Man himself therefore had a "double" or

counterpart in the Divine Idea, a sacred "type" of which the festival is celebrated in the Ritual, and which is masonically expressed within the niche of the Chamber of New Birth. Hence it was that the ideal counterpart possessed such divine sanctity, and the monarch offered sacrifice to his own double. For in the intelligible, no less than in the mechanical world, the expressed form is ever the counterpart of the impressed force ; while conversely, in the mechanical world, the material form is due to an immaterial motive-power. For can any mathematician define the very nature of force, otherwise than as that which sets matter in motion ? But if force be that which sets matter in motion, it cannot itself be material, if the fundamental law of motion be true that matter at rest remains at rest. Unless, therefore, the motions of the material universe— and it is of the motions of the heavenly bodies, and not merely of their existence that the Ritual continually speaks—be the result of an immaterial force impressing itself upon matter, our whole conception of dynamical science is wrong from the beginning. And reason itself becomes the mockery of reason ; for there is not an achievement of the engineer, not a prediction of the astronomer, not an application of the mathematician, which does not prove the truth of a principle radically false. So, on the other hand, no philosopher can long maintain any substantiality as underlying the phenomena around him, who does not recognize them as the expression of creative thought impressing itself upon created matter ; nor can poet or artist present new types of character unless he is gifted with the supreme power of the imagination, the faculty of perceiving and defining the unexhausted forms of human personality potentially existing in the sole creative mind. For genius is the power of giving form to potentialities.

Pursue Egyptian theosophy in which direction we may, the things of time speak ever of

eternity, the self-existent Deity is always
secretly reflected in his creatures. Accordingly each phenomenon of nature conveyed to
them a corresponding manifestation of the
divine personality, and according to the Ritual
it was the Deity indwelling in the soul, which
confers upon the man the power of perceiving
these relations. "I am perception," we read,
"the imperishable soul." In the noonday
glow of the sun they beheld the splendour of
Ra; in his setting the death of Osiris; in the
new dawn his resurrection as the incarnate
Horus; in the glowing fire the creator-spirit,
Ptah; in the harmonious proportions of the
universe the Eternal Wisdom, Thoth, "the
mind and will of God;" in the starry firmament crowned by Alcyone and the Pleiades
(the sacred bull and attendant cows) the ineffable beauty of Athor,* the living tabernacle
of the sacred Light.

* Properly Hat-hor, The House of Horus, the Risen
God of Light.

Bearing now carefully in mind the extreme complexity of this secret parallelism, and the strict analogy between the visible and invisible worlds which constitutes the basis of the political organism, we have little difficulty in perceiving the importance of the function in regard to the Hidden God, discharged by the House of Osiris. Viewed independently, the great temples of Egypt present to us a heterogeneous collection of miscellaneous deities, amongst whom now the sun, now the moon, now the earth, now the river, now the orbit, now the horizon, is predominant without any apparent reason or purpose; while the Ritual breaks up into a chaos of broken images and grotesque distortions of astronomical conceptions. Seen by the inner light of the great house, where the Path of the Hidden Places reflects the river of celestial light, the great temple system of Egypt reveals itself as an organic whole with a simple majesty not unworthy of its unrivalled shrines. For since

the chief localities on the material Nile represented the different stages on the Path of
Light, so do the various worships naturally
arise of the spirits exercising the corresponding
functions—somewhat as among ourselves the
water of the Jordan is peculiarly consecrated
to the rite of baptism.   Thus with regard to
Annu, the divine birthplace, reference is constantly made to the new birth; Thebes is
peculiarly connected with Amen, the Hidden
God; while at Memphis, the key of the
organism was the House of Osiris itself.   And
a knowledge of the spirits exercising special
powers in these places, formed a conspicuous
portion of the Ritual in the preparation of the
Initiate for enduring the ordeal.

Had the case been otherwise, indeed; had
the real objects of Egyptian worship been a
mass of deities local and unrelated; then inasmuch as the form of government was well
nigh a pure theocracy, the authority of the
monarch being derived not merely from his

descent but from his personal union with Ra, and inasmuch as heresy was punished with excommunication and even, as M. Maspéro states, with death by fire, it would have been inevitable that each successive dynasty, as it proceeded now from This, now from Memphis, now from Thebes, now from Sais, should have torn up by the roots the religion established by its predecessors; and the annals of Egypt would have been as full of religious discord and confusion as those of our own Tudor princes. History however has produced, so far, but one instance of an endeavour on the part of the king to introduce novelty into the religion. Amenoph IV., who married a foreign princess, adopted the title of Khu-en-Aten,*

---

* I have adopted the translation of the word Khou, given by M. Deveria in the passage above quoted, the hieroglyphs being identical; but the name, according to Mr. Flinders Petrie, is more correctly pronounced Akhenaten. That diligent explorer, in his interesting work on Tel-el-Amarna, the site of the palace built by Khuenaten, on the borders of Middle and Upper Egypt, has abundantly illustrated the theory that the monarch's object

or "Illuminate of the Disc"—a title which,
as we may see, clearly outrages the Ritual
which we have seen embodied in the masonry.
For as the disc of the sun is but its visible
surface, so the "disc" of the tomb was but its
entrance gate which was lifted by Shu (the
Light) "when the sun sets from the world of
life;" and to place the illumination therefore
at that point was to ignore all the grades of
the Postulant, the Initiate, and the Adept, and
to destroy the most essential conditions of
illumination.   In the same way the expression
"Living in Truth," which, as Mr. Petrie points
out, was constantly employed by Khuenaten,

was to substitute the solar disc (Aten) as an object of
worship for the personal Deity—Ra, the Hidden God and
Uncreated Light, Amen—previously worshipped under
various symbols.   This attempt, as well as the distinction
between the disc and the rays—which he also considers
Khuenaten to have introduced—Mr. Petrie characterizes
as a striking advance in philosophical truth : though it
is difficult to understand in what way the adoration of a
material object in place of a Personal and Unseen God
can be philosophically regarded as an advance.

indicates, when applied to the disc, the same
degraded and idolatrous conception, since it
substitutes a material and visible object for
that Truth which in the older worship was
spiritual, interior, and unseen. And thus,
under the succeeding monarch, while the word
Aten was preserved, the offending title, Khu,
was sedulously obliterated.

In the masonic record therefore, the House
of Osiris, we have a key to the whole politico-
religious constitution of the country—a key
which none could imitate, none could alter,
none destroy; which no man could comprehend unless initiated, nor any forget or mistake, who had once received illumination.
Accordingly, in that masonry we find the
originals of many of the mystic symbols,
whereby the priests so expressed the divine
and the royal authority as to be intelligible
to those and those alone who had been initiated
masonically. Thus, if we draw the groove of
the orbit in the Chamber of the Splendour, with

" The Wall of Earth " at the Northern end separating the Orbit from the Shadow, we shall have
the hieroglyph for the orbit "Sennen," which
is identical with the cartouche, ⊂⊐ surrounding the titles of the monarch. That familiar
symbol, by aid of which Champollion first
divined the secret of the writing, is therefore
nothing else than a masonic sign, signifying
that not the circumference, but the immensely
more extensive orbit of the earth is the limit
of the royal authority ; and indicating thereby
(since the orbit implies renewal from age to
age) its endurance no less than its universality. Again, if we represent the course of
the celestial Nile by the rays traced in the
roof of the same chamber, ⋀⋁ we have the
hieroglyph of the river, while the straight
floor-line descending from the throne gives
its hieratic equivalent. So if we draw the

Throne and axis.   Nuter Holy.

great throne in the Hall of Truth with the
central line of the light, running down to
depths of the rock on which it is built, we
obtain the hieroglyph denoting holiness; and
if we add to this the lower portion of the
building, the territory of initiation, there results
the hieroglyph for the territory of the holy
dead.

The Place of the Holy Dead.

Again, suppose that we represent the same
place interiorly by drawing the Well, where
the re-born soul is reunited to the postulant,
together with the line where the interior

Well of Life, Place of Initiation.

masonry is bounded by the natural rock
through which entrance or initiation into the
interior masonry is obtained from below—the

entrance impassable by the postulant until the
soul is restored to him.   Then, if we indicate
the image of the Well itself, shining in its
own living but invisible waters, as seen by
the soul from above, just as the Creator looks
down on His own image in the universe, we
obtain the symbol of the " Ank," or mirror

Ank, Symbol of Created Life.

of life.   So, if we represent the descent
traversed by the Initiate from the Head of
the Well to the Opening into the Chamber

Sceptre of Ptah, Spirit of   Opening from Well of Life to
Divine Fire.   Chamber of Divine Fire.

of the Fiery Ordeal, we have the Sceptre of
Ptah, the Spirit of Divine Fire.   And, if

we represent the passage of the horizon together with the masonry of the entrance, we

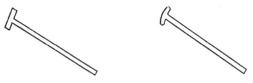

Passage of Pole-star.   Sceptre of Anup.

have the sceptre of Anup, the guide of the
soul.   Sometimes the whole hieroglyphic name
receives illustration at least, if not origination,
from the same pyramidal source ; as, for
instance, in the name of Hapi, the radiant
guardian of the Nile.   For if we draw the
Grand Arch of the highest chamber, imaging
the Grand Arch of the universe, the seat of
that luminous spirit, we shall produce the
initial of that word.   And if we add the
Entrance Gate (itself surmounted by the
Double Arch), together with the scored line
in the Passage of the Horizon, pointing downward to the foundation of the rock, we shall

have the complete set of hieroglyphs which com-
pose his name, and thus masonically
indicate his office as protector of the rock, the
mouth, and the fount of the River of Light.

But by far the most important expression of
these truths is contained in the kalendar, or
recurrent series of festivals, which reflected on
earth the rejoicings of heaven; and a full
understanding of which was one of the glories
reserved in the Ritual for the Illuminate.   By
means of that kalendar the " Mystery-Teachers
of the Heavens " co-ordinated not only the
political but the social life of the nation with
the theosophy of The Light, while through its
masonic expression the divine manifestations
and the personal attributes of the Hidden
Deity were at once communicated to the
instructed and protected from the profane.
To their sense indeed of the divine personality,
far more probably than to any artificial
pretension to a supposed exclusiveness which

does not seem to have had any real existence, may be ascribed the mystery enshrouding their religion.   For mystery is to God only what privacy is to man, our sense of which deepens with deepening intimacy.   And though three hundred years of continuous wrangling over the secret truths which most profoundly affect the heart and mind have gone far to coarsen and deaden our spiritual sense, the soul still resents, as the most unpardonable offence, the profanation of a vulgar touch.   For whether we acknowledge it or not, the springs of our entire existence are hidden.   From the darkness of the womb to the darkness of the tomb, the source of our every action is veiled from us.   Mystery is the beginning ; mystery is the ending ; mystery is the whole body of our life.   We cannot breathe, nor sleep, nor eat, nor move, far less think or speak, without exercising powers which to us are inconceivable, by means of processes which to us are inscrutable.   Who is so ignorant as not to

know these things ; who so learned as to make
them clear ?

Most powerful and most hidden of all is the
passion which grows the more reticent in
proportion as it is more enduring, the passion
which dominates at once the senses and the
spirit ; the master-mystery of Love.   But
Love himself was none other than the hidden
God.   In Greece, where some rays of Egyptian
wisdom penetrated with a brightness denied
to more distant lands, this truth was not
unknown.   Love was the third in the Trinity
of Hesiod.   And in Parmenides we read how
" strife has entered into the deepest places ; but
in the centre Love stands calm."   But in the
teaching of Egypt, the Creator's love so conspicuous in the sublime hymn already quoted,
is the motive power of the universe, the
secret energy of the Light.   " I am the
Inundation," says the Creator in the Ritual—
the fulness of the Torrent of Life.   And
again, " I am the Fount of Joy," the

inexhaustible source of happiness to the soul. Most striking too is the allusion which occurs in another hymn to Amen, where it speaks of the crown of illumination, or " Atf " crown of

" Atf," Crown of Supreme Light, Crown of Illuminate in
Burning Circle of the Orbit.

the monarchs, fashioned after the form of the light which sometimes crowns the Zodiac, the Burning Circle of supreme heaven, before the

Light of Supreme Heaven, Crown of Burning Circle of Zodiac.

summer dawn. That crown, we learn from the Ritual, was placed upon the head of the illuminate on his accomplishing the " passage of the sun," in the ascent of " the orbit," and the hymn proclaims that " North and South of that crown is Love." So when the Illuminate in the masonic Light after ascending the Chamber of the Orbit stood before the throne at its higher end, Northward and Southward of him was Love—to the Northward, the Love manifested in the starry guide which led him to the knowledge of truth in its splendour, and before him the Love concealed in the heights of heaven, the Secret Places of the Hidden God.

CHAPTER IV.

THE MYSTERY OF THE HEAVENS.

OF all the natural images familiar to the
mind none is more radiant, and none more
tranquil, than that of the rolling year as it
circles perpetually about the feet of God.
Even in the midst of cloud and fog, the mere
striking of a clock, that record of planetary
motion, serves to remind us how circumscribed
is the surrounding gloom, and how the dull
earth beneath our feet is, even as we gaze
upon it, shining to its far companions in the
fields of light.   As that lustrous orbit is
woven, revolution after revolution, with never-
failing beauty, cycle after cycle of age-long
periods, like golden serpents, twine themselves

around it, and span the gulfs of time with the years of the Most High.

Such a system of harmonious periods and of measured intervals, corresponding to universal, not arbitrary, standards, was a natural, and indeed an essential, element in the theosophy of a priesthood whose religious teaching was intentionally veiled under the analogies of astronomy.   In examining therefore the astronomical science of the " Mystery-Teachers of the Heavens," * to use the official title employed in the Court of Pharaoh, we may not unreasonably expect to trace the origin and signification of various familiar measures, of which the use is widely diffused, but the fundamental conception unknown. Nor shall we be altogether disappointed in

* For most of the facts here stated with regard to Egyptian astronomy I am indebted to the invaluable researches of the late lamented Dr. Brugsch upon the kalendar, as I am also to his history for quotations from the papyri, and allusions to the customs of the country.

this respect ; while a sudden and vivid interest
will be found to attach to the common units
of time and space, when we perceive that
they are not the fruit of any arbitrary
arrangement, however ingenious, but are the
products of universal concords, and represent,
so to speak, the beats and bars of the music
of the spheres.

That the moon was the sacred and, at
least in early times, the secret standard of

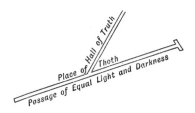

Balance before Thoth.

Egyptian science, there seems little doubt.
Thoth, the Great Lord of Wisdom and of
Measure, the divine recorder, before whom
stood the Balance of Justice, wherein the
light and darkness of man's moral life were

weighed, was lord, not of the sun, but of
the moon ; and to that latter orb we are
indebted for our fundamental standards both
of space and time, as we may easily see,
remembering always that we are dealing with
approximate measures, and " mean," or average motions.   For the position of a heavenly
body is, in general, not the same to an
observer on the earth's surface as it would
be if he were stationed at its centre, which
is the chief point of astronomical reference.
This difference, or parallax, must therefore be
always taken into consideration; and in the case
of the moon, when on the horizon, it is found to
be about * the three hundred and sixtieth part
of the circle of the heavens—that is, a degree ;
and conversely therefore the fundamental measure of the circle is given by the difference
between the moon's apparent position on rising

* It falls short by not quite three (circular) minutes,
or rather less than a seven-thousandth part of the circumference.

at any place as seen by an observer at the
earth's surface, and the position in which it
would appear at the same moment if viewed
by an observer at the centre of the earth.
Equally simple is the fundamental measure
of time, viz. the hour or period required by
the moon in her orbit, relatively to the sun,
to traverse a space equal to her own disc;
and this measure was peculiarly sacred in
Egypt, each hour of the twenty-four which
elapse during a single rotation * of the earth
being consecrated to its own particular deity,
twelve of light and twelve of darkness. "Explain the God in the Hour" is the demand
made of the adept in the Hall of Justification.
And that God in the Hour, we learn, was
Thoth, the Lord of the Moon, and "the
Reckoner of the Earth."

A singular relation of a similar kind exists

* The word "rotation" is always applied in this work
to the motion of a body about its own axis; "revolution," to its motion around another body.

between the lunar period and the risings of
the stars, which was also utilized by the
Egyptian astronomers. For whereas in regard
to the apparent position of the sun, relatively
to the rest of the heavens, the motion of the
earth in her orbit has a perceptible effect;
in regard to the stars, the distances are so
enormous that the orbit of the earth shrinks
into insignificance. The time therefore which
elapses between any two successive risings of
the same star at any given place will, on the
average, be a little less than that between any
two successive risings of the sun at that place ;
since in the first case the time depends only
upon the complete rotation of the place round
the centre of the earth, whereas in the latter,
the motion of the earth's centre during the
interval must be taken into account. This
difference is, on the average, about four
minutes in every twenty-four hours, and will,
therefore, in fifteen days, amount to an hour.
Accordingly, as we learn from a most interesting

paper published by Professor Renouf on a
kalendar of the XIXth dynasty, the observations of the stars were taken every fifteenth
day, thus correlating the sidereal period with
the lunar period of the hour.

Again, the interval which on the average
elapses between the moments in which the
moon successively comes to the full (always
in relation to a given place such as Memphis),
that is to say a lunar month or "lunation" is
about 29½ solar days.   Suppose now we take
as an unit of time thirty such solar days; then
each lunar month would fall short of that
period by half a day or one-sixtieth part, and
the lunar year, consisting of twelve such periods,
would fall short by six days, so that all the
measures would be proportionate.   Here, then,
we possess the key to a most singular correlation between the lunar motions and the solar
months (consisting always of thirty solar days),
which Dr. Brugsch has pointed out in the
Table of Edfu ; which was published in the

days of the Ptolemies, but never, apparently, while a native monarch reigned.   On the first day was celebrated the "conception of the moon," when that orb was on the meridian at noon (while still invisible to the observer)—a refinement unknown to our kalendar; on the second day its birth, or first appearance, and so on throughout the month of thirty days. During the first month, therefore, the lunar intervals would of course correspond more or less precisely with the solar days.   But whereas the two sets would grow progressively asunder, the lunar names remained affixed to the same solar days.   Thus the first day of each solar month was called the conception of the moon, and the second new moon, although neither phenomenon might have taken place anywhere near the time—a method of expression necessitating, it would seem, a double form of register, and simple enough to those who held the clue, but to a stranger hopelessly misleading.

Turning now to the motions of our own
planet we find, as Dr. Brugsch has shown, that
the Egyptian division of the solar, or to speak
more correctly, of the terrestrial year, depended
upon a knowledge of the $365\frac{1}{4}$ rotations
performed by the earth while completing (approximately) one revolution, around the sun—
an extra day being intercalated every fourth or
" grand " year.   But this method of regarding
the matter arises out of our own slovenly
method of expressing astronomical ideas, and
our habitual employment of language embodying the confused and confusing conceptions of the Greeks ; and it by no means does
justice to the Egyptian exactness.   The truth
is that a single year or revolution of the earth
is marked by no cosmic or universal correspondence.   Only in the fourth or " grand "
year, as it was termed, is a harmony established by the simultaneous (or nearly simultaneous) completion of the rotary and
revolutionary motions ; while at the same time

the sun himself, drawing with him the whole
planetary system, completes an arc of his own
mighty orbit, about equal to the whole circuit
of the course of the earth. Accordingly, every
year appears to have included (as it does in
reality) the three hundred and sixty-sixth day.
But adhering strictly to the fact, the last solar
day of the old year was identical with the first
of the new, the day of "completion-beginning;"
except in every fourth or grand year, when
the earth's revolution being completed simultaneously, or very nearly simultaneously, with
a rotation, the two festivals became distinct.
Moreover, since four minutes (of time) a day,
amounts in the course of a year to the time
occupied by a complete rotation of the earth,
it follows that the number of such rotations
or sidereal days in each year exceeds by one
the solar days; the difference being due to
the fact that the change in the earth's position
every twenty-four hours, owing to its orbital
motion, must be taken into consideration

in regard to the sun, but is imperceptible
when compared with the distance of the
stars.   By the method of reckoning therefore, above described, the solar or apparent
days are harmonized with the number of earth's
true rotations.   This being the principle, every
year admitted of division into two portions,
one consisting of an orbit of three hundred
and sixty days, of which the lunar year fell
short by the same number of days as the
solar year exceeded it; the other, that of the
sacred interval or " panegyric," as Dr. Brugsch
applies the term, consisting of six days, each
being a festival of special sanctity.

That orbit again of three hundred and sixty
days, was itself divided not only into twelve
equal solar months, but also into three equal
seasons (each of one hundred and twenty days),
corresponding, as Dr. Brugsch has shown, to the
three great physical divisions of the Egyptian
year—the season of the inundation (" Se "),
commencing with the rise of the Nile, about

the time of the new moon nearest the summer
solstice ; the season of winter (" Pir "), and
the season of heat (" Semou ") answering
more or less to our spring. Hence in every
year the period of three hundred and sixty
days was divided either into three equal
seasons, each containing twelve decades of
days, or into twelve equal months, each
containing three decades of days ; while the
sacred interval bore the same ratio to that
whole period (one-sixtieth) as a minute (of
circular arc) bears to a degree ; and the excess
quarter of a day upon which the whole
arrangement depended bore the same ratio to
the sacred interval (one twenty-fourth) as the
solar hour to the complete day. It is not
unworthy of remark also, that whereas in
the order of the seasons, as corrected by Dr.
Brugsch, their hieroglyphs have no correspondence with the physical year (as Champollion believed to be the case), and appear
therefore to be arbitrary and unmeaning ; yet

when we refer to the course of the soul in the
Ritual, we find them to symbolize three successive stages of its progress; the fields, ⌊ꝑ⌊ꝑ⌉
of Aahlu, into which it comes forth from the
Chamber of New Birth; the Enclosure, ⊏ ⊐
of the Hidden Lintel of Justice, the beginning
of Justification; and the source of the Celestial
Nile, ⋏⋏⋏ where it receives the crown of
Illumination.

For ordinary purposes and comparatively
short periods the reckoning of the Grand
Cycle suffices; but for long intervals the
correspondence is not sufficiently exact; the
real difference each year falling short of a
quarter of a day by nearly twelve minutes,
or the fifth part of an hour (less a certain
number of seconds). But the fifth part of
an hour will, it is obvious, in thirty years,
itself amount to six hours, that is, to a quarter
of a day; and accordingly, every thirty years
we find a special festival or Jubilee celebrated in
the Kalendar of Egypt: thus commemorating

the period said to have been occupied in building the Pyramid of Light. And in five hundred years, or the Egyptian Cycle of the Phœnix, the same difference will amount to between four and five days, that is, very nearly to the sacred interval; so that if that interval be omitted, the orbit of the coming year joins the orbit of the departing, and every five hundred years the Phœnix renews itself. All these cycles therefore centre round the adjustment of the quarter of a day; and so essential an element was that quarter in all calculations relating to the kalendar, that every fourth year, if we may trust Horapollo, the festival was celebrated by the addition of a quarter of an acre to the land belonging to the temples.

Of the three seasons, that of the inundation was the first and principal; and the flood of the Nile ran like a sparkling current through the religion of the country. " I am the Inundation," says the Creator in the sixty-fourth chapter, said to be the oldest of the Ritual, "the Light of the Second Birth." Every stage in the annual flood of the life-giving river was the subject of a special festival. Some little time before the summer solstice, the first symptom of the coming rise was given by the waters in Upper Egypt becoming suffused with a crimson colour. Of this singular phenomenon, which goes by the name of " Red Nile," Herodotus has left a very fine account ; and it is curious to note, as an instance of strong accord between ancient and modern travellers, that his description is quoted at great length by the eminent living Egyptologist, Professor Maspéro. The Red Nile is remarkable in every way ; but in none perhaps more than in the fact that the waters are at that time peculiarly sweet, while at " Green Nile," as another period is called, the reverse is the case. To the former condition, in connection with the midsummer sun, allusion seems to be made in the " Eye filled with blood," mentioned in the Ritual ; and to the

latter in the "intolerable stench" made by
Osiris in the river. About the period corresponding to our month of July, the waters
begin to rise; and the "Sailing of the Bark
of Ra" was celebrated, together with the
birthday of Osiris. A few days later was held
the great Assembly at the Nilometer, or sacred
"Tat," the most venerated symbol known to
their worship; and the first proclamation of
the rise was made. Towards the middle of
August took place the cutting of the Grand
Dyke, whereby the risen stream was permitted
to overflow into private channels; a ceremony
celebrated in more modern times as the
"Marriage of the Nile," but known to the
ancient world as the festival of the "Digging
of the Earth." No less a sanctity, in short,
attached to every phase of that stream of life
than to the "Celestial Nile" itself, of which the
earthly river was the image and counterpart.

It may now be not uninteresting or unin-
structive to compare for a moment the system

of Egypt with our own Leap Year, for which we are, in fact, indebted to that country, through the astronomer Sosigenes, who was imported by Julius Cæsar from Alexandria, to remedy in some degree the confusion of the Roman Kalendar. That famous Greek appears to have performed his task very much after a fashion not unknown to adapters. He cared —perhaps he knew — very little about the astronomical principle involved in the Egyptian reckoning, and nothing at all about the niceties of further adjustment which it demanded ; indeed, before half a century was passed, his own corrections required to be corrected. He took no heed of standard or of measure, of orbit or of sacred interval. But first he cut up the year into twelve unequal and unmeaning bits—to say he divided it into portions is far too scientific an expression—which rags bore indeed the name of the insulted moon, but of which that mighty measurer condescended to make no sort of recognition. And

then he threw the "odd day" in along with
the "odd month"; much as a child, who has
broken his toy-horse, glues a bit of tail to the
shortest of the legs, and calls aloud on creation
to admire his handiwork.

Nor is the difference between the Egyptian
and the alien treatment of the kalendar accidental or unimportant. On the contrary, it
suggests the key to its use in the ancient
country, as the great politico-religious instrument whereby the social economy of the nation
was co-ordinated with theosophy of the priesthood. Among modern nations monotony of
recurrence seems to be the single object
desired, so as to offer every facility for the
arrangements of business or pleasure, and to
confine within the strictest limits the diminutive period allotted to the life to come. Any
system therefore which breaks the regular
routine, more particularly if it be connected,
as in ancient Egypt, with the commemoration
of sacred events, provokes impatience much

more than admiration. And the various adjustments of the kalendar appear to be regarded as if they were odds and ends of time left littering about the heavens by the sun and moon, and requiring an ingenious astronomer—like Sosigenes—to fold together and put away tidily.

Very different from this narrow and ungracious spirit was the joyous temper wherewith the Egyptian " Mystery-Teachers of the Heavens " regarded those sacred intervals. Throughout the symbology of that country, life was the centre, the circumference, the totality of good. Life was the sceptre in the hand of Amen ; life was the richest " gift of Osiris." " Be not ungrateful to thy Creator," says the sage Ptah-Hotep, in what is perhaps the oldest document in existence ; " for he has given thee life." " I am the Fount of Light," says the Creator in the Ritual. " I pierce the darkness. I make clear the path for all ; the Lord of Joy." By them

therefore the intervals were gratefully accepted
as a kind of breathing-space, wherein time,
like the sun at the solstice, appears for a
while to rest, and man, like the immortals,
might enjoy, without impairing, the treasure
of life. Accordingly the panegyric, or time
of praise, separating, or rather uniting year
with year, took place not in the gloom of
winter as with us, but in the full height and
glow of summer ; at the period at once of
accomplishment and renovation, when the sun
was in his fullest strength, and the rising of
the waters of the Nile began to renew their
life-giving floods.   On the first day of the
sacred interval of continuous praise was celebrated the birth of Osiris, the Lord of Light,
Prime Mover of Creation.   On the second,
Horus ; God, of God ; Light, of Light ; the
eldest of creation, to use the expression of the
Egyptian Ritual.   On the third, Seb, Creator-
Spirit of earth.   On the fourth, Isis, with
her double relation of human and divine

motherhood. On the fifth, Neith, from whose
divine personality gushed the stream of life
eternal, who " gave to every mummy the
draught for which he thirsted, that his soul
might be separated from him no more for
ever." And on the sixth day was celebrated
the feast of " Hep-Tep," the crowning festival
of Completion-Beginning.

Such was the symphony of light and joy
which, for the Egyptian, preluded the glowing year ; and such also was its masonic
expression, wherein was struck the full diapason of lunar and solar, of terrestrial and
celestial, of temporal and of spiritual harmony.
As the lunar Chamber of New Birth, the
Habitation of Isis, " the Mother of God " and
the " Queen of the Pyramid," was originally
closed up, thus forming the trebly veiled and
most secret portion of the Hidden Places, so
in the eastern staircase of that chamber we
seem to discover the most secret masonic key,
both to the astronomical form and the spiritual

signification—the exterior and the interior
light. For in its fivefold gradation we have
the correlation of the lunar motion with the
sun, in the five degrees of the moon's ascent
and descent each month from the ecliptic.
Again, since the sacred quarter of a day
whereby the earth's rotation was harmonized
with its revolution exceeds the true period by
(very nearly) twelve minutes ; so in five years
does that annual excess make up $(5 \times 12 =) 60$
minutes, the lunar measure of the hour. And
thus we read in the Ritual of the " Chamber
of the Hour in Rusta," the territory both

Thrones of Isis and Osiris.

of death and birth. In the same staircase,
around the niche or " type," wherein the
regenerate soul is formed — the image of
the Queen of the Pyramid—we have the
fivefold regeneration of the senses ; and in
it too we may recognize, in such a form

as to preserve but not to betray this trebly hidden masonic key, the double throne of Isis and Osiris, pointing not improbably to a yet more secret staircase within.

Even this does not exhaust the fulness of this prolific symbol; but it gives a clue beyond its own immediate recess, and connects the Chamber of New Birth with the luni-solar Chamber of the Orbit, just as the New Birth itself connects Rusta with Aahlu; the place of Initiation with that of Illumination. For in the same ascent in the Chamber of Divine Birth, we have the five divine birth-days, which make up the sacred interval of the solar year. Immediately above is the great throne, crowning the lunar chamber, and masonically expressing the Egyptian "Hep-Tep," or crowning festival of completion-beginning; as the chamber which it surmounts represents the territory of both Death and Birth—the "Completion-Beginning" of mortal Immortality. By the over-lappings

of the roof are formed thirty-six rays or
indentations, marking the thirty-six decades
of the luni-solar orbit. The Southern wall,
impending about one degree North, points
to the Northern boundary of the zodiacal
belt; the lower line of overlapping wall to
its Southern boundary, and between are the
seven planetary spaces, with the groove of the
luni-solar orbit running down the space corresponding to that of the earth.

Still further illustrations of the relations
between our planet and her luminous assistant, as together they describe the doubly-
ruled Orbit of Light, are to be found in this
extraordinary Chamber of the Splendour. As
the wall points secretly to the Northern, and
the inclined floor to the Southern boundary
of the Burning Circle of the Zodiac (about
89° and 152° of North Polar Distance) respectively; so does the inclination of the
roof to the level passage (about 28° 30′)
secretly define the limiting inclination of the

lunar orbit (about 28° 30′) to the sacred plane of equinox. And the fifty-six ramp-stones, twenty-eight on either side of the gallery, give masonic expression to the fifty-six alternations of light and darkness which take place approximately in the period of the moon's rotation, twenty-eight of the ascent and twenty-eight of descent; the double position of the stones, partly horizontal, partly sloping, corresponding with the double attraction of the moon to the earth and the sun ; and the holes in their centres, with the crosses marked above them, indicating the lunar transits over the Grand Meridian of the House of Osiris.

Recurring once more to the Kalendar, it is evident that a system combining so wonderful a harmony with such perfect simplicity could never have been constructed without some definite starting-point in time, a Grand Epoch absolutely defined by some singular conjunction

of the heavenly bodies, and occurring only
after long and clearly measured intervals.
Such an interval is afforded by the famous
Cycle of Sothis, of high antiquity in Egypt,
and peculiar to that country, the principle of
which, being dependent upon the relative
rates of the earth's rotation and revolution
respectively, has by no means been always
thoroughly understood.*

Since the average interval between two
successive risings of a given star at a particular
place is determined only by the period of the
earth's rotation, whereas in the case of the sun
a period of about four minutes must be added,
on account of the motion of revolution in her
orbit during that period, it follows, as we have
seen, that the star will on the average rise at
that place about four minutes earlier every
day, making the round of the twenty-four

---

* As, for instance, by the famous scholar Scaliger, whose
misunderstanding was exposed by Professor Greaves, the
Oxford astronomer, in A.D. 1640.

hours every year.   Consequently there will be
in each year one day when that star will rise
at that place " heliacally," that is to say, just
so long before the dawn as to be visible for a
few moments on the horizon before vanishing
in the increasing splendour.   The position of
the star relatively to the earth and sun at
the moment of heliacal rising we may call its
orient ; and when the position is such as to
coincide with the summer solstice, we may
express that position as the Grand Orient of
the star.   Now the number of degrees by
which the sun is below the horizon when the
heliacal rising of a star takes place, is not
fully determined, and varies to some extent
with the locality ; but ten degrees below is
usually taken as the sun's position when the
star is lost in dawn, so that the time would
be about forty minutes before full sunrise.
Let us consider now the interval between
two such risings of some particular star ; and
for that purpose let us choose, like the

Egyptians, Sirius or Sothis, the most brilliant of the distant suns, the flaming sentinel
to us of the fiery hosts of space. Suppose,
then, that on some particular day (such as
that of summer solstice) Sothis is on the
horizon of Memphis when the sun is eleven
degrees below it, that is, one degree below the
point of dawn. On that day Sothis will rise
heliacally, and will remain visible on the
horizon for about four minutes (while the
earth rotates through one degree), after which
it will be lost in the break of dawn. On the
anniversary of that day it will again be on the
horizon, when the earth completes her 365th
rotation ; that is, when our planet is a quarter
of a degree less advanced in the orbit, since
the full revolution takes $365\frac{1}{4}$ rotations.
Hence, since the earth *rotates* through a quarter
of a degree in a minute (of time), there will
be the difference of a minute in the corresponding rising each year, and therefore of
four minutes each grand cycle. But since

four minutes makes the difference of a day in the star's first appearance, there will for every grand cycle be a difference of a day in the heliacal rising of the star : and consequently in $4 \times 365\frac{1}{4}$ (or 1461) years the whole orbit will be traversed. That lovely cycle, with its tetrachord of starry light just gleaming on the horizon and then vanishing, lost in the growing splendour, appears from the allusions to the dawn to have had its spiritual analogue in the festival of the " Shapes," or divine forms of beauty; when the departed re-created in the divine image rose gloriously from the grave, and shone for a while amid the company of starry spirits, before merging his lustre, though not his existence, in the splendour of the manifested Godhead.

From this highly important cycle we may draw some conclusion as to the grand epoch of the Egyptian Kalendar; the date, that is to say, when mere tradition came to an end, and systematic records, organized upon astronomical

principles, began to be preserved. Since in
the course of the cycle, the heliacal risings
take place on each day of the entire year, they
will run during the first half of the cycle in
one direction (relatively to the earth's orbit)
and in the latter half in the opposite. And
since there is also a corresponding series of
settings, subject to a similar change of direction, the two series would in each cycle
make up a double reversal, interchanging
positions not once but twice. When therefore
Herodotus tells us in a well-known passage
(Euterp. 143), how, according to the Egyptian
records, the risings and settings had been out
of their orders four times since their reckoning commenced; "the risings twice taking
the place of the settings, and the settings
twice taking the place of the risings," the
meaning becomes perfectly clear if referred
(as Rawlinson suggests) to the heliacal risings
and settings of Sothis, the determinator of
the Kalendar. And the very circumstance

that Herodotus himself in all probability did
not understand — and was not intended to
understand—the drift of the extract, strongly
favours its authenticity; since it is very difficult to conceive that a person, ignorant of
astronomy, should so misrepresent a statement
made to him by astronomers, as to blunder by
accident into the correct exposition of a
different astronomical relation. We learn
therefore that two Sothiac cycles (four reversals) had been completed since the institution of the scientific Kalendar; so that the
cycle then current would be the third. And
as there is evidence that that cycle was completed in A.D. 139, and therefore commenced
in B.C. 1322, we conclude that the commencement of the first Sothiac cycle and the
institution of the scientific Kalendar took place
$(2 \times 1461$ years previously, *i.e.*) at the summer
solstice of B.C. 4244; the moment of commencement being marked by the heliacal rising
of Sothis. In chapter lxiv., which describes

the new birth of the soul, and thus supplies
the key to the whole creed, or in its own
words gives "The Entrance on Light in one
Chapter," a passage occurs which appears to
refer to this dawning of another age. "The
twenty-four are passing," it says, "until the
sixth. He remains in the Gate." In the sixth
hour that is to say, reckoning from midnight
(as Professor Renouf has shown to have been
the custom), the march of the stars is stayed,
and the sun enters the Gate of a new cycle ;
in the same way as for the regenerate soul
the night is past, and he enters the Gate of
Everlasting Day.

That the date in question was the true
epoch of the institution of the Kalendar, to
which all astronomical allusions are to be
primarily referred whether in the Ritual or
in the Pyramid of Light, is confirmed by a
simple explanation which is thus afforded
of a very marked peculiarity (and apparent
anomaly) in its use. As is well known, the

"node" or point where the earth at Equinox
cuts the plane of the Equator, and consequently the point of solstice (which is always
90° from that of Equinox), is not invariable,
but year after year falls a little short of
(or precedes) its previous position, so as to
shift round in a direction opposite to the
earth's revolution.   And the rate at which
that precession takes place (about 50″ per
annum) is such as to carry the node, or point
of crossing, round the entire orbit in about
twenty-six thousand years.   Now attention
has been drawn by Dr. Brugsch, who has so
admirably illustrated the ancient kalendar, to
the circumstance that during the later dynasties, a double series of months was employed,
wherein, for instance, "The First of Thoth,"
that is, the first day of the first month, is given
in the time of Thothmes III. (about B.C. 1600)
both on the day corresponding to our 20th of
July, and on the 27th of August, and similarly
with the rest; but he has not offered any

solution.   Suppose now that in addition to
the current date of the solstice the archaic
date was also preserved—a suggestion entirely
in agreement with Egyptian custom and mode
of thought—that is to say, that a record was
kept of the day of the Grand Epoch on which
the earth arrived at the point in her orbit
which she had reached when the kalendar was
defined, then the peculiarity could be explained.   For since the date of Equinox, and
therefore of course of solstice, falls a little
earlier relatively to the orbit every year, the
archaic date will fall a little later.   And as
in twenty-six thousand years it traverses the
circle of the year, and falls again on the
anniversary ; in two thousand six hundred and
fifty years the archaic date would be thirty-
seven or thirty-eight days later ; so that if the
kalendar were founded at the epoch assigned,
the difference between the current and the
archaic date in the days of Thothmes III.
would just correspond to the difference which

we find.   Again, at the commencement of the
third Sothiac cycle, in B.C. 1322, the archaic
date would be later still, on the 29th or 30th
of August.   And this appears to have been
adopted in the later times as the fixed archaic
date, without further variation in the Alex-
andrine Kalendar.

By a similar reference to the archaic date,
we may throw some light on the peculiar
sanctity attaching to certain days of the
month, for which it is otherwise difficult to
account.   For instance, in the Kalendars of the
third Sothiac cycle, the fifteenth and the sixth
of the month appear to be particularly sacred ;
and in the Turin papyrus of the "Book of the
Dead" (the allusions in which would probably
not go back so far as the first cycle, but might
refer either to the second or third), command
is given no less than three times that the
most important festival of the year, the Birthday of Osiris, should be celebrated on the
fifteenth of the month.   But the Birthday of

Osiris was, as we have seen, the first festival of the New Year, and what connection could such a day have with any particular day of any month whatever? A very close connection if the archaic date is to be taken into consideration. At the commencement of the second Sothiac cycle the archaic date of Osiris's Birthday would fall twenty or twenty-one days later than at the foundation of the kalendar; and, remembering the five days for the sacred interval, we reach the fifteenth day of the first month; while a similar calculation, allowing in all forty-one days, brings us in the third Sothiac cycle to the sixth of the succeeding month. For a similar reason another great festival, that of the Bark of Ra, is ordered to be celebrated on the Birthday of Osiris, since at the foundation of the Kalendar that day coincided with the rising of the sacred Nile, the waters of which represent new life.

Hence, in order to preserve a true record of time, it is necessary to note the motion of the earth with reference to four, and only four, different standards; that is to say, in regard to the stars, to the moon, to the sun, and to the Equinox, the other relative motions of the earth having no perceptible effect upon our reckoning of time. All these standards, with their respective measures and harmonies, were known, as we have seen, to the Egyptians; and this accounts for the circumstance which Dr. Brugsch has remarked, that at a very early date the Kalendar of Egypt was kept upon four different reckonings. All these standards also, each with its spiritual signification corresponding with the Ritual, we have seen expressed in the masonry of the Grand Pyramid. For to the architect of the Egyptian Light, there was no celestial truth which was not manifested in the motions of the celestial orbs; nor was there any chamber among the Hidden Places of the Great House which did not secretly reflect the path of the just in the mystery of the heavens.

CHAPTER V.

THE MYSTERY OF THE DEPTHS.

LIGHT is the first principle of created life. There is no life without growth; there is no growth without light. Colour, perfume, savour, every varied object of sense vanishes if light be absent. Each beam is a separate celestial gift, direct from the hand of the Creator; as in the bas-relief on the tomb at Thebes, discovered by Mr. Stuart, where the diverging rays form a pyramid of light, and to each ray is attached a hand of blessing.

Universal too, as is the necessity for light in living nature, equally extended is its manifestation in the form of motion. Wherever life exists, in man or bird, or beast or fish, there also is that power which is denied to inanimate matter—the power to originate motion. To live and move and have our being are three states inseparably connected with each other. Mathematician and poet alike acknowledge the universality of motion in living form. "Motion, fount of beauty," exclaims Pindar in one of his loftiest odes. "All nature is in motion," says Professor Price in his lucid treatise on infinitesimals. So too, the unfailing harmonies of the heavenly bodies express themselves in the periods of their orbits. And through the correlations of those luminous circuits, as through a veil of glory, the correlations of interior truth were shadowed forth by the Egyptian "Mystery-Teachers of the Depths." Depth beyond depth, space beyond space, height beyond height, from the company of planets around our sun, to where the "clusters of countless stars are but a faint nebulous gleam," Light is everywhere the

Omnipotent Creator, the laws of Light the expression of infallible truth.*

But how to seize with material grasp the intellectual relations of the most ethereal element known to man? How imprison in stable form the flashes of the fiery spark as it darts with inconceivable speed from space to furthest space? How render palpable to the direct touch the distant courses of those flying orbs? In a word, how shall we build up the manifestation of Light, and find masonic expressions for the Mystery of the Depths? Light itself gives us a reply. For if, as in the bas-relief at Thebes, the diverging flood

---

* In the same way Moses, who never claims for himself direct revelation in regard to any matter contained in Genesis (though in subsequent books that claim is repeated again and again), and whose fame as an expert in Egyptian science was quoted hundreds of years after his death by St. Stephen in his address to his countrymen, commences his exposition of the Mystery of the Depths by the initiation of Light and Motion. "The Spirit of God moved upon the face of the deep. And God said, Let there be light : and there was Light."

of rays be represented as it pours down at
noon on the day of summer solstice, the opening day of the Egyptian year, we shall have
one face of the Pyramid of Light. Suppose
now that a quadrangular pyramid be erected
with four such sides facing respectively the
cardinal points of the heavens. Then since
each revolution of the earth is completed by
one quarter of a rotation later than the preceding, it follows that every fourth or grand
year the same face will be turned towards
the sun when the revolution of the earth is
accomplished; and thus the Egyptian Grand
Cycle (of four years) will be masonically expressed. Just such a form is found in the
quadrangular Pyramid of Light, its sides so
oriented as to have originally faced the
cardinal points, and its summit so truncated
as to permit the sun on one day in the
year to rest upon it " with all its rays,"
so that the building " devours its own
shadow."

The general form determined, what proportions shall the dimensions assume, or in other
words, at what angle shall the sides converge
towards the invisible vertex? The earth in
her orbit gives reply. For as that planet
moves around the sun in an (approximately)
circular path, while each ray travels towards
it in a direct line, the relation between the
illuminating force and the illuminated body
may be expressed by the relation between the
radius and the circumference of a circle. But
this relation is such that the altitude of a
pyramid when bearing the same ratio to its
base-circuit subtends an angle of about 51° 50'.
And that is the Angle of Elevation of the
Grand Pyramid. Nor is this most important,
and indeed dominating, measure due to accident; since the angle in question is the most
marked, and almost the only feature, which
the lesser and later Pyramids share with the
Pyramid of Light, so that it forms the
masonic sign whereby the inferior buildings

tacitly asserted their kinship with the Great House.

Although however, these general aspects of the radiance suffice to determine the general aspect of the building, yet a closer investigation of the light will disclose a more intimate relation. For since our atmosphere may be conceived as divided into successive layers of air, increasing in density as they approach the earth, each ray as it travels will be slightly deflected, or refracted, as it passes from a finer to a denser ring, the refraction being greatest when the body is on the horizon, and imperceptible when it is near the zenith. Conversely, if on any given day the position of the sun be observed at equal intervals from rising to noon, and from noon to sunset, the apparent place of the sun will, owing to refraction, be slightly different from its true position at any observation ; and a diagram representing their mutual relations will offer the appearance of a house having many stories, with a small platform at the summit, since near the zenith the true and apparent positions are identical (and the only motion is that of transit)—that is to say, we shall have the appearance of the Grand Pyramid when the casing-stones are removed.

If then, on the first day of the (Egyptian) new year—when the sun is about fourteen hours visible above the horizon at Memphis —an observation be taken every two minutes (four observations for the period occupied by any ray in reaching the earth from the sun) there will be altogether about four hundred and forty observations, making two hundred and twenty courses of ascent and descent, of which a certain number will be wanting at the top since at the zenith there is no refraction.   But this is precisely the case in the Pyramid of Light ; the number of existing courses being

about two hundred, and the number required
to complete it reckoned at about twenty more.
Further, since the moon in every two minutes
of time completes a (circular) minute of her
circuit relatively to the sun, and since at the
commencement of every Sothiac cycle she
commences a new lunation and comes (invisibly) to the meridian at the same time with
the sun at noon, it follows that these unit-
intervals of observation correspond with the
minute-intervals of her motion ; and each
course of the Grand Pyramid corresponds to
the change in the altitude of the sun for one
circular minute of the moon's motion relatively
to that body.

The true and apparent forms of the Grand
Pyramid being thus determined by the true
and apparent motions of light, we have now
to inquire with what scale we are to build up
the chambers of the house. The rolling earth
once more suggests the standard. The cosmic
unit of space—the Sceptre of Anup, the Guide

of the Horizon of Heaven—must be clearly
defined, and incapable of confusion; it must
be self-evolved, and yet immutable; it must
be within man's power to compass, but not
within his grasp to alter. Now these conditions are fulfilled by one line, and one only
known to man, the polar axis of the earth—the
line, that is to say, about which takes place
the earth's daily rotation, while itself performs
the annual circuit around the sun. Let that
line be carried far as the eye can follow or
thought can reach, the depths through which
it pierces remain for us for ever at rest.
That is the line which directs the axis of the
Sacred Horizon of the Point of Equinox, and
which indicated to the mind of Egypt the
entrance path for the holy departed as they
passed from the created to the Uncreated Light.
A beautiful allusion is made in the Ritual to
the illuminative action of the sun in reference
to this double motion of the axis, as the earth,
the vessel of God, performs her daily and

annual course in the heavens. For we read there how the holy departed " has appeared in the Bark of Ra in the course of every day ; " and how Thoth, the Divine Wisdom, " clothes the spirits of the justified a million times in a garment of true linen ; " of that substance, that is to say, which by its purity and brilliancy reminds us of the mantle woven out of rays of light wherewith the sun enwraps the earth afresh each day she rotates before him, just as the soul of man is invested with new radiance each time that he turns to the presence of his Creator.

How then shall we avail ourselves of this mighty measure, this rule of light and standard of space ?   This time the building itself answers through its familiar title.   According to Dr. Brugsch, the term Pir-am-us in Egyptian signifies the EDGE ; and on examining the base-circuit of the building, we find it to be composed of casing-stones with a bevelled horizontal edge, so exquisitely finished that,

according to Mr. Flinders Petrie, it is equal
" to the finest work of the optician." On the
occasion of the visit of the Empress Eugénie
to Egypt, in 1869, one of these casing-stones
was measured *in situ* by Mr. W. Dixon, and
found to contain just 25·025 British inches.
But the relation of this length to the polar
radius (or semi-axis) of the earth is of the
very last importance in universal measurement.
Several years ago Sir John Herschel pointed
out that our inch is contained in the earth's
polar radius just 250,250,000 times; so that if
that unit be increased by its thousandth part
(less than the fineness of the finest hair) it will be
contained in the polar radius just two hundred
and fifty million times. Since therefore this
stone contains twenty-five inches so increased,
it measures the earth's polar radius exactly ten
million times; and as the Egyptians were
certainly familiar with the decimal system,
expressing units, tens, hundreds, thousands,
and millions by distinct hieroglyphs, this stone

in the base circuit of the Great House supplies a simple masonic unit of cosmic length, a standard of universal measurement.

Were this ratio an isolated instance, some question might not unnaturally arise as to the accidental nature of the connection; but the intention of the architect is strongly confirmed by the kindred discovery due to Mr. Flinders Petrie. That acute observer has pointed out that the length of the raised pavement was a simple measure (one-twentieth) of a geographical mile. And since a geographical mile is a measure of the earth's circumference at the Equator, a knowledge of it implies a knowledge of the measurement of the polar radius.

Striking however as is the ratio which this stone bears to the cosmic standard, its relation to the Pyramidal Edge, of which it forms a part, is no less prolific of universal results. For, taking as the length of that base-line,*

---

* These results are as follows, expressed in our inches :—

the average of the results obtained by the
principal surveys executed since the great
Napoleon opened the dull eyes of Europe to
the inexhaustible treasures of ancient Egypt,
we find that the casing-stone is contained in
the line so measured just 365·25 times, and
consequently in the entire circuit $(4 \times 365\frac{1}{4})$
1461 times.   Hence, as the form suggests the

French Commission	9163
Colonel Howard Vyse	9168
Professor Smyth	9110
Royal Engineers, 1st survey	9130
„ 2nd „	9140
Mr. F. Petrie	9126
Mean	9140

This length differs therefore from that obtained by Mr.
Flinders Petrie. But, as for some reason, which is not
very clear, Mr. Petrie allows no less than $4\frac{1}{2}$ inches for
each socket to "play," a most extraordinary condition,
surely, in the case of workmanship "equal to the finest
work of the optician," it is difficult to place our usual
reliance on his accuracy. The average here taken, it will
be observed, of the whole results coincide precisely with
one of the measurements, and also with the mean of the
greatest and least.

Grand Cycle, so also does the measure of the
base-circuit; the number of times the cosmic
unit is repeated in that circuit, defining the
number of solar days in the Grand Cycle, and
consequently also the number of the solar
years in the cycle of Sothis.

It seems, therefore, not unreasonable to
conceive that before the casing-stones finally
shut up the secret, the relations of the sun and
moon to the position of Sothis and of the
pole-star should have been correlated with the
courses of the Pyramid in the manner above
described; and thus a starting-point for all
the motions of the earth, whether in relation
to the moon, the sun, the equinox, or the
stars, have been registered unalterably in the
masonic light.

To measure the motions of the earth however is the commencement, but only the
commencement, of the universal scale. That
which we need for the Mystery of the Depths
is nothing less than the span of solar or

measurable space. In other words, we require
to define the extreme limits on either hand
within which no fount of original light is
found except our own sun, since the distances
of the stars are beyond accurate measurement.
But the distance of the limiting point of solar
or measurable space, or rather the radius of
the limiting horizon (since the distance will
be the same in every direction) is about
twenty-five hundred million times the length
of the earth's polar axis; so that that axis is
contained in the radius of measurable space
two hundred and fifty times as often as itself
contains the edge of the casing-stone. Now,
if that casing-stone be divided into twenty-
five equal parts, each of such parts will, as
we have seen, contain our own inch increased
by its thousandth part. This unit, therefore,
which we may call the polar inch, measures
not only the axis of the earth, but of the
depths of solar or measurable space, being
contained in the former two hundred and fifty

million times, and in the latter two hundred
and fifty thousand billion times.   But in that
ancient chapter of the Ritual (lxiv.) which
claims to have been revealed in the days of
the IVth dynasty, we read that the Creator,
when revealing Himself to the new-born
soul as the Measurer of space, employs this
very ratio as standard.   " ' I who know the
Depths' is my Name," so runs the text of
this sublime chapter; " I make the cycles of
the shining millions of years; and billions are
My measurement." *

The mention of these cycles of the shining
years suggests a principle of singular beauty,
as the key to the architectural measures of
ancient Egypt.   Among the many valuable
results due to the industry of Mr. Flinders
Petrie is a collection of cubits of various
lengths, employed by the architects of the

---

* In the original : " Ari Kherti Khuu aha pu tefnut
pu krastuf."   The translation above given differs slightly
both from the version of Dr. Birch and that of M. Pierret.

IV^(th) and XI^(th) dynasties. These architectural
units are very numerous, and, unless referred
to cosmic principles, quite miscellaneous, having no apparent co-ordination either among
themselves or with anything else. When
however taking as our unit the polar inch,*
we compare them with the measures of light,
as expressed in the shining circuits and radii
of the celestial periods—remembering always
that the radii and semi-radii of the cycles of
years are both consonant with the angular
construction of the Pyramid and are secretly
involved in the analogy of Illumination—we
find a most remarkable correspondence in
measure after measure, not absolute indeed,
but different only by decimals of an inch.

Take for example, the number of polar

* This inch is of course the same as that adopted by
Professor Smyth, and called by him the " Pyramid Inch ; "
but he has so inextricably associated that name with views
directly opposed to Egyptological research, that I prefer
to use an expression which denotes an undoubted relation,
first pointed out by Sir John Herschel.

inches into which the casing-stone is divided, when considered as a measure of space, viz. twenty-five; a close approximation to which is found in two specimens * belonging to the IVᵗʰ dynasty, which were discovered at Ghizeh —that is to say, which were employed in the neighbourhood of the Grand Pyramid about the time of its erection. Again, taking as unit the semi-radius of the cycle of Equinox, the radius of which cycle is about 4122 years, and expressing an inch to a century, the half of it gives us the cubit of 20·6 inches; and this measure is the more common form of the Egyptian cubit, the standard employed for the sacred "Tat," or Nilometer, which measured the waters of life, the symbol regarded as the

* Mr. Petrie maintains this cubit to be "evidently an Egyptian edition of the royal twenty-five inch cubit of Persia;" but why a Persian cubit should be employed at Ghizeh, or what we know of Persia some thousands of years before the time of Darius, he does not tell us. It is difficult to see why he might not with equal reason pronounce the Capitol of Romulus to be "evidently an Italian edition of the Capitol at Washington."

highest expression of sanctity, and the final
ornament placed upon the holy dead. From
the moon also we (approximately) obtain two
standards of Egyptian measure. For the number of days in a lunar month gives closely, at
an inch for a day, the 29·3 inch cubit of the
IVth dynasty. And, at an inch for a year,
the number of years (about 18·6) in the cycle
of the lunar nodes—(that is, the interval
which elapses between two successive crossings
of the equinoctial plane by the moon at precisely the same point of her orbit)—yields
(very nearly) the 18·7 inch cubit of the XIIth
dynasty. And, once more, since the orbit of
the earth is not strictly a circle, but an
ellipse with the sun in one focus, there will
always be one point in the orbit which will
be in " perihelion," that is, nearer the sun
than any other. And this point is not
stationary, but makes a circuit of the earth's
orbit in about 114,000 years ; whereof the
half-circuit gives us the fifty-seven inch cubit

of the XIth dynasty (at an inch to ten thousand years), and the quarter radius the forty-five inch cubit of the IVth dynasty (at an inch to a thousand years). It would seem therefore, that a table of the cubits employed by the architects of those early times would represent a general system of cosmic measures, the scale being marked off upon the axis of the earth, the sole standard of immutable space, and the ratios of the different cubits being proportional to the immutable time-periods of the heavenly bodies. And thus, when the film is brushed away which the dust of ages has cast over these relics of antique science, their aspect remains no longer lifeless and repulsive ; but we recognize in them the glowing insignia of universal truth, the gems from the azure depths, sparkling with the lustre of intrinsic light.

No sooner do we apply this key to the Book of the Master, than a series of concealed significations begins to unclose. The famous

Urœus, or symbol of the snake—connected in some not very definite manner with solar phenomena—has always been intimately associated with the royalty of Egypt. But it appears to have escaped attention that in the Ritual are to be found several serpentine forms of various lengths, and—what is most striking in itself but easily explained by the results already attained, — that when those several lengths are expressed in inches, they prove to be proportional to the measures of the various serpentine curves traced by the motions of the earth and moon. For instance, in chapter cxxx., we read of "a snake seventy cubits in his coil." But taking the well-known cubit of 20·6 inches and repeating it seventy times, we obtain one thousand four hundred and forty-two inches; which is proportional (within the seven hundredth part) to the number of minutes of time (24×60) in the average daily rotation of the Equator or coil of the snake ; so that it expresses our own division of the heavens into twenty-four hour-circles, each divided again into sixty equal parts or minutes of time; both which measures, we have already seen, were familiar to the Egyptians. Moreover the number of the sun's rotations about his own axis is, approximately, one hundred and forty-four in a period of ten years, so that the snake expresses an axial motion common both to the sun and its satellite : and appears therefore to be "the chief Urœus, gleaming and guiding millions of years," of which we read in chapter xxxiv. On the other hand, in another passage of the chapter previously mentioned, an extent of seven cubits gives the length—not of the snake's coil but—of his back : and this length (one hundred and forty-four inches) just gives the back of the tropical snake, or spiral, that is, the distance of the sun at solstice from the Equator, at that epoch about twenty-four degrees, or one hundred and forty-four decades of circular minutes. Other examples of a more complex character might be adduced ;

but these may be sufficient to show that in
the inch we possess a clue to the secret significance of numerous symbols; and that for
very reason it was not openly set forth as the
standard, but its place was supplied by the
cubit, which betrays no meaning except to
one already so far initiated in the Mysteries
of the Depths.

Turning now to the Pyramid of Light, we
find the same principle conspicuous throughout
the building; the lengths of its various
passages and chambers, when expressed in
polar inches, being apparently proportional to
the radii (or semi-radii) of the celestial periods
corresponding respectively to the stages in the
progress of the departed. And so strongly
marked is the prevalence of this principle, that
while a mere knowledge of the measures, however exact, suggests nothing of the spiritual
meaning, the insight which we have already
attained into the co-ordination of the building
with the Ritual enables us to determine for

ourselves the dimensions of many of the parts. For throughout the teaching of Egypt progress in Light is effected by increased instruction and experience in Truth; and in the Wisdom of that ancient country, the measures of Truth were the years of the Most High.

At the very point of entrance, indicating the sacred horizon of the pole-star (as the hieroglyph of the star signifies the invisible world), we find that a consideration of the particular position occupied by the star, when in conjunction, so to speak, with the Pyramid, widens and elevates our view from an earthly to a celestial plane. For though to a dweller on our globe the great plane of reference is the plane passing through the celestial poles and containing the horizon of the point of Equinox; yet when we proceed to regard our companion orbs, circling around the same parent luminary, and when we take into account the influence which those members of the same luminous family exert upon each

other, we are compelled to recognize what is
called the Invariable Plane of the Planetary
System, the plane, that is to say, about which,
as La Place demonstrates, certain highly important relations between the masses and the
motions of the planets are always fulfilled.
Now this plane has never a greater inclination
than about 3° 6′ to the apparent ecliptic, that
is, the plane of the orbit of the earth.   But that
arc (3° 6′) measures within a few minutes the
distance of the pole from the pole-star when
in conjunction, so to speak, with the Grand
Pyramid.   When therefore the pole-star shines
down the entrance passage, its position in
regard to the pole (due allowance being made
for corrections), defines the limiting position
of the invariable plane to the plane of the
orbit.

Similarly in regard to the inconceivably
slow variation * in the inclination of the axis

* See the table and memoir published by the Smithsonian Institute of Washington.

to the ecliptic, a variation which, while never exceeding $2\frac{1}{2}°$ on either side, requires no less than thirty thousand years to accomplish. And from this majestic depression and elevation of the polar axis in its course around the sun— the inexpressibly stately obeisance made by the sceptre of Anup before the throne of Ra— we may determine relatively to each other the inclinations of the interior passages. The difference between the limits of the solstices (calculated at about $2°\ 22'$) gives the difference between the inclination of the roof and of the floor-line of the Grand Gallery, or Chamber of the Orbit, while the inclination of that roof to the level passage leading to the Lunar Chamber of New Birth ($28°\ 30'$) defines, as we have already seen, the limiting inclination of the moon to the Equator. The variation during one Sothiac cycle corresponds with the difference between the floor-lines of the upper and lower galleries. And if we may place the completion of the building at B.C. 3732 (only a generation earlier than the estimate of Dr. Brugsch, which is not designed to be exact), then, since it occupied thirty years building, the number of years from the foundation of the Kalendar to foundation of Pyramid will be about four hundred and eighty-two ; that is, will correspond with the number of inches between the entrance and the scored line which points to the foundation ; while the interval between the foundation of the Kalendar and the co-ordination of the Pyramid with the pole-star (viz. about eight hundred years), the difference during the inclination (about 4'), corresponds closely with the difference between the inclinations of the Lower Ascending Gallery and the Passage of the Pole-star : so that to such as understood the meaning of that inclination, the periods of the star's co-ordination with the entrance would be foreknown. If this were the principle employed—and considering the difficulty of obtaining exact measures, the points of correspondence are surprisingly close—none could understand the relation of the star to the building without first understanding the masonic relation embodied in the edifice, between the standard of space, as represented in the entrance passage, and the solar throne at the head of the Grand Gallery or Chamber of the Orbit. Nor could any one be instructed in that secret by the Master without acquiring masonic evidence of its truth, in the Path of the Horizon of Heaven, and its orientation with the hidden interior—the beginning and the ending of the Ritual of Light.

Penetrating now to the innermost recesses of the Hidden Places, let us review the celestial significance which we have attached to the various chambers, and (remembering always that we are dealing with approximations) let us note the proportion of their measures to the corresponding celestial periods ; the celestial unit varying in each case according to the nature of the celestial cycle (and demanding

in each case therefore a knowledge of the
connection of the Ritual with the particular
chamber) ; while the masonic unit throughout
is the polar inch, the twenty-fifth part of the
Pir-am-us, or edge of the base-circuit casing-
stone, the twenty-fifth ten-millionth part of
the polar radius of the earth, and the twenty-
fifth thousand-billionth part of the radius of
solar space. For "millions and billions are
the measure of things."

Commencing with the highest and most
secret source of life and light, the Eternal and
Self-Begotten Energy of the Hidden God, we
find it illustrated in the never-ceasing rotation
of the sun about its own axis, the energy of
which we know not the origin, and to which
we attribute the birth of the planets.   Of
such rotations about two thousand five hundred
and twenty-five are performed by the sun,
while the earth is performing one hundred
thousand similar rotations, and that number
gives the number of polar inches in the height

of the extreme point of the huge granite triangle * which dominates the secret places of the interior. Descending thence to the King's Chamber, where the birth of the Eternal Day is celebrated in the open tomb of Osiris, we have recourse to the measure of light, not in its interior energy, but in its emission ; and find that the cubit proportional to the radius of the cycle of equal Light and Darkness (20·6 inches) is a measure of that chamber, as it is also of the Chamber of the New Birth of the Soul.

As we proceed towards the outer portion, the manifestation of the splendour defines the proportions of the Chamber of the Orbit, the Upper Hall of Truth, where so many lunar and solar phenomena have already been noticed. At the head of that chamber is the great

* This is the number given of British inches ; and the correction for their conversion into polar inches will about be counter-balanced by the thickness of the granite apex.

throne, " the stone of God," to use the expression of the Ritual, surrounded on every
hand by masonified radiance.   The seat of
that throne (about 61·3 inches) measures the
number of times the radius of the earth is
contained in the radius of the orbit of the
moon ; while its height is proportioned to the
number of decades in the orbit of the Egyptian
year, the five divine birthdays being expressed
in the Chamber of New Birth immediately
beneath.   Above that throne at the higher end
of the chamber rises the seven-pointed arch of
the planetary heavens, its boundary lines defining the flaming belt of the zodiac.   And from
its foot runs downward the floor-line ascended
by the Illuminate, and measured by the radius
of the cycle of perihelion, or Circle of Nearest
Approach, formed by " the Assembly of Ministers of Truth," but along the midst of which
none might pass save the Illuminate alone.
And if we may estimate the distance of Sothis
(whose chamber lies beyond) to be 1,374,000

instead of 1,375,000 times the distance of the sun, the number of thousands of hours occupied by light in reaching us from that star (between 1881 and 1882), will be defined by the number of polar inches in the continuous floor-line of the Grand Gallery (1881–2) ascended by the Illuminate before passing to Sothis ; while the integral years (21) in the same period gives the number of the Gates of Aahlu corresponding to the (21) Stages of Judgment traversed by him in ascending the same Chamber of the Splendour.

As we descend yet further towards the outer world, the Chamber of the Shadow, where Truth is manifested in darkness, with its Seven Halls of Death leading upwards from the Hidden Lintel, and its final projection into the Place of Light (1561 inches), is measured by the number of lunations in seven cycles of eclipse $(7 \times 223 = 1561)$. And finally, as the Horizon of the Point of Equinox determines the entrance for the departed to the path of

light ; so does the radius of the equinoctial
cycle (about 4122 years) determine the descent
of the entrance passage (about 4122 polar
inches) on the side of the west, where " the sun
sets from the land of life."

With this brief survey of the celestial
periods and their masonic analogues, we take
up once more the Book of the Master, and approach the House of the Hidden Places, wherein
are concealed the Mystery of the Heavens and
the Mystery of the Depths. In every standard,
every unit, angle, ratio and multiple employed
by the great Architect of the Masonic Light,
we have seen reflected the proportions of the
house not made with hands, eternal in the
heavens, the house which the divine Horus
built for his father Osiris ; the " House of the
Great God," to which, as the papyrus of Amen-
Hotep tells us, Thoth, the Eternal Wisdom,
conducts the Illuminate. And as we gaze
around in silent contemplation, from every
corner of the universe the profound words of

the Ritual come echoing back to us : " Millions
and billions are my measurements. ' I who
know the Depths ' is my name."

NOTE ON CERTAIN MEASURES AT BABY-
LONIA AND EARLY CHINA.

Since, supposing the views put forward in the foregoing chapters to be correct, the Egyptian measures of ·
time and space are certainly the oldest on record, it may
not be amiss if, before passing to the inner mysteries, we
compare with them two other famous systems of antiquity,
and observe how certain anomalies which have hitherto
been incapable of explanation, become simple and intelligible when regarded as misconceptions of the Egyptian
reckoning. Take, for example, that of Chaldæa. That
the Babylonian astronomers measured their time by
periods of 60, of 600, and of 3600 years (the *soss*, the
ner, and the *sar*) is well known, and that they also divided
the circle into degrees, and again into sixty and sixty
times sixty measures. But upon what principle they
chose the sexagesimal measure, and whether they regarded
the two sets of multiples as possessing any connection
with each other, is not so clear. According to Lenor-
mant, they calculated their periods "on the great
astronomical cycle of 43,200 solar years, representing,

according to their calculation, the total period of
the precession of the Equinoxes" (!)—a theory which,
if true, does not say much for their astronomical
skill.

There is, however, another cycle, closely connected
with that of precession, which, while suggesting the
sexagesimal measure, will be found to yield a convenient
unit for both divisions. For since the two points of
perihelion and Equinox revolve gradually in opposite
directions, they will increase their distance from each
other every year by the sum of their annual movements,
which is reckoned at about $61.9''$, and is called the
Anomaly. Hence, neglecting the decimal of the second,
and remembering that $61'' = 1' 1''$, and $61' = 1° 1'$, we have
the following table :—

		Period.	Anomaly.
For	1 year	$= 1' 1''$
		$= 1$ (Circular) Min.
		$+ \frac{1}{60}$th Min.
1 Soss =	60 years	$= 1° 1'$
1 Ner = 10 Soss =	600 years	$= 10° 10'$
1 Sar = 6 Ner = 60 Soss =	3,600 years	$= 61°$
Half Cycle = 6 Sar = 36 Ner = 360 Soss =	21,600 years	$= 366°$
		$= 360° + 6°$
		$=$ Circle $+ \frac{1}{60}$th Circle.
$= 60 \times 60$ Anomaly for 6 years.

Now, as the cycles of precession and perihelion are
involved in the construction of the Egyptian measures,
so also would this cycle (which is a mere deduction from
the other two) also be known ; and, in fact, we find
standards of lengths in Egypt corresponding to this
cycle as to the others. Suppose then, that some visitor

or half-educated native should acquire a smattering of
the astronomy, so far as to obtain the measure of one
cycle and the name of another; then we should have the
confusion between Anomaly and Equinox contained in
the Babylonian measures. And suppose again, that the
same ingenious inquirer should hear, without understanding, of the double reckoning involved in the Sothiac
cycle; and in order to make things quite correct, should
apply it to the period he had devised for precession; then
we should have the 43,200 years $(2 \times 21,600)$ above
described. Whether or not this be the explanation, a
remarkable example of a very similar misconception is
supplied by the orientation of their buildings. For, as
the late Professor De Lacouperie pointed out, their cardinal points, though relatively correct, are all shifted
through one-eighth of a circle, their South really being
South-West. And this, it will be easily seen, is precisely
what would be done by any one who, having obtained his
notion of the cardinal points in Egypt without understanding the principle, should imagine them to be fixed,
and should use the Egyptian points while dwelling in
Babylonia.

Such an origin is quite in agreement with other points
connected with Babylonian civilization. That certain
of their principal measures, such as the standard of
Telloh, were derived from Egypt is undoubted. And
their tradition that the elements of their civilization were
imparted by Oannes, half man and half fish, who retired
every night into the sea, just answers the description of
an immigrant sailing up the Persian Gulf from the Eastern
coast of Egypt, and retiring to his ship each night; while

such a course itself would be a natural continuation of the course pursued by the ancestors of the Egyptians in their emigration from Poont in the South.

Far to the Eastward again, a problem, or rather a whole set of problems, given up for many centuries by the native archæologists, receive simple solution when we apply the same principle to the ancient Kalendar of China. From a highly interesting paper read in the Victoria Institute by the Rev. Dr. Legge, University Professor of Chinese at Oxford, and prince of Sinologists, we find that after the ninth century before the Christian era, the Chinese year was divided into periods of sixty days. These days were expressed in writing by means of two classes of characters, called respectively the ten heavenly stems and the twelve earthly branches, which were taken together in pairs, each branch being taken with each stem, but the stem always preceding, never following, the branch ; whereby each day of the cycle was represented by a different pair. And he observes that the sexagesimal cycle was of extreme antiquity, and that "how it arose is a mystery ; but that he would make little account of that if he could tell from whence the inventors got the component parts, the ten stems and the twelve branches." But a reference to the far more ancient Egyptian Kalendar naturally suggests the sexa-gesimal measure ; while the sixty alternations of light and darkness which constituted the Egyptian month easily resolve themselves in foreign hands into a period of sixty days. Again, the two hieroglyphs which express the year, the stem ("Se") for its totality, and the branch (Apu-ter) for its commencement, supply the titles of the characters; while the number of days in the sacred decade give the ten heavenly stems, and the number of months in the civil year the twelve earthly branches. There seems therefore little difficulty in conceiving that the elements of the Eastern calculations may have been obtained from that more central and far more ancient civilization, particularly if we consider, as many now admit, that the elements of religion and of science were first imported into China from the head of the Persian Gulf (the direct route from Egypt) * by the famous tribe which bore the name of Bak; which in the hieroglyphic signifies the land of Egypt.

Turning now for a while from Professor Legge's valuable paper to the oldest of the religious books of China, the Shu King, of which he has himself given a translation to the world, we are met by more than one passage referring unmistakably to a superior condition of culture formerly enjoyed and irrecoverably lost. At the end of

---

* The late Professor De Lacouperie, to whose labours is chiefly due the tracing of a connection between the civilization of China and the Bak tribe (proceeding, not from Babylonia itself, but from the country immediately to the Eastward of it), has detected a certain resemblance, in a considerable number of instances, between the archaic characters employed by the two countries. But if a further comparison be made with the corresponding characters of Egypt, the Chinese will be found to resemble the latter with at least equal, if not greater closeness, a circumstance which seems to point to a common origin from the source more ancient than either. And an immigration, it is to be observed, from the country East of Babylonia into China would be a natural continuation of an emigration to the head of the Persian Gulf; just as the latter course would be a natural continuation of the original migration from Poont.

the third Book the chiefs lament the loss of the " Standard Stone and the Equalizing Quarter,* formerly preserved in the treasury." A standard stone kept in the royal treasury as a reference for weights and measures is intelligible enough, and reminds us of the allusion in the Egyptian Ritual to " the Stone from the building of those who possess the Ark of Osiris." But an " Equalizing Quarter ! " A quarter of what ? And what did it equalize ? We know indeed of one quarter—a quarter of a day by which in the older country the rotations of the earth were equalized or harmonized with its revolutions, and which served as a standard for all manner of periods and measures. And this very quarter suggests at once a connection with the Standard Stone, since that stone itself, the throne of Ra in the House of Osiris, crowning the Chamber of the five Divine Birthdays, and containing the measure of the thirty-six sacred decades, represented the " Hep-Tep " or sacred Festival of Completion-Beginning, involving the secret of the Grand Cycle, and the equalizing quarter of a day.

That such a quarter had been lost we have proof from another part of the same sacred books of China. About

---

* Professor De Lacouperie, who favoured me with a discussion on this subject, pointed out that Midleton translates this expression simply by the general word " measure." To this I have no reply to make, except that Professor Legge is a very high authority, and that he can scarcely have been unacqainted with that translation. The expression, moreover, seems to speak for itself, for it is just of that peculiar character which no translator would be likely to assign gratuitously, while a very able scholar might fail to render it with precision.

twenty-two or twenty-three centuries before the Christian era, and some fourteen or fifteen hundred years before the earliest extant trace of the Chinese Kalendar, the Emperor of China was seized with a fit of archæological fervour, and instituted the first historical records of that country of which any traces remain. One result of his researches had an unfortunate effect upon certain of his subjects. Filled as he felt himself to be with the ancient wisdom, he summoned his astronomers and laid down to them the broad and simple principle that every year consists of three hundred and sixty-six days—a statement which is, as we have seen, more strictly correct than three hundred and sixty-five days if understood properly and as the Egyptians understood it ; but which, without the secret either of the sidereal day or of the Grand Cycle, inevitably leads to calculations which events would refuse to verify. Accordingly it is not surprising that the unlucky astronomers when next engaged in predicting an eclipse went altogether wide of the mark. But the Emperor rose to the occasion. He had been, he said, "searching into antiquity," and had no doubt what was due to so gross an ignorance of their office. Everything, he observed severely, "had been done which ought to have been done. The tom-toms were beaten ; the petty officers galloped ; the inhabitants ran about the streets." And yet when the sun took no notice of these proceedings, the astronomers sat like a log and did nothing ! It was disgraceful. However, the law was clear on the matter. If the astronomers predicted the eclipse too soon, off with their heads ; if too late, off with their heads. And as in this case it must have been either too soon or too late, their heads went off accordingly. No wonder the Chinese men of science lamented the loss of the Equalizing Quarter.

In these cases however, the suggestion of an Egyptian origin is only indirect, through that country supplying the clue which the later nation apparently lost. But there is another problem to which Professor Legge invites particular attention, observing that he looks forward to its solution with no slight interest; and that is the origin of certain " dissyllables and trissyllables," introduced in the place of the days of the month by the illustrious archæologist and reviser of the Chinese Kalendar, Szemâ Ch'ien, descended of a long line of imperial historiographers, who wrote towards the close of the second century B.C. Although all the terms which Ch'ien uses appear in a rudimentary dictionary of the time of the Han Dynasty, Professor Legge is strongly of opinion, or rather entertains no manner of doubt, that they are of foreign extraction ; and he states that a famous Taoistic scholar, Kwo P'o, who died A.D. 324, put the terms on one side as incapable of explanation. " A discovery," the eminent scholar goes on to say, " may be in store for the explorers in Sanskrit or Assyriology, or some other Eastern mine. But let it be borne in mind that the use of the cycle of sixty for the measurement of days, and possibly for other periods, was long—very long—anterior to Szemâ Ch'ien." Now it is a most singular circumstance, and one which testifies strongly to the penetration of that eminent scholar, that these same names when referred to the Coptic or vulgar tongue of Egypt, not only possess an intelligible meaning, but that in almost every case they signify an Egyptian festival, as follows :—

Titles employed by Szemâ Ch'ien.	Egyptian Phonetic Equivalent.	Signification of Egyptian Equivalent.	Corresponding Egyptian Festival or Doctrine.
Yu Chao	Ioh-Khaou	Moon-Day	Birth of Moon.
Chiang Wu	Chinka-Oue	Separation	Separation (celebrated twice a month).
Chû-Li	Khouo-Lai	Abundant Rejoicing	Great Festival (Kalendar).
Shun-Hang	Sheu-N-Ankh	Altar of Life	Fire Altar (Ritual).
Sheh-ti-Ko	Sheu-Ti-Koi	Altar of the Fields of God	Fields of Aahlu (Paradise).
Chao Yang	Khao-Ch'ink'	Separation of Day	Burial of Osiris.
Tan-eh	Tanghe	Preservation	One of the stages in the Path of Light.
Chih-Hsu	Khi-Shu	Dart of Shu	Dart of Shu (turn of the year).
Ta Mang-Lo	Taia-Maein-Laou	Panegyric of the Sail	Sail of the Bark of Ra (Ritual).
Ch'ih-Fun-Jo	Khi-Foon-Ioh	Dart of Hairs of Moon	Locks of Athor.
Kwan-tu	Koun-Tou	Within the Wall	Festival of "Hidden Lintel" (Ritual).
Hsieh Hsiah	Hsiohe Hssa	Measure the Fields and Regions	Fields and Paths of the Dead.

The expression "Within the wall" is particularly

notable, for its accordance with an Egyptian festival is in itself so extraordinary as to render it very difficult to regard it as a mere coincidence. Although therefore it is far from probable that a Chinese scholar should deliberately adopt foreign, in the place of native titles, yet, on the other hand, if the elements of the kalendar were imported into China by its first civilizers from the more primæval country, nothing is more likely than that a man so devoted to archæology as Professor Legge describes Szemâ Ch'ien to have been, should have hunted out these archaic titles from the earliest records of China, and should have endeavoured to bring them into use as more correct terms, although possibly he himself may have been unable to understand their meaning. In any case the table, wherein the strange titles employed by Ch'ien are paralleled with their phonetic equivalent in the Egyptian tongue, and the translation of those equivalents in the festival to which they seem to correspond, will enable the reader to judge for himself how far the Egyptian key avails to open the Chinese lock which for fifteen hundred years has been given up by the Chinese experts.

CHAPTER VI

THE INITIATION OF THE POSTULANT.

As the created light is the primary force
manifested in the system of creation, so also
is the Uncreate, or Self-Begotten Light
(Kheper-Ra), the prime mover and creator
whether of the visible or of the unseen universe. "Light Great Creator is his Name;"
we read in one of the chapters added to the
Egyptian Ritual at the Saite recension. And
again in another ancient papyrus : "The God
of the Universe is in the light above the
firmament; and His symbols are upon the
earth." Now it was with that divine Light,
immortal, invisible, intolerable to mortal eye,
the Light which none may look upon in the

flesh and live, that in the ancient creed of
Egypt, as in that of Christendom, the holy
dead was to be at last united, person with
person, and indissoluble bond.   No language
less universal than that of faith can enable us
to express this sublime belief.   For in no other
creed do we find that man never loses his
individuality which is yet united personally
with the Deity in so intimate an unity, that
in the Ritual the Osiris-soul can with difficulty
be distinguished from the Osiris-Godhead.
"The sun is worshipping thy face;" says
Osiris in the Ritual, to the soul new born into
the divine existence; that is to say, the very
splendour of creation, the source of light and
life to the visible world, bows down in worship
before him who has become a participator in
the divinity of its creator.   "He is I, I am
he;" the soul responds, almost in the actual
words of the Gospel.

Long and manifold was the process whereby, in the teaching of Egypt, the human

nature became united with the divine—an
union effected, through the God-Man Osiris,
not as in the gross and distorted myths of the
classic nations, by the conversion of the Godhead into flesh, but by the interior taking of
the manhood into God.   Without and within,
the transfiguration was complete.   The soul,
instantly illumined by the fulness of the
Godhead, became forthwith capable of corresponding with the divine Energy.   The
senses, restored to incorruption, were gradually
fashioned into instruments capable of expressing the soul's assimilation to that infinite
power, for which the bounds of space and
time exist not, but past and future alike stand
open in an endless present; that transcendent
freedom, wherein ·Act is coincident with Will,
and Will commensurate with Thought.   In
order then that the senses may be so quickened
and irradiated as to perceive the action of the
Creative Mind in the exterior universe, that
progress must be made by the departed in

person, which, while still unreleased from subjection to the senses, the student of science makes
dimly through the intellect. For whoever
would understand the framework of the
heavens, the structure of man's sacred dwelling place, must commence with the pole-
star, and tracing out the horizon of the
point of Equinox, which equally divides the
light from the darkness, must apprehend
how the axis of the earth is for man the
prime measure of space, and the standard
rule of the Depths. If he would learn the
secret of living form, the ocean will be his
teacher, as he passes from shore to profoundest
depths and fathoms the secret places of the
teeming waters. The measure of the celestial
orbits will be revealed to him by the moon,
as from that companion orb he watches the
rotation and the revolution of our planet. To
understand not merely the motion but the
evolution of our globe, he must dare the place
of the earth's central fire, undismayed by the

cavernous glooms of the lurid abysses. And there, gazing backwards for uncounted ages, he will trace amid convulsions and cataclysms inconceivable the " Lord of Law" and the "Words of Order ; " as the huge mountain chains rise higher and higher from the chaos, to prepare the surface of the globe for the dwelling-place of man. Before him next stretches the shadow of the earth, that dim and vast expanse ; where the majesty of the open heaven is enshrouded in night ; and he perceives how the conjunctions of eclipse are due to the same power as the orbits of illumination, and the hour of darkness is measured by the Giver of Light. That shadow traversed, a yet more awful vision, the terrible splendour of the solar fount in all its fulness, bursts upon his sight ; and as he mounts the sevenfold ascent of the planetary spheres, he gazes undazzled on the stupendous jets and sprays of flame that dart on a sudden thousands and myriads of miles on high. Then far beyond in the

infinite depths of space, his eyes, now radiant
"as the eyes of Athor," seek out the well-
loved Sothis, the harbinger of the new dawn,
the portal of the illimitable heavens, "that
land of a million fortresses." And in anticipation of each successive stage of this
amazing progress, this reconquest of the senses
to the dominion of the reason, we may watch
the course of the masonic postulant accepted
by the "Master of the Secret," as he is inducted, chamber by chamber, into the Hidden
Places in the Pyramid of Light.

Yet though a man understand the material
forces of the universe, though he know all the
phenomena of the heavens, and the composition
of the most distant suns ; nay, though he wield
with so masterly a grasp the wand of science
as to evolve at will an organic world from the
atoms of the abysmal depths, all this, in the
mind of Egypt, was not sufficient, even for
initiation into the inner mysteries of divine
realities. No mere expansion of the intellect,

however pure and lofty ; not even the scientific definition of absolute truth, could suffice to open the secret things of God, any more than the most exact acquaintance with the features and the proportions of the Pyramid would disclose their interior signification without the teaching of the hidden Wisdom. And hence, at the commencement of the Ritual, in the heading of the first chapter, before a word of doctrine has been revealed, we are told how it proceeds from Thoth, "The Mind and Will of God," as the inscription of Hermopolis entitles him.

Now there are three modes in which such knowledge may be communicated to those prepared to receive it ; namely, by simple instruction, by distant vision, or by personal participation. Each of these modes is, it is evident, an advance upon that which precedes, a preparation for that which follows it. No man can become a participator in the Divine Nature who has never been illuminated by its

contemplation. No man can contemplate the
Deity who has not been instructed in Truth ;
nor can any receive that initiation until he
be dead to the flesh. As, therefore, in the
masonic induction the catechumen could ascend
but a few steps in the light of common day,
and passed, when the disc of the starry heaven
was opened by the Master of the Secret, into
the profound darkness of the Descending
Passage ; so too, when the great preparation
of Death had been accomplished, when soul
and spirit had been released from the dominion
of the senses, when, by the sacred purification
of embalmment, the corruptible body had put
on incorruption, then " On the day of the
funeral," we read, the Unseen Master commenced to instruct the catechumen in the
stages which must be undergone preparatory
to his initiation. And so closely does the
masonic path in the Pyramid correspond with
the path of the departed in the Ritual, that
the traveller to-day who penetrates the recesses

of the mysterious building may follow, well-nigh step by step, the mystical progress of the departed through the unseen world. For to the Egyptian of old, to have mastered the secret of the House of the Hidden Places was to have mastered the secret of the tomb. For him the grave had no darkness, death held no terror; for he knew beforehand the starry path, wherein each step brought him nearer to the Creator-Light.

Ritual in hand, let us now take up our position once more at the foot of the exterior ascent, beneath the entrance of the star, along with the catechumen of the Secret; and with him let us forecast the time when, bereft of sense, of will, of life, he will go forth, dumb and helpless, to the mouth of the tomb, and commence "The entrance on Light" (chap. i.) while "borne to the land of the holy dead." Then, reciting chapter by chapter, as we mount step by step, we become informed, in the course of that brief but steep ascent, of the

preparation which awaits him when the last
glimpse of earth is hidden from his sight.
Thus we learn how (ii., iii.) * after death, the
departed comes forth into the light of immortality, even as the sun when he sets, bursts
forth in radiance on the world which is hidden
from our view.   Then, since the departed
cannot yet bear the judgment of interior
justice, he is warned beforehand (iv.) that
when he has commenced the descent, he must
" pass the Road above the Earth," the ascending passage concealed by the Hidden Portcullis
behind the fourth exterior course.   And behind
that secret portal in the vignette illustrating
the chapter, we descry the face of the Unseen
Teacher, that countenance of which the holy
dead, when initiation has begun, shall presently be strengthened to bear the distant but
unveiled vision.   Before that lintel can be

* If these numbers be placed on a print of the interior
of the Pyramid, in the order here indicated, they will show
how the titles here assigned to the different parts are
obtained from the Ritual.

passed, and the road above the earth be
traversed, many trials, he now learns, are
waiting for him. There are tasks of justice to
be fulfilled, if he omitted those good works on
earth, the memorials of which may be his
sponsors ("Ushabti") (v., vi.). Apep, too,
the dark serpent that devours the hidden
Light, as the winding darkness of the autumnal
equinox devours the light of the year, lies in
wait (vii.) to crush him in its multitudinous
folds, while he treads the path where Light
and Darkness balance. Still mounting upward,
and at each step approaching nearer the grave,
the catechumen is instructed how, when that
serpent shall be passed, the Gate of the West
(viii., ix.), the aperture of the western wall,
will conduct him into the Well, or Chamber of
the deep Waters, as the setting sun goes down
into the deep waters of the western ocean and
comes forth thence in triumph (x., xi.). Passing in silence over that which shall happen to
him in the Well, since that knowledge cannot

yet be imparted, the Divine Teacher directs him, when the mystery of new life is accomplished, to retrace his steps to the Passage of the Heavenly Horizon; and, after entering and coming forth from (xii., xiii.) the Chamber of Ordeal, to approach once more the Lintel of Justice. For then, and then only, can he set foot upon the threshold of justification, when "the stains have been burnt from his heart" by the raging fire (xiv.).

On the fifteenth course now high above the horizon of the earth, our eyes (two courses higher than our feet) already face the double-arched gateway defined by the pole-star, the outer entrance of the secret places revealing the path of the Horizon of Heaven. And similarly in chapter xv. the departed comes towards the land of Eternity. "May I proceed," he continues, "as thou dost, without halt, like thy holiness, Ra, thou who hast no master, great traverser of waters, with whom millions of years are but a moment." Then,

as he bends his head towards the entrance of
the Pyramid and gazes on the dark passage
now open within, "I proceed to heaven," he
says; "I kneel among the stars." And at the
conclusion of the chapter he learns the words
to recite when his sun is setting, and he kneels
with his hands towards the land (of the unseen), "O height of Love, thou openest the
double Gate of the Horizon."

With these sublime words of thanksgiving,
the instruction of the catechumen comes to a
close; sufficient knowledge having been imparted to direct his course as postulant to the
places of Initiation and Ordeal, until which
point be passed he can look no further into
the mysteries. In the following chapter (xvi.),
as we ascend the last course before quitting the
outer light, the divine voice is for a season
hushed; and the Ritual silently offers three
pictures for our contemplation. On one of
these the sole object presented is the sacred
Scarab, a symbol of the Eternal One, the

Self-Created Being who knows no beginning
and no end. On the second is the figure of the
departed standing before Amen, the Hidden
Deity. The third contains simply a blank
stele or Egyptian form of tombstone. And
that stele, as we learn from the very ancient
papyrus of Unas, the "prophet of the Pyramid," was fashioned in the form of a false door
for the pyramidal entrance, the entrance, that
is to say, which lies on the seventeenth course
of the northward face, and which is oriented
by the northern star.

In that moment of silence, the departed is
alone. The friends have left him. The sun
of earth, which from his earliest years has
greeted him, is for ever hidden. The " Gate
of the Earth" is passed (xvii.) ; and the
Catechumen of Wisdom has been accepted as
the Postulant of Immortality. Dense, utter
darkness is before him ; but under the direction of Anup, the guide of souls, he passes on
beyond that Gate of the Ascent, where the

divine Light lifts the disc of the tomb. " It is
the region of his father Shu " (the Light), the
Ritual continues : " he effaces his sins, he
destroys his stains." Then as the departed
advances through the darkness, and fearlessly
commences the Descending Path, the inner
Light, unseen by mortal eye, reveals itself in
vision. He beholds the lower world (xvii.), the
territory of Initiation, the entry of the Hidden
Places, concerning which the divine Wisdom
has instructed him, the place " wherein he
must enter and from whence he must come
forth," the transformations which he must
desire to make, that he may be transformed
into the likeness of God, the good works which
he must do, the " throne " of the regenerate
soul, and the blessed company of Osiris after
the body has been laid to rest. In that same
vision too he sees the whole lower world, the
" Angle of Fire ; " and " the Pool " or Well of
Life, with its summit opening into the Double
Hall of Truth (xvii.).

With the eighteenth chapter begins the "Book of Performing the Days," that is, the period of preparation for Initiation and Ordeal, the due performance of which entitles him to pass "the road above the earth" (xviii.), there to receive the Crown of Justification (xix., xx.), when his victory is assured.   As he pursues the descending Passage of the Heavenly Horizon, the reconstruction of the inner man, the new creation to life immortal, slowly commences (xxi.).   One by one his faculties are reawakened to spiritual life ; his mouth (xxii.) is opened, that he may respond to the teaching of the divine voice ; his mind and his name are restored (xxiv., xxv.) ; his heart (xxvi.) is given back to him, and he knows no more the icy numbness of the paralyzed affections.   Gradually the new-formed body gathers force and substance ; that is to say, not the natural body, which never bursts its sacred swaddling-bands till wakened in the last chapter of the Ritual and the last chamber of the building by the Grand Orient of the open tomb, but the spiritual or astral body wherewith the man, already raised in incorruption yet still awaiting the open manifestation of Osiris's resurrection, converses with the "Starry Spirits," the intelligences of the transcendent spheres. With the new life commences the attack of his spiritual enemies, now rendered palpable to his sight (xxvii.–xxxii.), the dread inhabitants of the under world, that wage in man the great battle of contending light and darkness. Sloth, the tortoise, strives to delay his steps; the asps put forth their venom; crawling reptiles infest his path. From every side the raging passions, the devouring crocodiles which inhabit the waters of life, rush furiously to the attack; but he repels all those creatures of darkness by the astral brightness of his starry nature. "Back, Crocodile of the South," he exclaims; "I am Sothis"—the star of the Eternal Dawn. His foes, defeated by the divine

protection (xxxiii.–xli.), the body raised in incorruption (xlii.) acquires in every limb and
every feature the seal of God. His hair,
from which the light glows forth in streams,
is as " the hair of Nu," the sacred Nile glowing with the streams of life ; his countenance,
shining as the sun, is radiant as the face of
Ra ; his eyes, glorious as are eyes of Athor,
gleaming with immortal beauty ; his fingers
are as the Uræi, the insignia of the royal
power ; his feet burn with the fire of the
Creator-Spirit Ptah ; his humanity is as the
humanity of Osiris, the incarnate God. " There
is not a member of him," says the Ritual,
" which is not divine."

Resplendently beautiful as is the astral body
assumed by the new being, he is not yet prepared for initiation ; but fresh trials still
await him as he approaches the granite block
which obstructs the descending passage. His
self-dominion, the head of his glory, may be
taken from him ; he may incur the second

death of defilement from the creatures of
darkness (xliii.–li.).   But still, by the same
guidance avoiding all these dangers, he comes
forth as the day through the Gate of the
West, to the passage which conducts him to
the Well of Life ; and as he passes that
threshold, he is fed with the celestial food
which they may not eat who are partakers
of defilement (li.–lii.).   " The enemies do not
eat of my body," says Osiris, in another part
of the Ritual.   Avoiding defilement through
the strength of that food (lii., liii.) he receives
the breath of Ptah (liv.–lviii.), and drawing
near to the Well of Life, is granted a first
draught of its refreshing streams (lix.–lxiii.).
In the depths of that well, wherein, as the
Sai-an-Sinsin tells us, approach is made to
Osiris, shall presently take place the regeneration of the renewed man (or " Ka "), by reunion
with the new-born soul amid the living waters.
" I give the waters of life to every mummy,"
says the Goddess Nout, who presides over

the waters, in the inscription on the vase
of Osur-Ur (given in " Records of the Past "),
" to reunite it with the soul, that it may
henceforth be separated from it no more for
ever. The Resident of the West has established
thy person amid the sages of the divine Lower
Region. He giveth stability to thy body, and
causeth thy soul not to distance itself from
thee. He keepeth remembrance of thy person,
and saveth thy body now and for ever."

During this arduous preparation, while the
departed passes from earth in absolute weakness to wage the prolonged conflict of light
and darkness, the imperishable soul, restored
to her native element, is born a second time
in the Chamber of the Queen of the Pyramid,
wherein was born the divine Osiris, at once
her Son, her Maker, and her Spouse. " I am
Yesterday," says Osiris, in the sixty-fourth
chapter, said to be almost coeval with the
Pyramid of Light ; that is, " I am He who
was before time began," since, however far

back in time a day may be, yesterday was always before it. " I am the Dawn," he continues, " the Light of the Second Birth, the Mystery of the Soul, Maker of the gods, by whom are fed the hidden ones of heaven." So in the inscription on the coffin of Anches-Ra-Neferab—that is, of her " whose life was the Sacred Heart of Ra "—we read concerning Isis, that is, she " who opens for thee the secret places by those mighty names of thine. Thy name is Infant and Old Man, Germ and Growth, Son of Heaven, who makes the road for thee according to his word. Thy name is Everlasting, Self-Begotten, the Dawn, the Day, the Evening, the Night, the Darkness. Thy name is the Moon, the Heart of Silence, the Lord of the Unseen World." And on another part of the coffin of the same holy queen, the spirits of Annu, called in the Ritual the " secret birthplace of the gods," are invoked as those " who preside over the sacred birth."

With the new birth of the soul comes also

the restoration of power in its original divine
image.   For as in the condition which is
subject to decay the corruptible senses
dominate and inform the soul, so according to
the theosophy of Egypt, in the condition of
immortality, does the illuminate spirit inform
and dominate the regenerate senses.   While
we are subject to the flesh, the external
universe impresses itself continually upon the
mind, dimming and imprisoning the original
" type " or image of the Deity, which feebly
struggles to express itself in the masterpieces
of poet or artist.   But when the soul is born
into new life, it regains that Creative Image,
and is endowed with the power of co-operating
with the divine Energy.   For, as we learn
from an exquisite chapter in the Ritual, it is
the fragrance of Innocence, which perfumes
the breath of the Creative Beauty.   Hence, in
the masonry on the eastern wall of that most
secret Chamber of New Birth, we find expressed the fivefold dominion informed by

the soul, new-born in the sacred type of the image of the Queen. Now thus the senses themselves become so essentially divine, that the departed pays worship to his own faculties. " I have adored Touch and Taste," he says later on ; for touch and taste are the channels whereby is communicated to man the food of immortality.   From that Secret Chamber, the regenerate soul comes forth glorious as the day (lxv., lxvi.), and " opening the door " (lxvii.), once so carefully concealed, comes forth in full radiance to the fields of Aahlu (lxviii.–lxxii.), the territory of illumination : to take its seat (lxxv.) upon the lower throne above the head of the Well, between the Chamber of the Orbit and the Chamber of the Shadow.   " The gates of heaven open to me," he says ; " the gates of earth open to me."

That solemn enthronization being witnessed by the postulant in the depths below ; he remembers that the time of ordeal draws near, and after praying, as instructed beforehand,

that his sin may be rubbed out, he celebrates
the "festival of the soul passing to his body."
But not immediately may that passage be
accomplished. Raised though he be in incorruption, glowing as he is in every member
with the immortal light, he cannot yet bear
unveiled the overwhelming glory of the soul.
Therefore, in the teaching of Egypt, around
the radiant being which in its regenerate life
could assimilate itself to the glory of the Godhead, was formed the "Khaibit" or luminous
atmosphere, consisting of a series of ethereal
envelopes, at once shading and diffusing its
flaming lustre, as the earth's atmosphere shades
and diffuses the solar rays.   And at each
successive transformation (lxxvii.–lxxxvii.) it
descended nearer to the moral conditions of
humanity.   From the form of the golden
hawk, the semblance of the absolute divine
substance, the One Eternal, Self-Existent Being,
it passes to the "Lord of Time," the image of
the Creator, since with the Creation time

began. Presently it assumes the form of a
lily, the vignette in the Ritual representing
the head of Osiris enshrined in that flower ;
the Godhead manifested in the flesh, coming
forth from immaculate purity. "I am the
pure lily," we read, "coming forth from the
lily of light. I am the source of illumination
(the nostril of the sun) and the channel of the
breath of immortal beauty (Athor). I bring
the messages (of heaven), Horus (the Eternal
Son) accomplishes them." Later the soul
passes into the form of the Urœus, "the soul
of the earth ;" the serpentine path traced upon
the earth irradiated by the vertical sun, as
the senses are irradiated by the supreme
illumination of the soul.

And finally it assumes the semblance of a
crocodile ; becoming subject, that is, to the
passions of humanity. For the human passions,
being part of the nature wherein man was
originally created, are not intrinsically evil,
but only become evil when insubordinate to

the soul. And thus the crocodile, which
attacked the departed before new birth, is
rendered divine in the regenerate form.
Therefore it was that the crocodile was held
in high reverence by the Egyptians, for it
spoke to them of the time when man should
regain the mastery of his passions, and when
the last barrier between himself and his
glorious soul should be removed for ever.

Immeasurable as is the distance which thus
separates the two beings which make up the
perfect manhood, there is no hesitation or
delay on the part of the soul. That radiant
creature in its glory has not forgotten the
frail companion in union with whom it dwelt
during the days of its humiliation. Restored
to its native purity, welcomed by the Almighty
to a participation in his own energy, throned
on its seat of absolute dominion, yet such is
the ardour with which that soul returns the
love of man, that like the Creator Himself it
cannot rest satisfied with its own inexhaustible

bliss; but hastens to come down from its seat of power, that it may raise and glorify expectant humanity. And thus the vignette shows us the winged creature flying towards the postulant. Meanwhile the latter, from below watching its flight, prays in an ecstasy for the reunion. "O bringer," he cries, "O runner in his hall!"—the Hall of Truth, where the throne of the soul is erected. "Great God, let my soul go where it desires (lxxxix.). O conductors of the bark of millions of years, led through the gateway, clearing the path of heaven and earth, accompany ye the souls to the holy dead."

The prayer is granted. Leaving its throne on high, and passing through its various transformations, the soul descends the ladder of the well, as in the papyrus of Ani. Then the divine protection is obtained (xci.); and, amid the living waters in the pool of the Persea, the Tree of Immortality (as the Ritual elsewhere calls it), the earnest desire of the postulant is fulfilled, and he is re-united with his living soul (xciii.) ; " My soul is from the beginning," he says, " from the commencement of time (reckoning of years). The eye of Horus " (the Divine Son) made for me my soul, preparing its substance. The darkness is before them ; the arms of Osiris hold them. Open the path to my soul and my shadow (Khaibit) and my spirit, to see the great Gód within his sepulchre the day of making up the souls." If that knowledge is possessed, the Ritual adds, he enters on Light ; he is not detained in the lower world.

That priceless gift conceded, the postulant, though he cannot yet participate in the divine splendour until his ordeal be passed, yet can he behold it openly from afar, and enter on his initiation into the sacred mysteries. Ascending, in the strength imparted to him by his soul, the ladder of the well, he offers a prayer to the Divine Teacher (xciv.), and, " holding in his hand the Sacred Mysteries," he turns his opened eyes successively in the three directions which we saw indicated by the hiero- glyph of the divine Initiator Thoth.   First he gazes down "the opening where Thoth is," the Chamber of the Shadow, now no longer closed to his view, though not yet accessible to his person; and he beholds the secret Wisdom which gives to Truth its splendour (xcv., xcvi.), the countenance of the Divine Teacher, whose voice instructed the catechumen, and whose power protected the postulant.   Then, as his eyes grow clearer, he offers a prayer to Anup (xcvii.), the starry guide, who has led him thus far towards his heart's desire; and, turning towards the Chamber of the New Birth, he discerns the Bark of Ra (xcviii.–cii.), the vessel of God, foretold to him before his entry on the path by the Divine Teacher—the vessel which shall bear him safely across the Deep Waters.   Even while he looks, the whole interior of the building is lit with a sudden glow; and the masonry, pourtraying each por-

tion of the sacred vessel, reveals their mystical
significance, which the Initiate must know
before permission can be granted to embark.
Within the Inner House the vast granite
Triangle dominating the secret heights assumes
for him the form of an " Anchor," with its
central axis indicated, but not delineated, by
the equality of the members : as we saw
the central mystery of the Supreme Secret,
the Unity of the divine Substance to be indicated but not defined by the equality of the
Persons in the Egyptian Trinity.   And that
" anchor " firmly fixed, not in the depths
below, but in the heights above the open
sarkophagus, speaks to him of Osiris, " the

The Anchor and the Coffin of the Lord of Earth.   (Sarkophagus
and highest chamber.)

Lord of the earth in his coffin ; " the vision

which awhile ago he prayed that he might
behold on the Great Day of Reckoning.   At
the head of the Grand Gallery is the " seat "
of the " Dweller in Space : " the radiant throne
at the top of the long incline to which the
Initiate now lifts his eyes.   Right through the
midst of the throne rises unseen the Axis of
the Great House, the Central Ray of the Grand
Light of Egypt, like a huge but impalpable
mast towering from foundation to summit of
the vessel of Light.   That axis passes through
the Chamber of New Birth below, and separates the Outer from the Inner House which
lies beyond the throne, as the central but
impalpable truth of Death separates the glory
which now is from the glory which lies beyond.
And in the truth of Death, to the Egyptian
the " Completion-Beginning " of the New Birth,
the Initiate discerns " the great bringer and
taker away," as the Ritual calls the mast of
the vessel of Ra.   Aloft upon the same axis,
above the solar throne, the roof of the

lustrous chamber, with its starry rays, images
to him whose eyes are opened, the "Sail of
the Firmament," which, by its starry grandeur,

The Sail of the Firmament.

draws the soul irresistibly to God. The Well
reflects to him the "Paddle" shining in the
invisible waters, as the image of the Creator
shines invisibly in the Waters of Life : the
"Planks," the rungs of the ladder whereby the
soul came down to visit him, each guarded by
a spirit of celestial intelligence. In the subterranean chamber he discerns the "hold" of
"darkness," and in the Chamber of New Birth
the Cabin, or Secret Place of the Divine Vessel.
A remarkable instance of pyramidal allusion is
supplied by the form of the cabin. For the
roof proper was surmounted by another roof of
the singular and apparently unmeaning shape
given in the text. But if above the Chamber

of New Birth we indicate the throne of Ra, which immediately surmounts it, we shall have

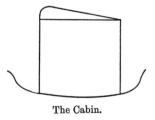

The Cabin.

the shape in question; so that the form implies the enthronization of the Uncreated Light upon the Mystery of the Divine Mother, Isis.

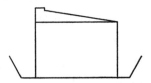

Chamber of New Birth, surmounted by Throne.

Upon that bark of safety take place both his present Initiation and the Illumination which is to come; and each of these ascents finds its appropriate expression in the masonry, the one in the place of New Birth, the other in the Chamber of the Splendour. And in the

vignettes of the Ritual, we see the vessel bearing upon it at one time a fivefold, at another
a sevenfold staircase ; the fivefold dominion of
the regenerate senses, and the sevenfold elevation of the illuminate intellect.

Yet one more vision opens out to the Initiate. As he raises his eyes more upward
yet to the extreme height of the Chamber of
the Splendour, far removed from the head of
the well, yet forming part of the same divine
structure, he discerns the "opening where
Athor is" (ciii.), the azure depths of ethereal
loveliness leading to the secret heights above
the Chamber of Grand Orient. For a moment
he gazes in silent rapture on the far-off
opening of the unimaginable vision, and then
calls to his aid "the Opener of the Great
Sanctuary" (cv., cvi.). "Oh, assistant—oh,
assistant!" he exclaims; "I am among the
servants of Immortal Beauty!"

Fortified then by that enduring remembrance, he turns from the scene of future

illumination, and descends towards the place
of impending trial.   Around him stand
revealed the "Gods of the Western Gate"
(cvii.), the Western opening to the Well of
Life, where dwell the spirits who came unseen
to his assistance at the hour when the sun of
earthly life went down into the West.   From
the "Chamber of the Waters of Heaven"
flows down the torrent of the "Celestial Nile"
(cx.), and mingles at his side with the stream
from the "Chamber of the Birthplace of the
Gods"—that stream which waters the fields
of Aahlu, the home of the regenerate.   And
high above, far as his quickened eyes can
pierce, are assembled the bright companies of
starry spirits from every quarter (cxi.–cxiv.)
to assist at his victory, his judgment, and his
coronation.   In the memory of that unfading
vision, and the strength of those protecting
spirits, the Initiate enters and comes forth
(cxvi.) from the subterranean Chamber of the
Fiery Ordeal.

CHAPTER VII.

THE ILLUMINATION OF THE ADEPT.

INITIATION achieved, and Ordeal undergone, the character both of building and of Ritual seem to undergo a transformation. Not that the air of mystery is in any way lessened, rather it deepens if possible, as we penetrate into the more secret parts. But the period of weakness and of expectancy once passed, a sense of power and triumph grows more and more distinctly perceptible as we enter the secret places of absolute "Truth." Turning back with the Initiate, now become the Adept from the "Meskwa" or Place of Ordeal, we retrace our steps upwards, under the direction

of the celestial guide, who conducts us to the
" Gate on the Hill " (cxvii.) ; the lintel hidden
in the roof far up along the Passage of the
Star.　In remounting the ascent the adept
once more " enters and comes forth " (cxx.)
from the Gateway of the Well, that he may
again receive strength for the coming judgment.　And as he approaches the hidden
portcullis, which now he is called upon to pass,
where sits in person the Eternal Wisdom, he
recites for himself (cxxi.) the unforgotten
words wherein the Divine Teacher warned him
of the hour now drawing near of entering into
(xiii.) judgment and of issuing from thence.
Arrived at the hidden portcullis (cxxii., cxxiii.),
carefully concealed within the roof, that
arduous " Gateway reserved for the Gods,"
the divine Osiris-souls, the gateway which
none can enter, except " after coming out "
from the place of initiation, obstruction meets
him at every step.　Alike in the Ritual, and
in the building, each portion of that most

mysterious gateway, the secret of whose masonry still remains undisclosed, refuses entrance to the upward path except to the adept. "'I will not let thee go over me,'" says the sill, "'unless you tell me my name.' 'The weight in the right place is thy name,'" is the profound reply of the adept. For, as the raising of the portcullis depends upon the true adjustment of the weight, so also is justice the virtue without which the path on high remains for ever closed. "'I will not let thee pass me,'" says the Left Lintel — so continues this strange dialogue—"'unless you tell me my name.' 'Return of the true is thy name.' 'I will not let thee pass me,'" says the Right Lintel, "'unless you tell me my name.' 'Return of judged hearts is thy name.'" For without truth, and without self-judgment, no step can be taken of progress in the Path of Truth (cxxv.). With that doctrine we may compare the "Golden Words" of Pythagoras, himself a pupil of the priests of Egypt—

" Do innocence ; take heed before thou act ;
  Nor let soft sleep upon thy eyelids fall,
  E'er the day's actions thou hast three times scanned,
  What have I done, where erred, what left unwrought ?
  Go through the whole account, and if the sum
  Be evil, chide thee ; but if good, rejoice.
  This do, this meditate, this ever love,
  And it shall guide thee into virtue's path."

But to him who has learned of wisdom, however long, however arduous the search, the entrance into Truth cannot finally be denied. The Hidden Lintel is crossed ; and the memory of that passage is for ever kept sacred by the grateful departed. " I have come through the Hidden Lintel," he cries triumphantly, later on, "I have come like the sun through the gate of the festival." The lintel crossed, the Person of the Divine Teacher is disclosed, having before him the true Balance of Light and Darkness (cxxv.). The " secret faces at the gate " unveil themselves ; and the adept stands within the Double Hall of Truth—of Truth in Death and Truth in Life, of Truth in Justice and Truth in Mercy, of Truth in Darkness and

Truth in Splendour.   Then, as he surmounts
each obstacle besetting the entrance to the
path which leads on high, and achieves the
triumph over Death, he beholds the long array
of the Judges of the Dead, the celestial powers
who take account of the moral actions of mankind, each supreme in his own province of the
holy land; and to each in turn the adept,
whose stains have been washed from his heart
in the furnace of the ordeal, pleads his innocence of the sin of which that power is the
special avenger.   Very terrible are the images
under which those heart-searching spirits are
presented—terrible as the moral effects of our
own transgression, when viewed by the inner
light of Truth.   "The Eyes of Fire," the
passion which shrivels the intellect; the "Face
of Smoke," the pride that clouds the judgment;
the "Crackler of Bones," the sin which corrodes
the entire manhood, these and such as these
are the fearful insignia of the supernal powers.
Most terrible of all is the spirit "whose mouth

is twisted when he speaks, because his face is
behind him," the spirit of conscience, which
keeps its dread eyes inexorably on our past,
and speaks to us with mouth contorted in the
agony of self-condemnation—like the cry of
the penitent, which echoes as bitterly now as
when uttered three thousand years ago, "My
sin is ever before me."

Undeterred by that august tribunal, which
as we learn at the threshold, none can endure
but he who has truly judged himself, the
departed, protected by the Divine Guardian,
ascends the Passage of the Shadow where the
light is eclipsed, and achieves through Truth
his victory over Death. Gradually, as he
draws near the low but unobstructed gateway,
the glow of the splendour begins to appear;
and he sees before him the Sacred Orbit of the
circling earth defined by the four burning
points of Solstice and Equinox, like a basin of
fire surrounded by four jets of flame (cxxvi.).
In front of each of those cardinal points of the

heaven, are seated four divine spirits having the assemblance of an ape, the form nearest akin to humanity. To those four universal guardians and heralds of truth, the justified prays, that he may be purified yet further from his transgressions. "O ye," he says, "who send forth truth to the universal Lord, nurtured without fraud, who abominate wickedness, extract all the evil from me. Obliterate my faults and annihilate my sins." "Thou mayest go," is the gracious reply of the four heavenly teachers; "we obliterate all thy faults, we annihilate all thy sins." In this manner, as the Ritual declares, is separation of his sins effected "after he has seen the faces of the Gods." From henceforth death has no more power over him, and in rapture he returns thanksgiving to the supreme judges, the Gods of the Orbit, towards whom he now advances, and to Osiris on his throne (cxxvii., cxxviii.).

As he stands at the entrance of the upper chamber, where the slight projection of the

lower floor bears witness to the passage from
death to life, the divine voice, which has
been silent till its first lesson is exhausted,
recommences his illumination, and he is " instructed " (cxxix.) how " to stand at the Bark
of Ra "—no longer in the lower portion of the
vessel, but free of every part. Obedient to
the divine command, he passes the " Gate of
the Gateway " (cxxx.), and celebrates the Birthday of Osiris, the Opening of the Eternal
Year. Then, as he advances a step and
stands within the hall upon the slight projection, he beholds the whole building before
him, the vast universe of space, in its immeasurable grandeur, now free to his immaculate spirit. And as at the Lintel of Justice all
is barred, so here every part lies open. " The
heaven opens," we read (cxxx.)—the Chamber
of the Splendour with its seven-fold rays around
the solar throne ; " the earth opens," the Chamber of the Shadow ; " the North opens " to the
Chamber of the Pole-star ; " the South opens "

to the Chamber of Grand Orient; " the West opens " to the Entrance of the Well; " the East opens " to the Chamber of New Birth, with its Eastern ascent of the regenerate senses; " the Northern and Southern Chapels open," the Ante-chamber and the Place of Grand Orient, the Northern and Southern chapels of the inner house. Here, too, is the " crossing of the pure roads of life," of which the coffin of Amamu speaks. Behind are " the roads of darkness," which the departed in the Ritual once prayed so earnestly that he might pass. In front lie the fields of Aahlu, the blessed country where the justified executes the works which he is privileged to do for Osiris.

A burst of triumph greets the justified, when having accomplished the Passage of the Sun, he enters the Chamber of the Orbit, the Hall of Illumination. " The deceased," we read, " passes through the Gate of the Gateway. Prepare ye his hall when he comes. Justify his words against the accusers. There is given

to him the food of the gods of the Gate.
There has been made for him the crown which
belongs to him as the dweller in the Secret
Place." In another place the justified himself
exclaims, "I have opened the gate of heaven
and earth" (at the junction of the Halls of
the Orbit and of the Shadow). "The soul of
Osiris rests there. I cross through the halls.
No defect or evil is found in me." And once
more the deceased prays that he may pass this
hall. "Place me before thee, O Lord of
Eternity. Hail, Dweller of the West, good
Being, Lord of Abydos. Let me pass the
roads of darkness; let me follow thy servants
in the gate."

A similar note of exultation marks the
passage in the Sai-an-Sinsin, where we read of
the great tribunal and the House of Light.
"Thou comest into the House of God with
much purity," exclaim the mourners, addressing the departed. "The gods have abundantly
purified thee in the great tribunal. Thou art

not shut out of heaven; thy body is renewed
in the presence of Osiris. Thou hast not been
shut out from the House of Glory. Thou
seest the Path of Beauty, completing every
transformation which thou desirest." And the
ancient coffin of Amamu bore on the outside
this inscription, full of desire and hope : " An
act of homage to Anup, who passes the
deceased over the distant paths, the fairest of
the Karneter "—that is, the land of the holy
dead. " Thine eyes," say our own sacred
writings, "shall see the King in his beauty ;
they shall behold the land that is very
far off."

The gateway passed (cxxx.), the divine
voice resumes its instruction ; and teaches him
of " going to the heaven where Osiris is ;" of
being " received into the Sacred Heart of Ra,"
the fount of life (cxxxi.–cxxxiii.), of " the
adoration which he must render," of the vessel
of eternity in which the holy souls for ever
move, of the rejoicings of heaven (cxxxiv.–

cxxxvi.) in the manifestations of the Godhead
to man, and of the names and places wherein
those manifestations are made (cxli.–cxliii.).

And now the justified stands within the full
glory of the orbit, and looks forth, not with
the vision of mortal seer, but as the deathless
spirits who encircle the throne. While he
stands gazing, splendour after splendour,
revelation beyond revelation, bursts upon his
sight. Down from the radiant throne, along
the floor, along the walls, along the roof,
streams, floods, rivers of light come sweeping
on like the torrent of the summer rays, like
the inundation of the overwhelming Nile. But
the justified breathes freely the air of opened
heaven. His senses "for ever vivified," pierce
through the utmost bounds of space; his
quickened intellect grasps each starry law and
harmony; his purified spirit, undazzled by
the blinding radiance, discerns the Hidden
Love that occupies the throne. No longer as
a stranger, or at a distance, but as a prince

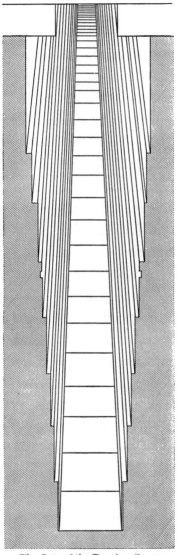

The Gate of the Burning Crown.

admitted to the highest honour of the court, the justified takes his place in the very line of direct approach ; while around and above him, the measureless expanse is filled with rank beyond rank of spirit-ministers. " He has passed his billions," we read, " the circle of flaming ministers is around him. His blessings follow him. ' Come,' says Truth ; and he approaches her Lord."

At that gracious word of Truth, the abysses of mystery reveal their most secret depths. First, the Chamber of the Shadow is lit by the irradiating brightness ; and the Illuminate discerns the nature of sin viewed in the light of truth. The Seven Halls of Death (cxliv.), each measured by its cycle of eclipse, lie open to him who has looked upon the face of God ; and each name of mystery betrays the form of darkness. " Babbling " Malice, that delights in " overthrow ; " " Fire-faced " Anger, " leaping on a sudden to the front ; " Envy, the " Eater of Dirt ; " Hatred, silent and "vigilant;" Lust, "the consumer, the over-thrower in a moment," that "lives off reptiles;" Pride, with its "face of stone;" Sloth, that hardens irretrievably the heart, the "final stopper of the rejected;" all these betray their nature to him over whom death has power no longer. And he discerns (as in the vignette) the seven avenging spirits, each armed with the two swords of physical and spiritual destruction.

Mounting then the steep ascent, he beholds the mystery of judgment disclose itself in successive stages as the twenty-one Gates of Aahlu—their spaces measured by the years of Light, as it speeds from Sothis, the gates which open only to "the meek-hearted" (cxlvi.) unfold before him. At each of the first ten portals flows a celestial stream of sparkling waters, which shed their undying lustre over the person of the Illuminate. Ascending still towards the throne of Ra, at the nineteenth portal he is clothed with robes of power; and at " the Gate of the Burning Crown," he stands beneath the Royal Arch of the Planetary Spheres.   Immediately beyond is the " Stone of God," where he receives from the Divine Occupant a " Crown of Illumination," the " Atf "-crown of Egypt, fashioned after the zodiacal light of highest heaven.   And behind the throne rises the final " Gate of Peace " with its seven crowns of joy.

But not as yet can the Illuminate attain the infinite serenity which lies beyond that gate.   Death and judgment are not the only secrets to be disclosed when the eye of faith becomes the eye of sight.   The place of the divine birth, the chamber in the " Fields of Aahlu," must be visited before the Illuminate become the Master of the secret.   And as he passes portal after portal of the fields (cxlvii.), he recites the titles of her whose habitation he now approaches: the " Mistress of Holy Awe," the " Mistress of Heaven," the " Regent of the Earth," the " Help of the Meek-hearted,"

VII.] *The Light of the Secret River.* 241

the "Mistress of Prayer," the "Light of the Secret River." Then, having learnt the majesty of its queen, he scans the sevenfold arch, the Mystery of the Transcendent Heaven (cxlviii.); to hold converse with the seven Supreme Intelligences who overarch the Splendour of Creation.

Yet once again must the Depths be sounded, and the Secret Places be traversed, before the Illuminate can pass as master through the Gate of Peace. One secret of death still remains, most terrible and most inscrutable of all. While we are yet imperfect, we can gain some knowledge of the effect of moral death upon ourselves, and even form a faint adumbration of its nature when viewed in the light of absolute truth. But the mystery of its divine permission who can penetrate? If the Omnipotent be all good, why did He ever allow of evil? If He be all-merciful, why does He permit His creatures to suffer? How can our actions be justly

" balanced " (cli.) when the forces which produced them were not of our own creation ?
Why are we to be made parties to the battle
of light and darkness, when no choice was
given whether we would exist or not ?   Why
are the souls of just men secretly snared and
overthrown ?   Whence comes the " foul flux "
which is purged from man, and which causes
all living creatures to shudder ?   Such questions as these we ask, and ask in vain.   Yet
if that darkest shadow, that horror which
forms the depth of human agony, the enshrouding of the Eternal Justice in the
blackness of utter eclipse, is still liable to
arise and overpower the soul, how can man
ever repose in safety ; and what revelation
or degree of glory will suffice to bring him
peace ?   But that it too is destined to pass
away in light, when the secrets are revealed,
and illumination is transformed into union,
who can doubt ?   So at least we read in the
creed of Ancient Egypt ; where, when the

other mysteries of death and of judgment have been disclosed to the Illuminate; when he has entered into the secrets of the new birth, and conversed with the Supreme Intelligences who " watch before the tomb of Osiris ; " when time exists for him no more, and he understands the design of the Eternal House, from foundation to consummation, he makes a final circuit of its Secret Places. Clothed in power, and crowned with light, he traverses the " Abodes " (cli.) or scenes of his former weakness ; there to discern, by his own enlightened perception, how it is " Osiris who satisfies the balance of him who rules the heavens ; " to exert in its supernal freedom his creative will, now the lord, not the slave, of the senses ; and to rejoice in the just suffering which wrought his illumination and emancipation.

Finally, when that grand progress through the Habitations of Humanity has been completed, the Master returns in majesty to the celestial company assembled in the Grand Lodge of the solar throne. Mounting beneath the Royal Arch of the Burning Crown, he treads the Stone of God itself, and passes through the Gate of Peace, with its seven crowns and titles of Victory. Then, outstripping in his flight the power of mortal thought, he passes beyond the shining orbit of the earth, beyond the vast expanse of solar glory, across the awful chasms of the unfathomable depths, to far-off Sothis, the land of Eternal Dawn, the ante-chamber of the infinite morning. He "has his star established to him in Sothis," says the Ritual. And here the Illuminate, now become a Master, is instructed in the last mysteries which precede the universal glory; the mysteries of the divine sorrow, the "tears of Isis" (clii.), whence comes the source of the celestial Nile, the fount of illumination to man. Here he passes within the triple veil, and is invested with the imperishable jewels of supernal lustre (cliii.–clxi.).

One chapter and one chamber yet remain—
the chapter of Orientation, and the Chamber
of Grand Orient beneath the Secret Places
of the Most High.   "Awake, awake, Osiris!"
so sing the mourners to the beloved departed,
now glorious in the House of Light, and
united indissolubly with the divine Being;
"awake! see what thy son Horus hath done
for thee.   See what thy father Seb hath done
for thee.   Raised is the Osiris."   "I have
opened the doors," replies the Osiris-soul, "I
have opened the doors. . . . Well is the Great
One who is in the Coffer.   For all the dead
shall have passages made to him through their
embalming," when their body in the flesh shall
be raised in incorruption.   Again and again
is celebrated the Mystery of the Open Tomb.
As the eclipsing planet which moves nearest
to the sun crawls like a tortoise across the
face of that orb, defacing it for a moment
by its own darkness, and then is swallowed
in the radiance, so also death, that dark spot

which crawls across the vision of the eternal splendour, is swallowed in the resurrection of Osiris-Ra, the Uncreated Light.   Four times is that Gospel of ancient Egypt proclaimed in the chapter which bears the title of the Orient.   " The   tortoise   dies ;   Ra   lives ! " Death is swallowed in Light ; God lives for evermore.   " O Amen, Amen," so continues that chapter of mystery, " Amen, who art in heaven, give thy face to the body of thy Son. Make him well in Hades.   It is finished."

Thus ends the strange and solemn dirge of ancient Egypt.   Once perceived, the intimate connection between the secret doctrine of Egypt's most venerated books and the secret significance of her most venerable monument seems impossible to dissever, and each form illustrates and interpenetrates the other.   As we peruse the dark utterances and recognize the mystic allusions of the Book, we seem to stand amid the profound darkness enwrapping the whole interior of the building.   All around

are assembled the spirits and the powers that
make the mystery of the unseen world : the
" Secret Faces at the Gate," the " Gods of the
Horizon and of the Orbit."   And dimly before
our eyes, age after age, the sacred procession
of the Egyptian dead moves silently along, as
they pass through the " Gate of the Hill " to
the tribunal of Osiris.   In vain do we attempt
to trace their footsteps till we enter with them
into the Hidden Places, and penetrate the
secret of the House of Light.   But no sooner
do we approach the passage and tread the
chambers of the mysterious Pyramid, than the
teaching of the Sacred Books seems lit up as
with a tongue of flame.   The luminous veil
itself melts slowly away, disclosing the Path
of Illumination and the Splendours of the
Orbit ; the celestial Powers and Intelligences
shine forth from beneath their enshrouding
symbols ; the spirits of the just grow lustrous
with the rays that proceed from the tribunal.
For though none may look upon these things

unveiled till the Guardian of the Starry Gate
has opened for him the Portal of the Light,
yet for the adept, who has been mystically
initiated in the deep waters, and illuminated
by the sevenfold Beauty, the invisible things
become manifest by the visible creation. And
a Light which is not of earth reveals in its
divine unity the full secret of the Hidden
Places ; the Entrance to the Path of Heaven ;
the Well of Life, the Place of New Birth, the
Ordeal of Fire, the Lintel of Justice, the
Victory over Death, the Judgment of Truth,
the Splendour of Illumination, the Throne of
Radiance, the Veil of Perfection, and the
Grand Orient of the Open Tomb, beneath
secret chambers of the Height, crowned by
the Grand Arch of the Supreme Trinity.

Thus only according to that primæval creed
could man fulfil his marvellous destiny ; and
thus only can that destiny accomplish his
heart's desire. No skill in the secrets of the
material universe, no dominion over the forces

of life and death, no power to pierce the veil
which hangs before the unseen world and
to hold communion with the spiritual intelligences, will satisfy his secret aspirations.
For the soul of man—so every form of creed
declares—can know no rest, nor can his spirit
ever be satisfied, so long as the thinnest
film remains to interrupt the unclouded vision
of the Hidden Love; until he stand face to
face, and eye to eye with " Him who knows
the Depths."

We quit that solemn monument of primæval mystery; and as we turn a farewell
glance upon the Gate of Heaven, the veil of
the majestic masonry once more hides from
view the interior splendour, and enwraps the
Secret Places of the Hidden God.

THE END.

TEMPLE OF THE VIRGIN MOTHER.
DENDERAH.

Frontispiece.

THE

BOOK OF THE MASTER

OR

THE EGYPTIAN DOCTRINE OF

THE LIGHT BORN OF THE VIRGIN MOTHER

BY

W. MARSHAM ADAMS

Formerly Fellow of New College, Oxford
Author of " The House of the Hidden Places, A Clue to the Creed
of Early Egypt from Egyptian Sources "

In Nature's infinite Book of Secrecy
A little I can read.
Antony and Cleopatra.

ILLUSTRATED

PREFACE

SOME years have now passed since I suggested, first in the columns of the *New Review* and afterwards in a separate book, a clue to the mysterious religion of ancient Egypt. That clue was afforded by a comparison of the secret passages and chambers contained in the Great Pyramid, or "Secret House," of Memphis, to which the Egyptians of old gave the title of the "Light," with the secret passages and chambers portrayed in the sacred papyrus describing the "Entrance on Light," which we at the present day call the *Book of the Dead* but which the Egyptian priests entitled *The Book of the Master of the Secret House.* And the correspondence which I pointed out to exist between them resulted in the two mysteries partially at least illumining and disclosing each other. Considering the difficulties naturally surrounding such a subject, the reception accorded to my work has been very encouraging. Here and there it is true some critic, impelled perhaps by an unwonted sense of injured omniscience, gave vent to utterances of a dark and oracular character. For instance in one famous weekly Review, the writer gave to the public and myself his personal and almost passionate assurance that, no matter what the appearances might indicate, no correspondence was ever intended between the building and the papyrus; as if he had been intimately acquainted with the authors of both, and a few thousand years or so were but an unconsidered trifle in his long and learned existence. But for the most part the book was freely recognised as the first attempt to give some consistent account of the hitherto uncomprehended religion of Egypt, taken solely from Egyptian sources; and the testimony borne by the highly distinguished Egyptologist, Professor Maspero, carries especial weight. " The Pyramids and the *Book of the Dead*," he wrote to me (adding at the same time that no Egyptologist had dealt with the subject before myself), "reproduce the same original, the one in words, the other in stone." And the prevalence of a tradition among the priests of Memphis (a fact which I learned later from the same authority) supporting my contention that that Secret House was the scene where the neophyte was initiated into the mysteries of Egypt, lends it a force which only direct evidence could rebut.

During the period which has elapsed since publication, I have not ceased to follow up that clue to the best of my power, more particularly by ascertaining the degree of accuracy which may be attached to the astronomical conceptions, which form so large a part of the imagery employed. For the directly religious portion of the teaching has engaged the attention of many experts in the hieroglyphic texts ; and our knowledge of the forms in which the divine ideas were conceived among that ancient priesthood, if not yet clear and consistent, is at least free in great measure from the distortion and misrepresentation wherein those ideas were involved, when filtered through the highly imaginative but singularly inobservant intellect of Greece. On the other hand, with regard to the scientific principles embodied in the Egyptian conceptions, except for the researches of the late Dr. Brugsch, no writer, so

far as I am aware, possessing a moderate knowledge of mathematical astronomy, and at the
same time some acquaintance with the hieroglyphic text, has devoted himself specifically to
the subject ; and hence it has naturally come to
pass that an amount of contempt has been
poured upon the science of early Egypt compar-
able only to the piles of filth which the ignorant
hordes of wandering Arabs heaped upon the
majestic monuments and temples themselves.
Yet surely it is not a little difficult to understand the position of those who, while recognising with a late astronomer, Professor Proctor,
that the temples of that country were erected
by " astronomers for astronomers," can nevertheless placidly regard those stupendous structures, which for thousands of years seem rather
to have defied assaults than to have needed
repair from the hand of man, as the mere
monuments of a folly even more stupendous
than themselves.   It is fairly amazing to think
that while even to this day the grandeur of
those marvellous ruins towers above the most
finished buildings of later nations, and while
every modern investigation only brings out
more clearly the profound skill and forethought
lavished upon their construction, yet even

scholars should be content to regard the whole
line of Pharaohs as animated by no other
spirit than that of Charles Dickens's happy-go-
lucky creation, Mr. Wemmick, in *Great Expect-
ations*. "Hallo!" said that casually minded
individual, "here's a church, let's have a wed-
ding." "Hallo!" according to these writers,
cries one Egyptian monarch, "here's a cataract,
let's build a temple." "Hallo!" cries another,
"here's a pole-star, let's put up a pyramid."
On the contrary, as we become more familiar
with the Wisdom of Egypt, so do we find that
wisdom to justify itself the more clearly to our
perception, and the stricter the precision required, the more closely do the scientific conceptions appear to respond. Here then at least
we are upon firm ground, and can apply the
severest tests at each fresh step of seeming
advance; while the inner or mystical doctrine
conveyed, that is to say, the presentation of
the Invisible Light therein shadowed forth,
will become far easier both to follow and to
check, if we rightly apprehend their mode of
regarding the manifestations of the light which
is seen.

Accordingly, when in the interval it was my
good fortune to visit the country for the second

time, I gave attention to both these points.
With the sacred writings in hand I went
through the secret places of the Great House;
and I greatly doubt whether anyone will do
the same, bearing in mind the tradition of the
priests, and picturing to himself the midnight
watch of the lonely neophyte amid the impenetrable darkness of those solemn chambers,
without recognising how apt was that awe-in-
spiring structure for the initiation into the
secrets of the unseen world.   With regard also
to the scientific aspect, I was so fortunate as to
detect certain points hitherto unnoticed which
seemed to throw much light on the astronomical conceptions; and on my return to England
I gave the result of my researches (if I may
be permitted so large a word) partly in a public
lecture which I was privileged to deliver in the
Hall of New College, Oxford, on the Scientific
Precision of the Astronomy of Early Egypt,
and partly in a letter which I published in *The
Times* on the geographical and astronomical
conditions fulfilled by the situations of the
principal temples.

Under these circumstances, it appeared to me
that the time had arrived when we may enlarge
somewhat upon our former horizon and enter

with greater freedom upon the nature of the doctrines inculcated in the sacred writings. But in executing this task it has been necessary, of course, to go over in some part the same ground as before; and where this has been the case I have not thought it advisable to rewrite that which I saw no probability of improving by revision, though even here the passages will, I think, be found to have gained in significance by the change of context. In especial *I have endeavoured to disencumber the subject from all the symbolism of whatever kind* in which it has been enwrapped, so as to throw some portion at least of the *Book of the Master* open to all the world. For they alone, it is true, will see the full bearing of such a record upon the development of mankind and the light which it throws on social problems, who have painfully traced back custom and rite and doctrine and law from age to age and from country to country by the laborious comparison of record and tradition and relic and monument, and can comprehend the almost indestructible tenacity which characterises the grasp of antiquity, and the vitality even now possessed by ideas and creeds long ago to all appearance buried in profound oblivion. But

who is there, however careless of such problems,
or disinclined for the study of history, who yet
does not feel some thrill at the thought of penetrating the very heart and mind of men whose
bones were mingled with the dust thousands
of years before the sacred plough traced out
the walls of Rome, or Abraham went forth
from Haran in the faith of the true God. For
the earliest known form of man's spiritual life
is fraught with a charm indescribable and in-
communicable. We cannot but be touched
with some feeling of pathos as we watch those
far-off generations looking forward to the mysteries of the tomb which they have solved for
so many ages, but which, to us, remain enigmas
still. We cannot but experience some sense
of awe when we find them expecting the same
immortality beyond the grave which forms the
hope of so many millions among ourselves.
And even such details as the construction of
the kalendar, or the reckoning of the years,
become irradiated with a sudden glow when
we recognise that as those long-departed students gazed silently and persistently into
Nature's infinite Book of Secrecy, their vision
pierced beyond the veil of sense ; and that for
every festival and every cycle, the outward

Preface xi

aspect of the earth and heaven imaged to
their mind some interior and eternal truth.
And that interest quickens with an ever-growing freshness as we pass from the celebration
and ceremonies of their common life to the
deeper doctrine of the Hidden God, and the
Instruction of the Postulant in the secrets of
the Eternal Wisdom.

But there is one feature in special which appears to me to possess an unique and pre-eminent interest. Commenting upon a review of
my book which appeared in *The Freemason*,—
a recognised organ of the famous brotherhood,
—a Roman Catholic professor of theology addressed to me the following letter, the contents
of which he courteously gave me permission to
publish, and which is the more worthy of consideration because the doctrines of that theology are as severely and systematically defined
as the most rigid conceptions of mathematics :

" Many thanks for sending me a copy of *The Freemason's* review of your attractive and remarkable book.
I, of course, know nothing of Freemasonry (though I
have followed what you say easily enough), but I have
been greatly struck with the notice in question. For
whereas the reviewer, writing evidently as an expert in
that subject, strongly commends your book as contain-

ing matter of deep interest to his fellow Masons, I, on
the other hand, as one whose special avocation is the
study of Catholic theology, have been surprised beyond
measure at the profound doctrines of the Catholic faith,
and the numerous illustrations of our own Scriptures,
which seem to me, in reading your book, to have been
foreshadowed beneath the symbols of that most mysterious religion, almost as though we had in it the very
' Word of God ' of which the Apostle speaks, the ' mystery which has been hidden from ages and generations.'
This double significance would be extraordinary enough
if your views on the subject were derived either from
the teaching of Catholicity or from the secrets of Masonry, but its singularity is enhanced a hundred-fold
when one reflects that they come neither from one
source nor the other, but from the records of ancient
Egypt."

Now with regard to the phrases and doctrinal allusions, current, as I believe, among the
Masonic brotherhood of the present day, which
in dealing with the building which was literally
the Masonic " Light" of Egypt I was led to
employ, I have in the present work reduced
them as far as I found it possible. For, although I was careful to explain that such expressions were designed to refer only to the
actual masonry of the building in question and
the analogous features in the Egyptian ritual,
yet in more than one quarter I found that the

book was supposed to be written on Masonic
principles ; an altogether erroneous view except in so far as those principles may be in accordance with the doctrines which we find in
the papyri. On the other hand, a notable instance wherein the deeper study of Egyptian
theosophy brings out with increased force the
analogy dwelt upon by the Catholic professor
will be found in dealing with the temple of the
Virgin Mother Hathor, from whose womb came
forth the divine Horus, the second member of
the Egyptian Trinity. More startling still,
when we turn to the Gospels themselves, we
find their teaching echoed by the Egyptian
Ritual with a directness even greater than in
the sacred writings of the Old Testament.
Thus, though the Hebrew scriptures reveal
many of the names of God, they do not assign
to Him the name of the Light. But the
Light is the very term by which the mystical
Evangelist designates the Second Person ;
while in the first ages of the Church the Illuminate was the title conferred upon those who
were permitted to assist at the Christian " mysteries." So, also, the title of Master, of such
great significance in the Ritual of Egypt, is
nowhere given in the Old Testament to the

Almighty, but it is the single title of authority claimed for Himself by the divine Master in the Gospel; and it is twice employed by Him in a mysterious manner when giving commandment for preparing the divine mysteries in the upper chamber.   Again, the second birth of the soul is nowhere, by open expression at least, taught in the writings either of Moses or of the prophets; and if those scriptures therefore contained the full teaching revealed to the Jews, why should Nicodemus have been rebuked for ignorance of that doctrine?   But Moses, nevertheless, whose skill in all the wisdom of Egypt was famous fifteen hundred years after his death, must have been well acquainted with it, for it formed a most important element in that creed, and was indeed the very act whereby the departed was rendered capable of initiation into the mysteries.   And thus we are brought face to face with a most profound and fascinating problem, which would solve a thousand anomalies.   Was there along with and even before the existence of a recorded revelation an unwritten and inscrutable mystery handed down by the "Sekhem Ur am Sekhemmu," the Grand Master among the Masters, generation after generation, from the earliest ages to which our own scriptures refer,—the time when the prophet Enoch who foretold the scepticism of the latter days walked the path of God and was caught up bodily into the hidden Light? To my own apprehension, I confess, there is much to render it far from improbable that such a view may be correct; and that in searching for the key to the *Book of the Master* we may have chanced upon nothing less than the revelation of a revelation. But upon this point, of which all can form their own judgment, I have entered into no discussion, preferring to leave the analogy to speak for itself. And I have confined my efforts to attempting to express in a clear and popular form, which all may easily follow, an outline of those deeply veiled doctrines of which I may have caught a glimpse; and thus to present such an account of the earliest recorded religion as may afford to all some conception of its transcendent majesty and supernal beauty.

CONTENTS

Contents

Contents

CHAPTER VIII

THE SECRET SCROLL

CHAPTER IX

THE SECRET HOUSE

CHAPTER X

THE ENTRANCE ON LIGHT

CHAPTER XI

THE INSTRUCTION IN WISDOM

Contents

N. B.—Unless express mention is made to the contrary, the quotations throughout the work are taken from the Egyptian texts.

ILLUSTRATIONS

Illustrations

THE BOOK OF THE MASTER

CHAPTER I

THE RESURRECTION OF EGYPT

NUMBERLESS as are the changes and catastrophes of world-wide influence which have crowded this century of revolution, none is more startling or universal than its revelation of secrets and publication of that which has been sedulously hidden. It is not merely that the Röntgen rays of the press penetrate every corner of our lives and pierce through well-nigh every veil; that what is done at home to-day is to-morrow accurately known in the streets; that the counsels of statesmen are scarcely determined in confidence before they are published and discussed in every town and village; but the secrets also of the past have yielded themselves up, and we can plainly read the motives which our fore-fathers successfully concealed from the men of their own generation. From the long-forgotten archives of our own state papers, from Venice, from Genoa, from I know not where, light has poured in upon motives and trans-actions buried in oblivion not for decades but for centuries. On every side we have been de-luged with private letters, private memoirs, private despatches on affairs of state, private reports from ambassadors and confidential agents, private instructions from ministers and monarchs, documents of every kind never in-tended but for the eye of the person addressed, until curiosity has become an extinct sentiment, and it is almost impossible to realise that not so long ago the most cherished of all our personal privileges was privacy. Nay, the tomb itself has burst open its hiding-places, and civilisa-tions which perished thousands of years ago have unrolled themselves before our eyes. We may tread the streets of Pompeii, which had already been hidden from mortal eye for one hundred and fifty years when the fathers of the first General Council met at Nicæa to define the Christian faith. We may gaze upon the

gems which went down into the tomb at Mykene
with the ill-fated house of Atreus. We may consult in the heart of London the very tablets
which made up the famous library of the Assyr-
ian Assur-Banipal. Alike in space and time,
the ends of the earth have come upon this generation. As the distances upon our globe have
shrunk until we hold daily and familiar inter-
course with the farthest corners of the world,
so the chasm of the ages has been bridged
across by the newly opened records of the past.

Amid all this busy scene of revival and revelation, the resurrection of primæval Egypt
stands out with peculiar eminence. For more
than a thousand years from the day when the
barbarous Omar entered the capital of the ancient kingdom, and the funeral rites of the
classic learning were celebrated in the flames
of the great library at Alexandria, to the day
when Champollion, like another Sirius, heralded
the dawn of a new era of Egyptian brilliance,
an ever-growing obscurity buried the entire
land. Less than a century has elapsed since the
most appalling penalties in this world and the
next were fulminated by the Sultan against
the official who should dare to allow a Christian " to approach the sacred port of Suez, the

starting-point of the Holy Haj." To-day that port is the crowded entrance of the most cosmopolitan highway on the globe. For centuries past, Egypt, as it was the earliest so it was the most jealously guarded seat of Moslem law. To-day its courts recognise a multiplex jurisdiction of alien nations, for which no precedent exists in the history of any other state. Within living memory, its hieroglyphs were an enigma hopelessly abandoned ; its temples hidden beneath the accumulated filth of generations of Arabs ; the very age of its ruins unguessed within thousands of years. To-day the mighty buildings stand clearly forth to attest their pristine majesty ; the canons of the kings may be consulted in their original records, and the errors ascribed to careless scribes, who thought no mortal eye would ever look upon the papyri concealed within the grave-clothes of the mummy, are controverted by the hieroglyphic scholarship of Europe.

A peculiar fascination surrounds every detail of life in early Egypt. For all other empires, except perhaps the Babylonian, can be assigned with more or less certainty some point of historic origin. The days of the founders of Rome or of Athens are but the middle ages

TEMPLE OF LUXOR.

of history when compared with the days of
Khufu or of Mena.   India does not claim for
her earliest Vedas an antiquity exceeding four
thousand years.   The sacred writings of China
count less than a thousand more.   A thousand
years earlier still, the beginnings of Babylonia
become very dim.   On the banks of the Nile
alone do we find, centuries before the date of
the Accadian Sargon, a settled monarchy and a
constituted state, an elaborate ritual and
organic hierarchy, a specific architecture and a
copious alphabet.   Hence it is that the principal anomaly which usually blurs our conception
of antiquity, namely, the interference of an
element alien to the environment, in the formation of the customs of a race, more particularly
when that race has been transplanted from
some wholly diverse soil, is absent from the
horizon of Egypt ; and the picture which we
may draw of Egyptian civilisation has its source,
its development, and its consummation in the
conditions of Egypt alone.   No feature of
attraction is wanting in that remarkable scene.
The stately river, the source of perennial life
and freshness to the entire land, the long line
of majestic temples crowning the banks, the
laughing population crowding its waters, the

dances, the games, the songs, the wrestlings, the perpetual feasts, the boats of pleasure jostling with the sacred boats of the dead,—all these things make up a picture which, set in the dazzling clearness of the cloudless sky, leaves a charm that can neither be rivalled nor forgotten.

That picture, too, demands no painful effort of the imagination to fill up for ourselves from broken and disjointed details. We are not called upon, as in classic writings, to piece out into such consistency as we may, the fragmentary hints of social life laboriously gathered from chance allusions hidden in a score of different writers. Nor need we content ourselves with descriptions of events written centuries after their occurrence. We can go straight to the fountain head, and consult the original records. On the huge gate-towers of the temples, on the walls, on the enormous sarkophagi, on the architraves, on the pillars of the immense buildings, we find the deeds of the princes set out in the sacred hieroglyphs. For the battle of Lake Regillus we must trust to the traditions preserved by Livy. For the first great battle of Megiddo, which preceded by hundreds of years the famous encounter wherein Josiah perished long before ever

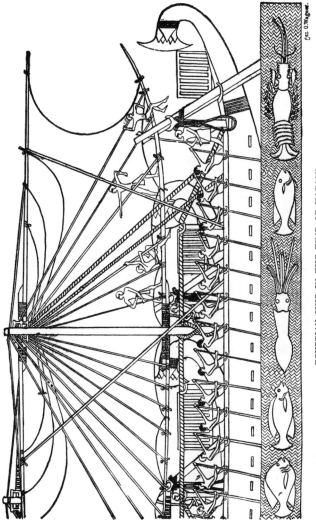

EGYPTIAN SHIP IN THE TIME OF HATASU.

Regillus was fought, we have the cotemporaneous account of the conqueror Thothmes
and the lists of the spoils drawn up by royal
officers.   Nay, more, the monuments of Egypt
give us not descriptions alone, but actual re-

Bust of Thothmes I.

presentations of the
scenes.   Of the tri-
umphs celebrated by
the renowned Julius,
what trace is left for
posterity to gaze upon?
But the triumphs of
Rameses and of Seti,
which took place well-
nigh as long before
the time of Cæsar as
Cæsar's day was before
our own, live yet in
every detail.   The gar-
ments, the ornaments,
the countenances, even the colour of the hair
of the different races which took part in
those processions, all may be seen to-day upon
the walls of the palaces which witnessed
them.   Of Moses and of Solomon, of the
founder of Rome, nay of the great apostle
of the Gentiles, we possess not even a tradi-

tional likeness.   But the features of Pharaoh
may be as familiar to us as they were to his
adoring subjects.   A triple enclosure formed
by massive columns, of infinite pathos in their
lonely grandeur, is all that is left to tell us how
the earth-shaking Poseidon was worshipped in
his home at Pæstum.   But every feature of
the procession which trod the long aisles of
Karnak, the vessel of purification, the wings
on the sacred scribe, the company of the singers, the quadruple ranks of priests, the sacred
ark borne upon their shoulders, the cherubim
with outstretched wings shadowing the Deity
enthroned between, have all been preserved
for our inspection, no less than the words of
the solemn litany which the worshippers addressed to Ra, the unseen Light.

Two marked peculiarities characterise the
records of the earliest times.   Nothing is more
striking than the knowledge of science which
the priests of Egypt are more and more generally admitted to have possessed, in proportion
as the facts are more carefully investigated.
What architect of the present day would undertake to erect a building, more than four
hundred feet high, full of chambers of the
most elaborate description which should never

need repair for six thousand years? What
other nation not only discovered the tran-
scendental relation between radius and circumference—the foundation of all curvilinear
measurement—but utilised it as a principle of
architectural construction? Where else shall
we find a building oriented with such perfect
accuracy that, if Mr. Flinders Petrie be correct, the minute displacement wrought in the
course of ages represents (and consequently
measures) the secular variation due to a recondite cosmical force? Where else shall we find
an antique kalendar based on a correct knowledge of the motion of the earth? What other
people knew, as Dr. Brugsch and M. Maspero
aver, the proper motion of the sun in space;
or who devised the lovely cycle of the herald
star, which measured whole ages by the rising
light as it dawned for a moment on the eastern
horizon?

Equally striking and even more distinctive,
perhaps, is the perpetual presence of the life-
giving river. From end to end of its territory,
from age to age of its history, in the religion,
in the commerce, in the honours of the dead,
wherever we may turn and on whatsoever object we may fix our eyes, we never for a mo-

ment lose sight of the blue waters of the Nile.
That beautiful stream, flowing tranquilly for
hundreds of miles beneath the serene sky, alone
gave verdure and plenty to the long and narrow
strip of fertile soil which lines its borders, cut
off by deserts on either hand, and alone permits the very existence of an Egyptian people.

According to ancient tradition and agreeably
also to the records, the ancestors of the race in
very remote times were not of northern but of
southern extraction,[1] being originally natives
of Poont, situated near the Equatorial sources
of the Nile.   In harmony with this tradition,
we find that the central point of the Egyptian
universe was the Aptu, or southern " Apex of
the Earth," in the " Holy Land of Khent," mentioned by Dr. Brugsch, that point on the Equator which is intersected by the meridian of
Memphis, just by the western shore of the
great Equatorial lake from which the famous
river derives its streams.   From that point of
origin, we may mark out the four cardinal
points of the universal sphere, the thrones of
the four Egyptian spirits of the Light, with

[1] Some Egyptologists still cling to the superstition (for of record in
its favour what is there ?) that the Egyptian race came into the
country from the North.   Not so, Prof. Maspero nor Prof. Petrie.

Hāpi in their midst, protecting the southern
fountains of the Nile. These four bright
spirits, the guardians of the heavenly dome,
were imaged to the Egyptians under the form
of the cynocephalous ape, the creature which
bears the closest resemblance to humanity.
And from them, as the four living creatures
before the throne of Ra, assistance was invoked
by the holy Departed in the Ritual of Egypt
at the moment when the full splendour of the
orbit was bursting upon his illumined sight.
From that country, the earliest immigrants appear to have followed a twofold route. In
part, according to a very ancient tradition mentioned by Dr. Brugsch, they proceeded along
the banks of the river, sojourning for a while,
it would seem, at Meroe, where the hoary temple of Amen and the ruins of Assur, discovered
in that island by Caillard, attest their ancient
presence ; while others appear to have come
down by the Red Sea, as Mr. Petrie's discoveries indicate, and thence to have crossed the
desert to Coptos. From this most important
circumstance, it is essential to bear in mind
that to the Egyptian the south was the " Great
Quarter," to which especial reverence was due.
And this explains why it was that every year

the sacred images were carried into the ancestral country.   An echo of the same tradition is found in the visits of the gods of Homer to the "blameless Ethiopians," for blamelessness would be the essential note of the reverence due to the parent race.   Consistently with this, we read in the ancient inscription on the coffin of Amamu, how the holy dead, "after flying over the whole face of heaven," is "established among the blessed company in the south."   And in that same archaic papyrus we are told of the celestial land of Khent, or Khent-Amenti, the habitation of the hidden God, imaged on earth by the " Holy Land of Khent" at the Aptu, or southern apex of the earth.   Hence also the most sacred portion of the temple was placed toward the same quarter ; and the Great Pyramid from the entrance to the innermost chamber was oriented north and south.

In truth, to the mind of the Egyptian the whole bed of the immense river was but the sacred image of the unseen land watered by the " Celestial Nile," of which the Ritual speaks ; the " Nuter Khart," or holy land of the dead, with its triple division into Rusta, the territory of Initiation, Aahlu, the territory of

Illumination, and Amenti, the place of union with the unseen father.   At the northern extremity of the river, where the ocean gives an entrance to the country, was the mouth of Rosetta, or Rusta, imaging, as we learn from a papyrus of the time of Khufu, the mouth of the tomb.   All along the valley of Upper Egypt as we ascend the stream, at Denderah, at Abydos, at Thebes, were the great shrines sanctified by the manifestation of the Deity. At the southern limit of the kingdom, immediately below the tropical arch traversed at that epoch by the sun in the height of summer, is the Cataract, or " Gate of the Nile," through which the forefathers of the race entered the country, imaging in the Ritual the point in

Atf-crown of Illumination.

Zodiacal Light of Supreme Heaven.

Aahlu, or territory of illumination, where the holy dead, when he has achieved the " Passage of the Sun," opens the gate of the celestial Nile and receives the "Atf-crown of Illumination," fashioned after the form of the zodiacal light, the glory of the supreme heaven.   And far towards the south lay the sacred land of

Poont, the distant fatherland, like Amenti, the unseen home of God their father. The same celestial origin and end, thus reflected in the entire country, were concentrated and epitomised in the capital. At the junction of the two kingdoms of Upper and Lower Egypt, where the Nile branches out into the great angle of the delta, stood Memphis, more properly " Men-nofer," the " Holy Foundation," the seat of the double government of Egypt, with its palace dedicated to the Creator-spirit Ptah, its cemetery bearing the title of " Blessed Immortality," like our own " God's Acre," and its canal called after the Voyage of the Unseen Waters. There, too, was the territory of " Sochet Ra," the Fields of the Sun. And close to the sacred city on the western bank of the river, upon a lonely rock, rose the Great Pyramid, that house of Osiris, to which, says the papyrus of Amen Hotep, Thoth, the Eternal Wisdom, " conducts the Illuminate."

From every portion of that country the past has yielded up its records. Egypt, for so many centuries the land of the buried, has suddenly become the land of the risen, dead ; and the message which the long-silenced voice proclaims as with a tongue of fire is the primitive

belief in the divine origin and end of man.
Everywhere and always throughout ancient
Egypt is heralded the same doctrine of eternal
Day.   From the orbit of the earth, from the
pole-star of the heavens, from the dawning of
Sirius, from the radiance of the sun, from the
renewal of the moon, from the waters of the
river, from the palaces, from the temples, from
the very cere-cloths of the rifled dead, comes
forth a voice which for ages has been hushed
in the grave; and that voice with startling
clearness bears testimony to a judgment beyond the tomb, and the Fatherhood of the
unseen God.

GREAT HALL OF COLUMNS AT KARNAK (RESTORED).
(BUILT BY SETI I.)

CHAPTER II

THE RELIGION OF LIGHT

TO whatever quarter of the globe we may turn our attention, tracing out the earliest records of the inhabitants, there is no community, " literally from China to Peru," as Sir H. Maine has observed, over the customs and constitution of which religion has not exercised a potent and permanent influence. But the country where, beyond all others, that principle prevailed in its fullest and most creative force was undoubtedly the land of Egypt. Highly complex in its structure and regulated in its every detail by the strictest observance of custom, the constitution of Egyptian society presents, nevertheless, a very clear appearance, if we regard the nation as a patriarchal family, founded on a hierarchical basis, and organically settled throughout the country upon a system dictated by religion.   The whole land was divided into the same number of provinces (or nomes as they are somewhat affectedly called after the Greek fashion) as the divine spirits who, according to the Egyptian creed, composed the tribunal by which the dead were judged.   In each province the capital was a sacred city, being the territory attached to a great temple, which itself constituted the enclosure around a shrine of the Deity.   To every temple a distinctive priesthood was assigned, the members of which could not enter the priesthood of another district ; while the monarch, though practically obtaining his throne by descent, appears to have undergone a form of election and to have been consecrated to his office by the high-priest of the patriarchal province.   Nor were the temples alone dedicated to sacred things, but the structures of daily life shared the divine significance.   And for every division of the country, as De Rougé has shown, the palace and the canal, no less than the temple and the district, bore a name of mystery, and reflected the region of the Holy Dead.

Most characteristic of all was the omnipotent and all-dominating sense of the fatherhood of

God, producing the familiar and in some respects even joyous aspect which the Egyptian imparted to the idea of death; ever regarding our present existence only as an antechamber of one to come, and our occupations in this life as a foretaste and counterpart

Osiris.

of a life beyond the tomb. Hence in theory, as M. Maspero informs us, every Egyptian had a right to an eternal mansion. And when the Christian apostle wrote that we have a house not made with hands eternal in the heavens, he only gave expression to the same image as the Egyptian priests when they spoke of the eternal house which the divine

Horus.

Horus built for his father, Osiris. For the same reason the ancestor of a family never withdrew his presence.   Hence temples were palaces, and palaces were temples.   And the greatest work which the greatest sovereign could achieve was to build for himself an imperishable tomb.

But though the influence of their religion was spread thus widely, and though the ranks of the priesthood appear to have been open to all who could endure the training, the inner doctrines were not taught publicly nor expressed in plain and definite language.   On the contrary, they were carefully hidden from the uninitiated, and were conveyed in terms of studied obscurity and by means of illustrations which themselves could not be understood without previous instruction.   To the sense indeed, which the priests at least possessed, both of the divine personality and of their own ultimate union with the personal deity, far more probably than to any artificial pretension to a supposed exclusiveness, may be ascribed the mystery enshrouding their religion.   For mystery is to God only what privacy is to man, our sense of which deepens with deepening intimacy.   And though three hundred years of continuous wrangling over the secret truths which most profoundly affect the heart and mind have gone far to coarsen and deaden our spiritual sense, the soul still resents as the most unpardonable offence, the profanation of a vulgar touch. For whether we acknowledge it or not, the springs of our entire existence are hidden. From the darkness of the womb to the darkness of the tomb, the source of our every action is veiled from us. Mystery is the beginning; mystery is the ending; mystery is the whole body of our life. We cannot breathe, nor sleep, nor eat, far less think or speak, without exercising powers which to us are inconceivable, by means of processes which to us are inscrutable. Who is so ignorant as not to know these things; who so learned as to make them clear?

Of the various forms and symbols in which the priests enwrapped the mystery of Egypt, there is one class which at once conceals and reveals the secret wisdom as with a radiant veil. No ordinary image, it is clear, no mineral, no plant, no animal, though they may shadow forth partially the particular attributes or actions of the Deity, could suffice to convey the full expression of the relation between God and man. Only the orbs of heaven, obeying in their lustrous course the laws which know no change, could adequately express the living energy, the illuminative power, and above all the illimitable endurance of the divine attributes ;—a form of imagery which suggested itself with great facility to the mind of Egypt.   Bathed in a cloudless and translucent atmosphere, with all the unfaltering mechanism of sun, moon, and stars perpetually opened before them, the priestly astronomers of that country, or the " Mystery Teachers of the Heavens," as they were officially called, pictured the invisible glories of the unseen creation to be reflected in the serene and luminous orbit of our own planet amid the firmament, as that firmament itself with all its radiant beauty is reflected in the clear waters of their own familiar river. And hence it is that in their sacred writings we find well-nigh every religious idea to be conveyed by some astronomical analogue ; while with each astronomical conception and conjunction there appears to correspond some manifestation of the Deity.   A beautiful allusion, for example, is made in the Egyptian Ritual to the illuminative action of the sun as the earth, the vessel of God, performs her daily rotation and annual circuit around in the heavens.   For we read there how the holy departed

has appeared in full splendour in the vessel of
Ra; and how Thoth, the Divine Wisdom,
clothes the spirit of the justified a million
times in a garment of true linen, of that substance, that is to say, which by its purity and
brilliancy reminds us of the mantle, woven out
of rays of light, wherewith the sun enwraps the
earth afresh each day she rotates before him;
just as the soul of man is invested with new
radiance each time that he turns to the presence of his Creator.   From their profound
theosophy, each phenomenon of nature conveyed to them a corresponding manifestation
of the divine personality, and according to the
Ritual it was the Deity indwelling in the soul
which confers upon the man the power of perceiving these relations.   " I am perception,"
we read, "the imperishable soul."   In the
noonday glow of the sun they beheld the
splendour of Ra; in his setting, the death of
Osiris; in the new dawn, his resurrection as the
incarnate Horus; in the glowing fire, the creator spirit Ptah; in the harmonious proportions of the universe, the Eternal Wisdom,
Thoth, "the Mind and Will of God"; in the
starry firmament crowned by Alcyone and the
Pleiades (the sacred bull and attendant cows),

the ineffable beauty of Hathor, the living tabernacle of the sacred Light.

Thus, in the religion of ancient Egypt, the
deepest and the most fascinating mystery of
antiquity, the visible creation was conceived as
the counterpart of the unseen world.   And
the substance consisted not of a mere vague
belief in a life beyond the grave, but in tracing out the Path whereby the Just, when the
portal of the tomb is lifted up, passes through
the successive stages of Initiation, of Illumination, and of Perfection, necessary to fit him for
an endless union with Light, the Great Creator.
That Path it was, through the secret places of
the universe, which appears to have been the
subject of the secret mysteries which were
communicated to the postulant, according to
Egyptian tradition, by the Master of the Secret
Scroll, in the secret chambers of the House
which bore the mystic title of the Light.   And
in order to follow his instruction, we must
commence by raising our eyes to the heavens
around us, and understanding how our earthly
sphere is itself a member of the starry host.

CHAPTER III

THE FESTIVALS OF THE SUN AND MOON

TIME, the most powerful factor in the determination of human affairs, is also the most impalpable. Of everything else which forms the subject of measurement, for instance of the velocity of the wind or of the extension of space, we can conceive, by analogy at least, some kind of mental picture; but of time we find it equally hard to pronounce whether it have or have not any distinctive existence. If there be any one mental fact which man accepts for himself as unquestionable, it is that we know our past and are ignorant of our future, yet between past and future who shall define the point of separation? So subtle, so imperceptible, is that infinitesimal and ever-moving barrier between the two limitless expanses, that atom of existence which we call the present moment, that it eludes even the

grasp of thought. If a man says "I am"—
the simple declaration of his own existence,
and as short a sentence as he can well utter,—
when he pronounces the word "I," the word
"am" is in the future; when he says "am,"
the word "I" is in the past. Yet alike from
the moment which has just gone by, and from
that which is even now at hand, we are separated by a gulf as absolutely impassable as that
which divides us from the days of the Pharaohs,
or from the future of a thousand years to come.
"God himself cannot undo the past," says Pindar. "Shadow forever veiled, forever near,
Thou who art called To-morrow," cries the
French poet in a well-known ode. "I am
Yesterday," says Osiris in the Egyptian Ritual,
signifying that he for whom the past is still in
existence is freed from the conditions of time
which limit the mortal intellect.

But time, though in itself inconceivable, pro-
duces effects which are both palpable and universal; for none can overlook the changes
which time works on all visible things, and
more particularly in the two most potent forms
of change, namely, those of growth and motion.
Wherever either the increase in magnitude or
the change in position in any given body dur-

ing a given period can be measured, there it is
evident that time can be measured along with
it.   Thus the varying aspect of the flowers or
the direction of the falling shadows marks the
passing hour.   The recurrence of certain well-
known scents and sounds proclaims the advent
and departure of the seasons.   The gradual
alteration in ourselves or in our friends tells us
of the lapse of years.   Nor can we measure
time except by change.

How then to find a definite and constant
standard, never altering and never ceasing,
whereto we may refer this most fugitive and
elusive element ?   In the mechanism of the
heavens alone—that is to say, in the relative
changes of the celestial bodies, constantly varying yet ever renewed after fixed intervals of
time—can such a measure be found, which will
continue to recur unfailingly though ages pass
away.   Chief among such periods is that of
the orbit of our own planet, the motion which
gives the key to all the varying aspects of the
universe.   From that orbit, the line of the
Pharaohs derived one of their proudest titles,
" Neb Sennen," Lord of the Orbit (⬯), proclaiming at once the universality and the endurance of their dominion ;   and from it the

Initiate in the Egyptian Ritual obtained his
Illumination in celestial things.   That motion
also is invested in no slight degree with the
serenity of the heavens ; and no natural image
is fraught with greater radiance or tranquillity
than that of the rolling year as it circles perpetually about the feet of God.   Even in the
midst of cloud and fog, the mere striking of
a clock, that record of planetary motion, serves
to remind us how circumscribed is the surrounding gloom, and how the dull earth beneath
our feet is, even as we gaze upon it, shining to
its far companions in the fields of light.   As
that lustrous orbit is woven, revolution after
revolution with never-failing beauty, cycle after
cycle of age-long periods, like golden serpents,
twine themselves around it, and span the gulfs
of time with the years of the Most High.

Such a system of harmonious periods, and
of measured intervals, corresponding to universal, not arbitrary, standards, was a natural,
and indeed an essential, element in the theosophy of a priesthood whose religious teaching
was intentionally veiled under the analogies of
the Light.   And the celebration of certain sacred festivals, dependent for their date upon
the recurrence of the various phenomena, pre-

sents the most significant and the most pictur-
esque feature in the social life of Egypt.   Singularly enough also, in tracing the periods and
festivals familiar to the Mystery Teachers at
the Court of Pharaoh, we shall sometimes discover the key to certain conceptions which we
familiarly employ, but of the origin of which

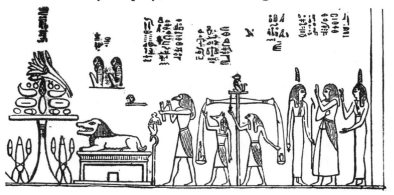

The Balance of Thoth.

we can give no account.   And we shall perceive, not probably without some pleasure,
that they are not the fruit of any arbitrary
arrangement, however ingenious, but are the
products of universal concords, and represent,
so to speak, the beats and bars of the music of
the spheres.

That the moon was the sacred and, at least

in early times, the secret standard of Egyptian science, there seems little doubt.   Thoth, the great Lord of Wisdom and of Measurement, the divine recorder before whom stood the balance of Justice, wherein the light and darkness of man's moral life were weighed, was lord, not of the sun, but of the moon ; and to that latter orb we are indebted for our fundamental standard of time.   For if we consider the motion of the moon relatively to the sun, we shall find that the time that orb takes in covering a space equal to its own disc is just an hour ; and thus we have a practical definition of that important unit.   Now, that measure of the " Hour " was peculiarly sacred in Egypt ; each of the twenty-four which elapse during a single rotation of the earth being consecrated to its own particular deity, twelve of light, and twelve of darkness.   " Explain the God in the Hour," is the demand made of the adept in the Ritual when standing in the Hall of Truth.   And that God in the Hour, we learn, was Thoth, the " Lord of the Moon [1] and the Reckoner of the Universe."

Turning now to the motions of our planet, we find, as Dr. Brugsch has shown, that the

[1] See Note A, page 193.

Egyptian solar kalendar employed a double principle, one for the civil, the other for the sacred, reckoning. In the former, the year came to a close at the end of every three hundred and sixty-fifth day, so that the opening of the new year ran round the entire circle of the seasons in the course of 4 x 365 or 1460 civil years. But in the sacred kalendar a day was intercalated at the close of every fourth, or Grand Year. Hence, therefore, as in our own kalendar, the four great turning-points of the year, namely, the Spring and Autumn Equinoxes (or days when light and darkness are equal all over the world), and the Summer and Winter Solstices, when the sun attains its greatest northern and southern declination, would alway fall on a fixed day of the sacred kalendar. And these festivals were represented in the Ritual by four jets of flame encircling the basin of solar fire, at each of which was stationed one of the divine spirits which "proclaimed forth Truth before the Lord of the Universe."

This reckoning being established, the midsummer solstice was chosen for the opening of the sacred year, the time, that is, when the sun attains the northern limit of his tropical dominion, amid the full lustre of his summer

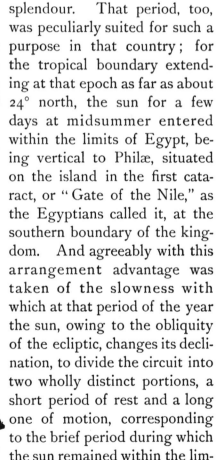

Pillar from Philæ.

splendour. That period, too, was peculiarly suited for such a purpose in that country; for the tropical boundary extending at that epoch as far as about 24° north, the sun for a few days at midsummer entered within the limits of Egypt, being vertical to Philæ, situated on the island in the first cataract, or "Gate of the Nile," as the Egyptians called it, at the southern boundary of the kingdom. And agreeably with this arrangement advantage was taken of the slowness with which at that period of the year the sun, owing to the obliquity of the ecliptic, changes its declination, to divide the circuit into two wholly distinct portions, a short period of rest and a long one of motion, corresponding to the brief period during which the sun remained within the limits of the kingdom, and the prolonged interval

between the departure and return.   The latter
period, or "Orbit," consisting of three hundred and sixty days, was symmetrically
divided according to two different forms,
namely, into twelve equal months,[1] each consisting of three decades of days, and into three
equal seasons, each consisting of twelve decades of days, namely, those of the Inundation
(Se), or rise, of the river, the Winter (Pir), and
the Heat (Semou), answering more or less to
our spring.   The shorter period, consisting of
the sacred interval, or Jubilee, lasted in the ordinary year for five, and in the grand, or fourth,
year for six days, and was entirely taken up
with a series of special festivals.   Hence every
half-orbit, or passage from summer to winter,
or from winter to summer, contained eighteen
such decades of days, and these decades, each
headed by a solar snake,—the spiral curve
traced out upon the surface of the earth by
the vertical sun in the course of each half-
orbit,—are depicted in a striking representation
of the kalendar on the walls of the famous
temple of Denderah.

It may now be not uninteresting or unin-
structive to compare for a moment the system

[1] See Note B, page 195.

of Egypt with our own leap year, for which
we are, in fact, indebted to that country,
through the astronomer Sosigenes, who was
imported by Julius Cæsar from Alexandria,
to remedy in some degree the confusion of
the Roman kalendar. That famous Greek
appears to have performed his task very much
after a fashion not unknown to adapters. He
cared—perhaps he knew—very little about
the astronomical principles involved in the
Egyptian reckoning, and nothing at all about
the niceties of further adjustment which it
demanded ; indeed, before half a century was
passed, his own corrections required to be
corrected. He took no heed of standard or
of measure, of orbit or of sacred interval.
But first he cut up the year into twelve unequal
and unmeaning bits—to say he divided it into
portions is far too scientific an expression—
which rags bore indeed the name of the
insulted moon, but of which that mighty
measurer condescended to make no sort of
recognition. And then he threw the " odd
day " in along with the " odd month " ; much
as a child who has broken his toy horse, glues
a bit of tail to the shortest of the legs, and calls
aloud on creation to admire his handiwork.

Nor is the difference between the Egyptian and the Roman treatment of the kalendar accidental or unimportant. On the contrary, it suggests the key to its use in the ancient country as the great politico-religious instrument whereby the social economy of the nation was co-ordinated with the theosophy of the priesthood. Among modern nations, monotony of recurrence seems to be the single object desired, so as to offer every facility for the arrangements of business or pleasure, and to confine within the strictest limits the diminutive period allotted to the life to come. Any system, therefore, which breaks the regular routine, more particularly if it be connected, as in ancient Egypt, with the commemoration of sacred events, provokes impatience much more than admiration. And the various adjustments of the kalendar appear to be regarded as if they were odds and ends of time left littering about the heavens by the sun and moon, and requiring an ingenious astronomer (like Sosigenes) to fold together and put away tidily.

Very different from this narrow and ungracious spirit was the joyous temper wherewith the Egyptian " Mystery-Teachers of the

Heavens" regarded those sacred intervals.
Throughout the symbology of that country,
life was the centre, the circumference, the
totality of good.   Life was the sceptre in the
hand of Amen; life was the richest "gift of
Osiris."   " Be not ungrateful to thy Creator,"
says the sage Ptah-Hotep, in what is perhaps
the oldest document in existence, "for he has
given thee life."   " I am the Fount of Light,"
says the Creator in the Ritual.   " I pierce the
darkness.   I make clear the path for all; the
Lord of Joy."   By them, therefore, the intervals were gratefully accepted as a kind of
breathing space, wherein time, like the sun at
the solstice, appears for a while to rest, and
man, like the immortals, might enjoy, without
impairing, the treasure of life.   Accordingly
the interval of Jubilee, or time of praise, separating, or rather uniting, year with year, took
place not in the gloom of winter, as with us,
but in the full height and glow of summer,—
at the period at once of accomplishment and
renovation, when the sun was in his fullest
strength, and the rising waters of the Nile
began to renew their life-giving floods; and
each of the days stood prominently out as a
celebration of some distinct form of divine

manifestation. As at the commencement of each year is renewed the divine gift of life, so on the first day of that period of continuous praise was celebrated the birthday of Osiris, the God of Light and Life, Prime Mover of Creation. On the second, the birthday of Horus, God, of God, Lord of the New Dawn, as the dawn itself is renewed at each fresh rotation of the earth. On the third, the birthday of Seb the Creator-spirit of earth, as our planet enters upon a fresh circuit round the parent orb. On the fourth, the birthday of Isis, with her double relation of human and divine motherhood ; as all nature was reawakened to fresh life and vigour on the renewal of the river. On the fifth day was celebrated the birthday of Neith, the Lady of Waters, from whose divine personality gushed the stream of life, who "gave to every mummy the draught for which he thirsted," as the parched lands thirsted for the waters of the Nile. And every fourth, or Grand, Year, was celebrated a sixth festival—that of "Hep-Tep," or "Completion-Beginning," when the revolution and the rotation of our planet were simultaneously completed and begun afresh ; while at the same time the sun himself, in his mighty march through space, drawing with him our whole planetary system, completes an arc of his enormous orbit about equal in length to the course of our planet around him. Such was the symphony of light and joy which for the Egyptian heralded the opening of the glowing year.

CHAPTER IV

THE RISING OF THE RIVER AND THE ORIENT OF
THE STAR

WHILE the periods of the sun and moon lent their harmony to the kalendar of Egypt, there was another cycle of a nature wholly distinct and far more peculiar to the country, which defined its seasons, and gave occasion for its chief festivals. In Egypt alone among inhabitable countries, the single source of life is the river. That narrow strip of land, abundantly fertile as it is wherever irrigated by the waters of the Nile, is itself but a part of the barren and boundless deserts which stretch on either hand from ocean to ocean ; and were those fertilising streams from the distant sources of the equatorial mountains to fail, Egypt as a populated country would cease to exist. These are the conditions which continually and inexorably impress themselves upon the minds of the

The Waters of the Nile.

inhabitants, and which distinguish the land,
not only from our Northern climates but from

all other lands ; for nowhere else is there to be
found a highly cultivated and populous nation
so wholly dependent for its daily bread upon
rain which falls not within their own borders
but upon far remote and even unknown regions.

Like the other institutions of the country,
its festivals were racy of the soil. Pregnant
too as they were, like other Egyptian conceptions, with mystical significance, the external
events which they celebrate are marked by
the stages in the annual rise and fall of those
waters, which figured to them the perennial
streams of the " celestial Nile." For their
river, as they maintained, " came down from
the southern heaven," being the outflow of the
tropical rains in its distant reaches of the
south ; and from that quarter, as ancient tradition and modern research unite in testifying,
the forefathers of their race set forth to their
more famous home. Accordingly the flood of
the Nile ran like a sparkling torrent alike
through the religion and the science of the
country ; and as the gradual rise and fall of its
never-failing stream marked the course of our
planet in its circuit round the parent orb, the
celestial festivals which celebrated the phenomena attendant upon its advance were mingled

with rejoicings which hailed the progress of the reviving waters.

Of the three seasons, each consisting of a hundred and twenty days, the Inundation ("Se"), which commenced at the close of the sacred interval of divine birthdays, was undoubtedly the principal. But the approach of that season had been heralded for many weeks beforehand by various signs in the higher reaches of the river, and these anticipatory

The Solar Eye Impersonated.

symptoms appear to have been celebrated during the close of the previous year. As early as the end of March, and far into April (the beginning of the Egyptian month Epiphi), the Khamsin wind commences to blow with violence, forming the breath of "Typhon," the destroyer. Then comes the vernal equinox, the "Eye of the Sun," which looks forth once more from its winter obscurity. Later on, the tropical rains, sweeping before them

the mass of decaying matter accumulated in
the river from the vegetation of the previous
year, turn the waters of the Nile for a few days
green and unwholesome ; when Osiris, as the
Ritual says, makes such a stench in the river
that gods and men and the very devils stand
aghast,—a marvellous image when applied to
the moral cleansing of all mankind by Osiris,
and the absolution pronounced upon the Justified in the Ritual by the " four Ministers who
proclaim truth before the Universal Lord." A
few days after "green Nile," as that phase is
called, follows the period when the river turns
red, at which time the waters are peculiarly
sweet.   This remarkable phenomenon invari-
ably accompanies the returning flood and is to
be witnessed at this day, while Herodotus has
left us a very fine account, quoted at great
length by Professor Maspero, whose endorsement of it is a singular proof of the unchanging
character of the Nile.   In the upper reaches
of the stream it takes place about the beginning of May, which is the time assigned in the
kalendar of Denderah to the sailing of the
bark of Ra, but it does not reach Philæ till
the middle of June, so that in Lower Egypt it
appears to be connected with the solstice, and

celebrated in the festival entitled the " Eye
Filled with Blood."   About five days before the
summer solstice (for we count always with
reference to that epoch), occurs the festival
now known as the " Night of the Drop," which
appears to have been celebrated under the
title of the " Tears of Isis."   Then comes the
period of lowest level, the death of the river,
when Osiris is wrapped "in his bandages,"

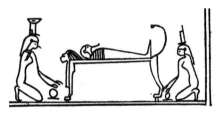

Mummy Laid out between Isis and Nephthys.

shortly followed by the birth of the Deity at
the solstice, and the other divine birthdays
which succeeded it.   On the day after the
close of the sacred interval, was celebrated
the opening of the New Year, or the first of
the month Thoth ; and on the second of that
month, when the rising of the river became
perceptible at Memphis, took place the festival
of the " Rose Crown of Hapi," the presiding
genius of the Nile, and guardian spirit of the

Holy Dead on their entrance into the new life.
About fifty days afterwards, the water has risen
sufficiently in the river for the public sluices to
be opened in Upper Egypt, to which process
allusion would seem to be made in the festival of
" Opening the Doors " ; and two days later we
arrive at the festival of high Nile and the
" Erection of the Tat," or sacred measure of
the waters—a ceremony of which a survival has
been preserved until very recent times.   Fifty
days still later, the flood reaches its greatest
height ; and the water festival of ten days' du-
ration took place.   To the season of Inundation
succeeded that of Winter (Pir), when the period
for the important operation of Ploughing, or
" Digging the Earth," commenced ; during
which season the waters gradually return to
their normal level, the subsidence commencing
at Philæ and ending in Lower Egypt.   Then
came the season of Semou (or Heat), when the
harvest was reaped ; in the course of which
the preliminary festivals begin for the coming
year.

In this blended chorus of rejoicing from
heaven and earth, the stars also had their
voice.   Inconceivably distant as are those
burning suns so far transcending our own

luminary both in size and power, their very
remoteness enables them to discharge certain
functions in regard to celestial measurement
which are denied to the nearer and more conspicuous orbs.   For instance, the interval between two successive transits of the sun at
noon over the meridian of any given place (or
in other words, the length of the solar day),
depends not only on the time occupied by the
earth in rotating round her own axis, but
partly also on the change in the earth's position which has taken place during that interval ; and as the rate of that motion is subject
to a slight variation, now quicker, now slower,
the interval between two such transits differs
slightly from day to day, and consequently
does not afford a constant measure of time.
But in regard to the stars, so enormous are
their distances that the immense orbit of the
earth shrinks, when compared with them, into
a mere point of space ; and the interval between two successive transits of the same star
(or the length of what is called a sidereal day)
depends solely on the time occupied by the
earth in performing a complete rotation round
its axis.   But that rate of rotation never undergoes, so far as is known, any appreciable

change; and hence the successive transits of
any given star over a given place will furnish
the prime requisite for celestial measurement,
i. e., a definite and never-failing measure of
time. For the same reason, the solar day will
be a little longer than the sidereal day; the
difference being on an average about four
minutes every day, or the time the earth
takes to rotate through one degree of the celestial sphere. And anyone who has watched
a given star for several nights together will
have noticed that its rising takes place about
four minutes earlier every evening, and that at
any fixed hour on each night it is one degree
more advanced in the heaven than on the previous night. In fifteen days, therefore, this
difference will amount to an hour, and, accordingly, as we learn from a most interesting
paper published by Professor Renouf on a
kalendar of the Nineteenth Dynasty, the observations of the stars were taken every fifteenth day. From this relation, when taken in
conjunction with a phenomenon of singular
beauty, we derive the key to the most celebrated form of the Egyptian reckoning.

Since a given star rises at any particular
place, such as Memphis, about four minutes

earlier each day, it follows that there will be in each year one day when the star will rise at that place just so long before the dawn as to be visible for a few moments on the horizon before vanishing in the increasing splendour; which phenomenon is astronomically described as the "heliacal rising" of the star, but which we may more shortly and conveniently call its Orient.   Now the number of degrees by which the sun is below the horizon when the orient of the star takes place is not fully determined, and varies to some extent with the locality; but ten degrees below is usually taken as the sun's position when the star is lost in the dawning light, so that the time would be about forty minutes before full sunrise.   Let us consider now the relation between two successive orients (which will of course be a year apart) of some particular star; and for that purpose let us choose, like the Egyptians, Sirius, or, as they called it, Sothis,[1] the most brilliant of the distant suns, the flaming sentinel to us of the fiery hosts of space.   Suppose then that on some particular day (such as midsummer day) Sothis is on the horizon of Memphis when the

---

[1] The true name employed by the Egyptians was Sopht, but the form Sothis is here preserved as being more familiar.

sun is eleven degrees below it, that is, one
degree below the point of the dawn. On that
day the orient of Sothis will take place, that
is, it will rise just before the dawn and will remain visible on the horizon for about four
minutes (while the earth rotates through one
degree), after which it will be lost in the break
of dawn. But on the anniversary of that day
(owing to a relation between the earth's motions of rotation and revolution somewhat too
complex to enter upon here) that phenomenon
will take place one minute later, so that the
star will be visible for three minutes, on the
next for two, and the next again for one. On
the fourth anniversary, therefore, it will come
to the horizon only at the break of dawn, and
consequently will not be visible at all that day;
but its orient will take place on the following
morning, when it will remain visible for four
minutes, and the same phenomena will again
recur.[1] Hence for every grand cycle (four
years) there will be the difference of a day in
the orient of a star, and consequently of three
hundred and sixty-five days in a cycle of 4 x 365,

[1] The problem has been worked out mathematically in a treatise
published by Professor Graves, the astronomer of Oxford, in A.D.
1640.

or 1460 civil years.   But that difference of a
day corresponds exactly with the day intercalated in the sacred kalendar every fourth, or
Grand, Year; exactly as in the case of our own
Leap Year.   And that arrangement, therefore,
was not the result of mere convention, but was
founded on a definite astronomical relation.[1]

That lovely cycle with its tetrachord of
starry light just gleaming on the horizon and
then vanishing, lost in the growing splendour,
appears from the allusions in the Ritual to
have had its spiritual analogue in the festival
of the "Shapes," or divine forms of beauty,
wherein the departed was re-created in the
image of the starry spirits, before merging his
lustre, though not his existence, in the splendour of the manifested Godhead.

[1] See Note C, page 195.

CHAPTER V

THE SACRED LANDMARKS OF THE AGES

AMONG the various peculiarities character-
ising the Nile, it has, I think, generally
escaped attention, that of all countries
Egypt is the one peculiarly suited, not by its
atmosphere alone but far more by its situation,
to provide a natural basis for universal measurement.   For it alone among inhabited regions affords certain positions on the earth's
surface so correlated with the great planes of
celestial reference as to render the periodic
motion of our planet among the heavenly bodies
easy to measure and to record.   To the students of most countries, those fundamental
planes, such, for instance, as the Ecliptic and
the plane of the moon's orbit, present themselves merely as viewless tracts of the infinite
expanse upon which the mind of man has built
up the intellectual measurement of the material

universe. They are recognised indeed as intersecting certain portions of our globe ; but for the most part, sea, and mountain, and desert claim the lonely regions through which they pass, too remote from the neighbourhood of man for us easily to realise that the position of a monument, or a particular bend in a river, may mark, for example, the tropical boundary, and thus may tell us where the plane of our own planet's orbit passes through the surface of the earth. Very different is the case with the fertile strip of land called into being by that strange river, the Nile, which, taking its rise from the great lake of the Equator, intersects in its lower or Egyptian course the planes in which the earth and moon respectively move, and other great planes of astronomical reference. Upon the banks of that river, therefore, and there alone, could man erect substantial and enduring monuments to be the landmarks of ethereal and illimitable space ; while by the shadow of a column or the direction of a shaft he could fix forever the celestial bearings of our planet in its ceaseless motion. For it must not be forgotten that, numerous and complex as are the variations of the celestial bodies, the laws which determine them are fixed

and incapable of caprice ; so that if the relation
which a single point on the surface of the earth
bears to the heavenly orbs at a single precisely
defined moment of time can be precisely measured and unalterably recorded, the precise position of every other heavenly body, and of all
the celestial planes, whatever be their variations and oscillations, becomes definite and cal-
culable in relation to it (so far as the limits of
human science extend), for every moment of
time past, present, or to come.

Now a precisely defined moment of time is
afforded by the commencement of the Egyptian kalendar, which dates not from a particular year or month, but from the exact moment
of the orient, or heliacal rising, of a particular
star.   And with regard to a place, we find that
the position of the capital of the kingdom at
the period is distinguished by peculiar relations
both in regard to Egyptian and to universal
measurement.   Situated close to the apex of
the Delta, the most distinctive point in the
long course of the parent river, and marking
the junction of the northern and southern kingdom, lies Memphis, or Men-nofer, the famous
city built by the equally famous Fourth Dynasty of Egypt.   And on a rocky eminence

not far from that spot, commanding the immense desert which stretches far away to the Western Ocean, rises the Great Pyramid, built by the astronomer-monarch Khufu, about 4235 B.C., that is to say, within a very few years of the foundation of the hieroglyphic kalendar.   Distinctive, too, as is the situation of this building with reference to the conformation of the country, it is equally remarkable in its relation to the two principal points to which all human measurements of space must be primarily referred, namely, the centre and the pole of the earth ; since its distance from the pole is just equal to its distance from the centre.[1]

A notable feature in the building which has been the subject of much speculation strikingly illustrates this relation to the pole.   For the single shaft which gives entrance to the interior does not run horizontally, nor does it open level with the ground ; but it emerges at about fifty feet from the bottom, being inclined upwards from within at such an angle as to point, according to the measurement confirmed by Prof. Flinders Petrie, to the position occupied by the pole-star between five and six thousand years ago.   Nor again was that di-

[1] See Note D, page 197.

rection unintentional, as the building itself
bears witness. For if we turn to the sacred
texts of Egypt, and compare them with this
sacred monument, we find them to be full of
allusions to astronomical conceptions, and
more particularly to what is called in the papyri the " Horizon of Heaven,"—a circle evidently entirely different from what we mean
in speaking of the celestial horizon of any
given locality, and occupying a definite and
important position in the universal sphere.
Now more than two years ago I drew attention to the identity of this circle, hitherto un-
defined by Egyptologists, with the great circle
forming the celestial horizon of an observer
stationed on the Equator, and having in his
zenith the point of equinox (or, in other
words, with the circle which we call the solstitial Colure). But, as that circle passes
through the pole, the orb by which its position would be indicated was the pole-star,
towards which the entrance shaft of the Great
Pyramid is astronomically directed, and which
imaged to the Egyptian the entrance to the
unseen world. Accordingly, during my late
visit to Egypt, one of my principal objects
was to test this relation ; and I confess that

the confirmation I obtained afforded me nothing less than amazement. For, in common
with the rest of the world, I had always believed that no hieroglyph is to be found on the
exterior of the building.[1] But on arriving at
the fifteenth step (the very step I had specially
mentioned), where the entrance shaft, hidden
from an observer standing immediately below,
lies fully exposed to the view, I saw a single
immense hieroglyph, deeply sculptured, immediately above the entrance ; and that hieroglyph was no other than the hieroglyph of
the " Horizon of Heaven " (⬜). Had
the founder of the building desired to confirm
my views by a single stroke, in his own silent
and absolute fashion, he could not have adopted
a more efficacious plan than by placing that
particular hieroglyph in that particular position.

Looking now to the other extremity of the
upper kingdom at the south, we find that on
the island of Philæ, at the " Gate of the Nile,"
there is an ancient inscription, a passage in
which lays stress on the "great vault of the

[1] I do not speak, of course, of those modern impertinences which a
distinguished Egyptologist, now dead, whose name, *honoris causa*, I
shall not mention, thought fit to inscribe some thirty years ago.

TEMPLE OF PHILÆ.

sun according to his time," as a characteristic
feature of the spot, and of an enclosure over
which " the sun stood in the centre." Such a
description could not be true at the present
day. For as the latitude of the island is a
little more than 24°, while the tropical boundary is less than 23½°, the sun could not be
vertical to any part of it. But since, for a
very long period, the obliquity of the Ecliptic
has been gradually lessening, the tropical
boundary must have been greater in former
ages ; and the phenomenon would have been
visible, and very noticeable, about the time of
Khufu. For calculating the diminution at the
rate given by Airy, viz., about half a minute (of
arc) per century, we find that the obliquity at
that epoch was very nearly 24°. The position
of Philæ, therefore (or more properly Pilak),
would be almost vertically under the sun at
the summer solstice, and consequently would
mark for all time the position of that orb relatively to the earth, at the epoch from which the
hieroglyphic kalendar dates its reckoning.

Similarly, if we calculate the position which
would be occupied by the moon at the epoch of
the opening of the kalendar, when at the farthest distance from the Ecliptic compatible with

eclipse, it will be found to be vertical to the latitude of Luxor.   And what is even more remarkable, as relating to an epoch long antecedent to the foundation of the kalendar, the farthest limit [1] ever attained by the sun through the variation of the Ecliptic is about 24° 33′; and that latitude is marked by the venerable temple of Ombos.

But besides the relations of our planet to the sun, moon, and stars, there is yet one motion which affects the entire orbit and which we find more especially illustrated by the position and design of one famous temple.   That motion is the extremely slow revolution performed by the axis of the celestial sphere around the axis of the Ecliptic in about 26,000 years, which is called the cycle of precession, since its effect, as is well known, is to cause the point at which the earth cuts the plane of her own Equator slightly to precede each year the position which it occupied at the previous revolution.   That this cycle was familiar to the astronomers of early Egypt [2] is, I think, sufficiently clear (though it will be confirmed by other considerations in

---

[1] According to the calculations published by the Smithsonian Institute at Washington.

[2] See Note E, page 197.

the later chapters) from the solution afforded
by it to certain apparent anomalies, which Dr.
Brugsch, the eminent authority on the hieroglyphic kalendar, has plainly stated, but without attempting to explain. For example, during
the later dynasties, as he mentions, a double
form of reckoning was employed; the same
day appearing, for instance, in the reign of
Thothmes III. (about 1500 B.C.) under two distinct dates no less than thirty-eight days apart.
Such a circumstance in our kalendar would be
wholly unintelligible except upon the hypothesis
of some confusion; but when we consider the
continuity of the Egyptian reckoning, extending through hundreds and thousands of years,
it admits of a simple explanation as follows.
Since the rate at which that precession takes
place (about 50″.2 in a year) is sufficient to
carry the point of equinox round the circuit of
our orbit in about 25,800 years, it follows that
in the three hundred and sixty-fifth part of that
period, that is to say, about every seventy-one
years, it will fall one day earlier. Hence it
follows that when we speak of the same day
(such as the thirtieth April) occurring in two
different kalendars seventy-one years or more
apart, we imply that the earth occupied on those

two days a similar position in regard to the
point of equinox, but not the same position on
the orbit, and consequently not in regard to
the celestial universe ; the node itself, or point
of equinox, having in the interval travelled a
short space along the orbit in a direction contrary to the motion of our globe. Suppose,
then, that, in addition to a kalendar having reference, like our own, to the equinox of the
current year, a second record were kept relative
to the equinox of the epoch at which the kalendar was commenced,—a suggestion entirely in
agreement with Egyptian custom and mode of
thought,—then the peculiarity would be explained. For since the point of equinox falls
a little earlier relatively to the orbit every year,
the archaic date will fall a little later. And as
in nearly 26,000 years it traverses the circle of
the year, and falls again on the anniversary, in
2,650 years the archaic date would be thirty-
seven or thirty-eight days later ; so that if the
kalendar were formed in the time of Khufu,
the difference between the current and archaic
dates in the days of Thothmes III. would just
correspond to the difference found in the two
kalendars. Such a form of reckoning also
would be made the more easily, because at the

epoch of the foundation of the kalendar the vernal equinox appears to have been marked by the orient of another brilliant star well known to Egyptian astronomers, and called by them Sah, namely our Betelgeux, the first in the constellation of Orion ; so that that star would supply a fixed point from which to measure the precessional motion. And it is interesting to note that in an ancient Egyptian manuscript, called the Sai an Sinsin (which has been translated by Dr. Brugsch), describing the transformation of the soul in the unseen world, we find that in the opening passage where the mystical conditions surrounding the entrance of the Holy Dead into the splendour of the invisible light are imaged forth by the conjunction of the heavenly bodies, special mention is made of that same orb, Sah, in that same position on the horizon.

By a similar reference to the archaic date we may throw some light on the peculiar sanctity attaching to certain days of the month for which it is otherwise difficult to account. For instance, in the *Book of the Master* to which reference has been already so frequently made, and the papyrus of which probably belongs to the third cycle, command is given no less than

three times that the most important festival of
the year, the birthday of Osiris, should be celebrated on the fifteenth of the month, and twice
on the sixth. But that birthday was, as we
have seen, the first festival of the sacred interval ; and what connection could such a festival
have with any particular day of any month whatever ? A very close connection, if the archaic
date be taken into consideration. For at the
commencement of the second cycle the archaic
date of Osiris' birthday would fall twenty-one
days later than at the original epoch ; and remembering the six days of sacred interval in
the Grand Year, we reach the fifteenth day of
the first month of the year, while a similar calculation for the third cycle brings us to the sixth
of the second month. For a similar reason,
another great festival, that of the bark of Ra,
is ordered to be celebrated on the birthday of
Osiris, since that day coincided with the rising
of the sacred Nile and the beginning of the
new life.

Now it is this principle which we shall find
in especial to pervade the design of the celebrated temple of Hathor, the mother of Horus,
which illustrated to the Egyptians the divine
beauty of the starry universe.

CHAPTER VI

THE TEMPLE OF THE VIRGIN MOTHER

SOME four hundred miles from the apex of the Delta, higher up along the Nile, lies the city of Annu, or Denderah, wherein was situated the temple dedicated to Hathor, identified in the sacred texts of the temple with Isis, the Queen of Heaven, whose most ancient and distinctive title was the Virgin Mother. This latter name still bears the trace of its original meaning, being a corruption of the words Ta M Ta Rer or " Place of the Orbit." [1] And the name becomes highly significant in itself, and throws no little light on the title which the Pharaohs bore of " Lord of the Orbit," when we observe that the length of the river in its course through Upper Egypt is just one millionth part of the orbit of the

[1] See Note F, page 198.

earth,[1] and that Denderah is little more than two degrees from the tropical boundary, where the plane of our orbit intersects the Nile. That the design of this temple was of very ancient date the records leave no manner of doubt. It is probable indeed (although some of the evidence adduced is not very convincing[2]) that the structure as it now stands is due to a comparatively late epoch, some authorities maintaining that it was not completed until the Christian era had begun. But of the antiquity of the original building there can be no question. For while, as Prof. Dumichen has observed, the religious ceremonies depicted on the walls belong to a very remote period, the inscriptions recount how Thothmes III. (more than 1500 years before the time of Christ) gave command to rebuild the temple according to the ancient design, so

---

[1] Reckoning the radius of the earth's orbit (or in other words the distance of the sun) to be between 92½ and 93 millions of miles.

[2] For instance, a considerable amount of argument in support of a date not anterior to the time of the Romans has been expended on the presence of a certain Greek inscription, which states that in the time of the Emperor Tiberius a portion of this temple (there called after the Greek fashion the Pro-Naos) was dedicated to a Greek goddess. With equal justice might one of our own grand mediæval churches be ascribed to the close of the eighteenth century, on the strength of an inscription recording in gilt letters the important circumstance of its whitewashing by the churchwardens.

that at that period the plan was already reckoned as antique.   Further, the same records
tell us how that original building was erected
by Pepi, a monarch of the Sixth Dynasty, who
reigned nineteen centuries before the time of
Thothmes, and how even that was not the
farthest point to which the history of the
structure ascended.   For the plan upon which
Pepi religiously carried out the ancient design
did not originate in his own mind, but was
brought to light by him from a crypt, or secret
chamber, being written "in archaic characters," say the records, by Khufu himself, the
astronomer-architect of the Fourth Dynasty,
and buried by him on the spot eight hundred
years before the days of Pepi.

In this temple of the great Mother of God,
structure and situation alike appear designed
to illustrate that starry universe of which she
was the queen.   Thus the fundamental principle of precession stands out with great clearness when, in accordance with the principles
laid down in the last chapter, we examine the
position of the temple.   For, since the locality
is close to the verge of the tropics, where the
plane of our orbit (or, which is the same thing,
of the ecliptic) passes perpendicularly upwards

through the surface of the earth, the sun at midsummer would nearly occupy the zenith of the place. If, then, an observer at Denderah should stand with his face towards the north, as the temple records inform us that the founder stood when on the night of midsummer he laid the foundation-stone of the building, he would have the plane of our orbit rising immediately in front of him, while the pole of the ecliptic would lie at his feet at the farthest verge of the celestial horizon. Now it is around that pole of the ecliptic that (in the course of about 25,800 years) the celestial axis describes the precessional circle. Hence, then, alike to the builder of the temple, and to the long line of pontiffs who took up their position, year after year, and generation after generation, to celebrate the chief festival of the temple, the stars in their nightly revolution around the axis of that horizon would trace out the same circle as in the mightier movement of precession ; while the gradual change in the hours of their rising and setting, as the centuries passed away, would measure the age-long hours, each spanning over a thousand years, of a single circuit of the axis,—the vast precessional day. Now, that this relation was essential to the plan is evi-

dent from the prominence given in the inscriptions to the pole of the ecliptic, or " Turning-
point [in Egyptian the Akh] of the Circles of
Light," as it is there called ; and again from the
emphatic stress laid in another part of the records upon the same central point.   " He saw
the Akh as the Akh, which is in the heaven of
Hathor, the Lady of Annu," say the records,
speaking of the founder.   That is to say, he
saw the pole of the earth's orbit as the turning-
point round which during his midnight watch
he beheld the heavens revolve, exactly as an
observer standing in the same position would
behold at the present day.

Another illustration, or rather application of
the same principle becomes evident when we
compare the temple and the Great Pyramid,—
those twin buildings of mystery due to the
same primæval astronomer, Khufu, the one
erected by him, the other only designed, but
left to his successor, eight hundred years later,
for accomplishment.   For the position of the
pole-star which, we saw, was indicated by the
entrance shaft of the Great Pyramid was 26°
7' above the horizon of that building ; and 26°
7' is the latitude of Denderah, that is to say,
its distance measured along a meridian from

the Equator. But in that position the star's true distance from the pole was 3° 53′; and 3° 53′ is the meridional distance between the temple of Denderah and the Great Pyramid. Thus while the celestial relation between the star and the horizon of the Great Pyramid measures the terrestrial relation between the Equator and the temple of the heavens, the terrestrial relation between the temple and the Pyramid measures the celestial relation between the star and the heavenly pole. The same relation, moreover, suggests a singular connection between the position of the star and the erection of the temple. For the date at which the star occupied the position thus indicated was about the year 3440 B.C., that is to say, not in the time of Khufu but of Pepi. Eight centuries, therefore, it would seem, after the epoch when Khufu secretly designed the celestial plan of the universal temple, his royal successor, Pepi, who himself bore the title of Grand Master (Sechem Ur), recognised the signal that the hour had arrived for the manifestation of that design, when the star which indicated the celestial pole illuminated the dark masonry of the twin building, and he saw the point " shining in the great house of watch-

ing," as it says in another part of the inscription.   Until that hour should come, the Grand
Architect concealed the design for the temple
of the universe; when the predetermined
measure of time was accomplished, the Grand
Master erected the building on the spot measured by the star and the pole of the heavens.

From that same measure also arises another
relation illustrating at once the connection of
the temple with the precessional motion, and
the meaning of various expressions in the temple records.   For that measure (3° 53′) is
within a few seconds just the sixth part of the
space contained between the Equator and the
ecliptic, and conveniently divides it therefore
into six equal parts on either side of the Equator; and that is the space through which, owing
to the effect of precession, the heavenly sphere
appears to be shifted, once northward and once
southward in the course of the vast cycle.
Hence, then, we have the meaning of a remark-
ably beautiful image contained in the records,
describing the temple as " The Seat of the
Heavenly Dances in the Six Heights of Osiris,"
that is to say, of the space-sweeping motions of
the starry host through these six heights of
the tropical heaven, as now advancing, now re-

ceding, they weave their never-ending measures, led by the star that marks the heavenly pole.[1]

A similar reference to the structure of the heavens is manifested everywhere throughout the temple. On one side of the vast entrance-hall, or "Khent," the walls are covered with a representation of the fourteen ascents of the moon, leading up on the fifteenth to the throne of Thoth, the Lord of Measurement, and corresponding to the number of days between new and full moon. On the opposite side are depicted eighteen boats, each led by a solar serpent, or spiral, representing the eighteen decades which, as we have seen, made up the half-orbit. And in the area of the same entrance-hall rise eighteen enormous columns, divided into three rows, each containing six columns, corresponding with the number of decades of days. To these columns, therefore, in the " Habitation of Horus," and to the foundation of the building at midnight, as the records relate, it would seem that allusion is made when we read in the papyrus of Ani, of " the night of setting up the columns of Horus and making him to be established as heir to the things which

See Note G, page 199.

belonged to his father." And again in the
Book of the Master we read that Horus himself gave the command, "Let the pillars be
here"; that is, in his own Habitation.

In the centre of the temple is the hall of
the Altar, with entrances opening east and
west; and beyond it lies the great hall of
the temple, entitled
the "Hall of the
Child in his Cra-
dle," from whence
access is obtained
to the secret and
sealed shrine en-
tered once a year
by the high-priest,
on the night of mid-
summer.   From

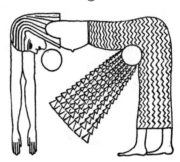

Hathor with the Splendour Proceeding
from her Womb.

that shrine the image of the holy Mother
was on that night conveyed by the priests
in procession up a secret staircase to an open
chamber on the roof, there to hold communion with her divine father Ra.   And
upon the walls is depicted the figure of the
Virgin Mother with the rays of the divine
splendour streaming from the circle of her
womb, forcibly recalling the striking vision of

the prophet Ezekiel, when he beheld a "great
cloud coming up from the North," and the
"splendour within the circle," and "the fire
enwrapping," and the "amber in the midst of
the fire,"—the sacred Mother retaining her
virgin purity transparent as amber in the midst
of her fiery espousals, and surrounded by the
great cloud of the heavenly host coming up
from Nazareth in the north of the Holy Land
to the place of birth, bearing the Eternal Splendour in her womb.

But of all the astronomical features presented
by this deeply interesting building, by far the
most remarkable is the celebrated wall-paint-
ing which was transferred bodily, early in the
present century, from the temple at Denderah
to Paris, where it formed the subject of the
liveliest and most prolonged discussion among
scholars, and where it may still be seen.   The
subject of this picture is somewhat difficult to
convey, but its appearance may be described
as follows.   Suppose a panther's hide to be
cut square, the spots to be filled up with sacred
symbols, interspersed with stars, and the figures
to be grouped into a kind of spiral which,
opening out from the centre, gradually widens
into a circle surrounded by a square border,

then we shall have a general conception of
the form of the picture. In the space between
the circle and the square rim is depicted at
each of the four principal points, in a double
form, the divine Horus, the child of Hathor,
Queen of the starry Universe, to whom the
temple was dedicated. The two forms, precisely similar, face each other, at each of the
four points of the orbit, thus representing the
equalisation of light and darkness all over
the earth at the two equinoxes, and at the poles
for each half of the year. Midway between each
quarter is the figure of the holy Mother, under
the form of Nut, the mistress who presided
over the waters, the celestial giver of those
heaven-descended rains which fed their life-
giving river. And the whole is enclosed by a
hieroglyphic inscription which runs round the
border.[1]

To this representation, sometimes most in-
accurately called a " Zodiac," the scientific
writers in the *Description de l' Egypte* assign
the more correct title of a Planisphere. Astronomically speaking, in fact, it represents the
aspect of the heaven as it would revolve before
the eyes of the monarch as he stood with his

---

[1] See Note H, page 200.

face to the north on the night of the foundation
of the temple ; while an examination of the
mystical figures and symbols thereon inscribed
shows immediately their intimate connection
with the celestial path of the holy departed.
For, numerous as they are, there is scarcely one
which does not appear in the vignettes and
illustrate the text of the sacred papyri ; and
more particularly of the *Book of the Master*,
that most jealously guarded papyrus wherein
the Divine Wisdom set forth at large the path
of the holy dead on their entrance into light.
In a word, the picture affords a representation
of the visible heaven as seen from the dwelling-
place of the Virgin Mother, whose very name
Hat-hor implies that she herself was the Habitation of the incarnate Horus ; while the mystical
symbols representing the starry groups, image
forth the supernal powers and spirits which
the holy departed, according to the creed of
Egypt, encountered in his progress through
the heights as he mounted from the plane of
earth to the burning throne of Ra.

To effect a comparison between the chambers of the building and the different parts of
the planisphere, and through them with the
constellations of the heavens, is not a difficult

task.   For, as in other great temples, the various halls and chambers in that of Hathor had
each its distinctive name, and sometimes a good
many names, bearing reference, for the most
part, to the mysteries of the Light and of a divine
Birth.   The " Hall of the Golden Rays " was
the title of one of the great halls.   The Chamber of Gold, the Chamber of Frankincense, the
Chamber of Birth, the Place of the Altar, the
Dwelling of the Golden One, the Chamber of
Flames, and the Throne-room of Ra, are among
the hieroglyphic titles attaching to the various
portions of the temple.   Now, as the planisphere contains the hieroglyphs which indicate
the northern and southern points, we are enabled to correlate the parts of that picture with
the various parts of the temple, and thereby to
discover a striking correspondence between the
different parts of the inscription and the titles
of the chambers and halls occupying the same
relative positions.   Commencing with the
northern entrance leading to the Hall of the
Golden Rays, we read " Head of the Circles of
Annu " (or Denderah), " Horus the Entrance
of the Golden Heaven."   Opposite the two
openings, one towards the rising, the other towards the setting sun, we have the hieroglyph

(Khut Su) signifying " Horizon of Light."
By the Chamber of Incense, we read " Palace Chamber of Holy Adoration " (Tuat),
"Palace Chamber of Supreme Light" (Tes Su).
By the Chamber of Birth, we find mention of the
" Head of the Nurse of Ra, Meeting-place of the
Region of the Gods."   In the same way, by
the Chamber of Flames, we have " Heavenly
Flame of Burning Gold," and by the Chamber
of Gold, the " Golden Heaven of Isis."   And
as the chief hall of the temple was the Hall
of the Child in his Cradle, so the chief representation on the planisphere is the holy Mother
with the divine Child in her arms.[1]

Conceive now that the monarch, standing
with his face to the north and keeping watch
from midnight to midnight, should project
upon the surface of the heaven that sacred design.   Then every portion of the celestial surface before him will be divided into groups of
stars or constellations corresponding to the sacred images depicted upon the planisphere, and
consequently with the various chambers of the
temple to which those images themselves correspond.   Thus the whole field of the watch-
er's view would be marked out with precision

[1] See Note J, page 202.

into well-defined groups or constellations, each
represented by its distinctive symbol, immediately recognisable by those, and those alone,
who should understand the nature of the temple plan and should be acquainted with the
temple structure.   And as each midsummer
came round, opening a fresh Egyptian year,
the hosts of highest heaven gathered around
the " Child in his Cradle," and the festival of the
starry universe was fitly celebrated in the temple of Hathor, the Mother of God, herself the
" Habitation " of the holy Light.

Deeply solemn must have been the scene
surrounding the Grand Master, Pepi, on that
memorable night when, obedient to the star-
given command of his long-departed predecessor, he stood and measured the earth.
Every feature, every detail, every ornament,
speaks with a silent eloquence which echoes
through space and time.   There lay before
the monarch the archaic design, traced out in
characters telling of an age already bygone,
and, itself new risen from the tomb, giving expression to the eternal destiny of man beyond
the grave.   In his hand was the royal " Khus,"
the masonic rule of ancient Egypt.   Upon his
head sparkled the luminous tiara of Hathor,

figuring forth the supernal beauty wherewith the Illuminate should be crowned in the day of immortality.   Far in the northern horizon the pole-star shone before his feet, proclaiming the advent of the long-appointed hour.   All round, throughout the immensity of the illimitable vault, burned amid the profound stillness of the night the countless multitudes of infinitely distant suns, recalling the sublime passage in the *Book of the Master :* " I make the shining circles of the years ; and billions are my measurement."   Upward from out the darkling depths of the unfathomable abyss, stretching like boundless wings on either hand, and high aloft by the zenith of the translucent dome, rose, invisible to the common eye but present ever to the mind of the astronomer, the plane of our planet's orbit,—that celestial plane of man's earthly course,—girt by the zodiac, like an azure belt of gleaming gems,

> " Those lights most lustrous of the firmament
>   Which through the heaven lead the gliding Year."

Then when the circuit was accomplished, and the surface of the heaven grouped into constellations according to the sacred plan, the monarch gave the signal for laying the foundation of the temple, and, fixing his eyes upon the northern centre of the revolving heaven, commanded the attendant ministers to stretch out the measuring cord in the predetermined direction, which he as Grand Master, and he alone, foreknew.

From that mysterious temple of the Holy Mother, with its shrine of secret birth, wherein the relations between the heavens and the earth are so sedulously embodied yet so jealously concealed, we proceed to contemplate the deeply veiled teaching of the Egyptian priesthood as to the universal fatherhood of the Hidden God.

CHAPTER VII

THE HIDDEN GOD

DEEPLY embedded in the heart of some ancient forest, we find here and there a massive and hoary boulder, its antiquity far exceeding that of the venerable trees, and its whole appearance telling of a distant soil and a bygone day. As we sit upon the granite block with the branches waving high above our heads, our wonder at its presence is deepened by the quiet scene. For countless ages that great stone has lain motionless, lifeless, changeless, amid all the infinite movement of changing life around it. No human power brought that huge mass where it lies, no eye can trace the path along which it was driven by the forces of nature. And not until we have traced the mighty variations and convulsions which in the recesses of time our whole globe has undergone, and have looked

priests of back far beyond the earliest seed-
time of the forest, to the days when the surrounding country for hundreds of miles formed
the bottom of an immense ocean, through
which the icebergs bore the huge rocks torn
from its frozen shores, can we understand the
position of that primæval stone.

Something of a similar character may not
infrequently be discerned in regard to the religious belief and worship of a nation, when a
tradition or custom survives the convulsions
and changes of the centuries and remains
firmly embedded in the national life, though
every trace of significance is long buried in
the past. Most superstitions, it is probable,
had once an intelligible meaning, even if that
meaning were founded on a mistaken belief;
but such survivals are by no means due to superstition alone. Who, for instance, can explain the Latin titles used for the psalms in the
Prayer-book of the Church of England, without going back more than three hundred and
fifty years to the time when England used the
same language in her public worship as the
rest of Christendom? So in the Latin Mass
the Kyrie Eleison betrays its connection
with the Greek, and the word Hosanna, in the

office for Palm Sunday, carries us back to the Hebrew.

But there is one word in particular which is employed, not on any special occasion, but in every service ; not once or twice, but after every petition ; not as a portion of the prayer, but as its summary and its seal. If a stranger stand outside the closed doors of a church while service is going on, there is one word, and probably but one, which he would hear distinctly repeated again and again. "Amen," "Amen," "Amen," that is the aspiration which, time after time, comes rolling forth with the full strength of choir and congregation. That is the word by which the apostle denotes the absolute nature of the Deity as compared with created matter. "In Him all things are Amen." Amen is the single word which the seer of the Apocalypse heard the Four Living Creatures utter before the throne in response to the chorus of universal adoration. And that is the title under which the same writer invokes the advent of his Divine Master at the conclusion of the vision : "Amen, Veni Domine Jesu." That, too, is the name which the Master assumed to Himself : "Amen, I say to you." And that is the name by which the Egyptian

old addressed the secret Deity—Amen, that is
to say in Egyptian, " The Hidden One."

That the existence of the one God was
widely known, by some classes of men at least,
among the nations of antiquity there can be
little doubt.   Among the Chinese, according
to the eminent authority, Dr. Legge, the word
Ti represented the same idea as we express by
the word God ; and its assumption as a title
by the earliest dynasty of the Emperors of
China would be quite in accordance with the
ancient belief that the monarch ruled as the
divine representative.   So,   in   the   sacred
books of India, when the disciples of Manu
approached that sage to beg for instruction
in the wisdom which afterwards formed the
foundation of Indian law, they addressed him
as follows : " For thou, O lord, alone knowest
the purport [or rites] and the knowledge taught
in the whole ordinance of the Self-Existent
[Svayam bhu], which is unknowable and unfathomable."   And their master, in his reply,
laid down the principle of the one uncreated
God, the Giver of Light.   " The Divine Self-
Existent," he said, " indiscernible, making the
elements and the rest discernible, appeared
with creative force, dispelling the darkness."

Again in the *Mahabharata*, the earliest production of post-Vedic literature, a translation of which, as well as of the laws of Manu, is given in the magnificent series of the *Sacred Books of the East*, the most enduring monument to its illustrious editor, a similar doctrine is ascribed to Vyasa. "In the commencement was Brahman, without beginning or end, unborn, luminous, free from decay, immutable, eternal, unfathomable, not to be fully known."

Equally explicit are the utterances of some of the Greek poets.

"One Self-begotten, from whom all things sprang," is one of the lines attributed to the famous Orpheus.

"To God all things are easy, nought impossible," so sang Linus, a brother of the same bright band. A fuller but not less accurate description is given by Xenophanes :

"One God there is, greatest 'mongst gods and men ;
Not like to mortals, or in form or thought.
In full he sees, he hears, in full he knows,
And without labour doth his mind move all."

Another poet, Cleanthes, strikes at the root of the exclusiveness arising from the characteristic principle of ancient idolatry, that a

deity listens to no prayers except from his
own descendants, by proclaiming that all men
are the offspring of God, and that consequently
the right of prayer to him is universal :

> " O thou most glorious and immortal one,
>   O many-titled, O Omnipotent,
>   Zeus, Lord of Nature, ruling all by law,
>   Hail, whom to worship is the right of all,
>   Since all of us are of thee."

So Aratus, whom St. Paul quotes in his famous speech to the Athenians. "God is the
source of our song and God is beginning of
all things. We too are offspring of God."

A similar passage, though capable of a more
pantheistic interpretation, is contained in the
Orphica.

" God First ; and God the Lord of Thunder last ;
  God head, God midst and all things are of God ;
  God Male and God immortal Womanhood.
  God the great stay of earth and starry Heaven,
  God breath of all, God fire's unwearied rush,
  God Ocean's root and God the Sun and Moon.
  God King himself the Patriarch supreme
  One strength, one Lord, one generator of all,
  One King, one mould the base of every form.
  Fire, Water, Earth and Air and Night and Day
  And Wisdom Firstborn and Exhaustless Love
  All have their Being in the Godhead vast."

Even the Roman mind, dim-eyed as it was for the invisible world, was not altogether without a glimpse of this truth, to which Horace has given expression when speaking of the supreme Deity :

" From whom none greater than himself is born ;
  Nor doth his equal or his second live."

But the truths which sparkle here and there in the teachings of India, China, or of Greece, fade and vanish before the blaze of Egyptian theosophy. Take, for example, the following extract given by Mr. Budge from the hymn to Amen-Ra, the hidden Deity, the self-existent Light :

" Hail to thee, Ra, Lord of Law, whose shrine is hidden ; Master of the Gods, the God Kheper Ra (Self-Existent Light) in his boat ; by the sending forth of his Word the gods sprang into existence. Hail, God Atmu (Light), Maker of Mortals. However many are their forms, he causes them to live ; he makes different the colour of one man from another. He hears the prayers of him that is oppressed ; he is kind of heart to him that calls unto him ; he delivers him that is afraid from him that is strong of heart ; he judges between the mighty and the weak.

" O Form, One, Creator of all things. O One, Only Maker of existences. Men came forth from his two eyes, the gods sprang into existence at the utterance of his mouth. He maketh the green herb to make the cattle live and the staff of life for the (use of) man. He maketh the fish to live in the rivers, the winged fowl in the sky ; he giveth the breath of life to the germ in the egg ; he maketh birds of all kinds to live, and likewise the reptiles that creep and fly ; he causeth the rats to live in their holes and the birds that are on every green twig. Hail to thee, O Maker of all these things, thou Only One."

Nor was the unity the only truth concerning the Godhead known to the priesthood of Egypt. Throughout the extent of the kingdom, at Thebes, at Ombos, at Denderah, at Memphis, at Annu (or On), a Triune God—of whom some knowledge seems to have been attained by Greece—invoked by many names, but everywhere consisting of three persons, consubstantial and coeternal, was worshipped as supreme. "I am Tmu in the morning," says the Creator, in a well-known passage, "Ra at noon, and Harmachi in the evening"; that is to say, as the dawn, the noon, and the sunset are three distinct forms co-existing perpetually and co-equally in the substance of the sun, so also did the three divine persons co-exist perpetually and co-equally in the substance of the Uncreated Light. Thus after declaring the sacred Unity in the most emphatic and explicit terms, the hymn already quoted proceeds to invoke the three persons by name, using, nevertheless, the singular pronoun for the collective three.

"He is of many forms," so the hymn proceeds. "O Amen, establisher of all things, Atmu and Harmachis, all people adore thee, saying, Praise to thee because of thy resting among us, homage to thee because thou hast created us.   All creatures say, Hail to thee, and all lands praise thee.   From the height of the sky to the breadth of the earth and to the depths of the sea art thou praised."

Thus as the whole body of Egyptian temples prove upon inspection to form a definite and co-ordinated system based upon astronomical relations, so also does the worship of Egypt, when seen in the light of the universal fatherhood, reveal itself with a majestic unity not unworthy of its unrivalled shrines.   Had the case been otherwise indeed ; had the real objects of Egyptian worship, been a mass of deities local and unrelated, then, inasmuch as the form of government was well-nigh a pure theocracy, the authority of the monarch being derived not merely from his descent but from his personal union with Ra, and inasmuch as

heresy was punished with excommunication
and even, as M. Maspero states, with death by
fire, it would have been inevitable that each
successive dynasty, as it proceeded now from
This, now from Memphis, now from Thebes,
now from Sais, should have torn up by the
root the religion established by its predecessors ; and the annals of Egypt would have
been as full of religious discord and confusion
as those of our own Tudor princes.

If the divine Trinity, however, were the only
secret of the Ritual, there would not be so
great a difficulty in following its symbols.
But there is a depth of mystery beyond, a
mystery the greater because manifested in
a visible form.   Throughout the sacred writings of Egypt, there is no doctrine of which
more frequent mention is made than that of a
divine birth.   " I am thy nurse, thy dandler,"
says Isis to the divine Horus in the inscription on the coffin of the queen who bore the
name of Ankh N.es Ra Nefer Ab (signifying
" Her Life is the sacred Heart of God ").
And the figure portrayed upon that coffin six
and twenty centuries ago, and now to be seen
in the British Museum, with its sacred seals
impressed upon the secret parts of the body,

its incision in the womb, and the rays descending upon the head, proclaims unmistakably the birth from a virgin mother beneath the overshadowing of the supernal light. And nowhere is that celestial birth more vividly expressed than in the temple of Hathor, the great hall of which speaks of the holy Child in his Cradle, in the midst of the vast company of the heavenly hosts. Nor do we read in the Ritual only of an incarnate, but of a suffering and a dying, God. We are confronted with the tears of Isis, and with the agony of Osiris. Moreover, not only is the twofold action of the same sacred person as man and God recognised, but it is embodied in an animal symbolism; just as among Christians the symbol of the lamb is used for the divine person, the calf and the eagle for the evangelists. Take, for example, the vignette of the Ritual representing the resurrection of Osiris as taking place in the presence of the Egyptian Trinity. The human form, being the highest available, is required by the supreme three; and in order to represent the lower nature, or divine humanity, it is necessary to take a lower creature whose characteristic should indicate that of the divine person represented. Of

such a nature was the cat, whose eyes, varying
in form like the sun with the period of the
day, imaged to the Egyptian the splendour
of the light. And thus we have the cat cutting off the head of the serpent of darkness,
in the presence of the sacred three. And
when the original meaning of that symbolism
was lost, that is, when the knowledge of God
was no longer retained in their science, it
would naturally give rise to the foolishness
of animal worship.

No less profound was the relation between
the Creator and his works, as intimated in their
well-known symbol for created life,
called the Ankh,[1] or sacred mirror,
wherein every great deity contemplates perpetually his own image;
but which is rarely grasped in the
hand of any except Amen. But how
should the universe be represented by a mirror, and, if it be, why should the heavenly
powers behold themselves reflected in it?
Since Egypt gives only the symbol but affords

The Ankh; or,
Sacred Mirror
of Creation.

[1] Another signification, that of a fisherman's knot, has of late been
adopted by some authorities ; but the shape of the knot differs essentially from that of the Ankh, the head of the latter being upright upon
the stem. And again, how should a fisherman's knot stand upright
on the knees of the gods ? And if it could, why should it ?

no clue to the connection, and since that
profound relation is not affected by the lapse
of ages, let us hear the great master of mediæval philosophy. According to the teaching
of Aquinas, the universe exists in a twofold
manner, first ideally in the mind of God, and
secondly materially, externally to him, so that
in creation the Almighty contemplates his
own mind as in a mirror. As a dramatist,
before he gives living expression to his characters, conceives in his own mind their forms,
their countenances, their actions, passions, and
conditions of life, with all the details of their
environment, and as his work reflects the
image of the author's mind, so in the theosophy of Egypt did the entire cosmos, embracing all space, all time, and all orders of created
being, reflect a single thought in the mind of
the Creator. Man himself, therefore, had a
double or a counterpart in the divine idea,
the sacred " type," the festival of which is
celebrated in the Ritual, and which possessed
such sanctity that the monarch himself is represented as sacrificing to his own " double."

　　Thus in the theosophy of Egypt the divine relations of the invisible creation were made manifest by those of their visible counterpart.   And

the same relation of the material to the immaterial world will be found to underlie our own
scientific conceptions, wherein the expressed
form is ever the counterpart of the impressed
force.   For can any mathematician define
the very nature of force otherwise than as that
which sets matter in motion ? But if force be
that which sets matter in motion, it cannot itself
be material, if the fundamental law of motion be
true that matter at rest remains at rest.   Unless therefore our whole conception of dynamical science is wrong from the beginning, the
motions of the material universe (and it is of
the motions of the heavenly bodies, and not
merely of their existence, that the Ritual continually speaks) must be the result of an immaterial force impressing itself upon the material
world, the mind of the Creator giving form
to his creation.   And it is in the perception
of that action that the supreme gift of the human mind, the imaginative faculty of genius, is
most fully exercised ; for genius is the power
of giving expression to the unexhausted forms
of creation potentially existing in the mind of
the Creator.

Most powerful and most hidden of all motives is the passion which grows the more

reticent in proportion as it is enduring, the passion which dominates at once the senses and the spirit, the master-mystery of love. But Love himself was none other than the hidden God. In Greece, where some rays of Egyptian wisdom penetrated with a brightness unknown to more distant lands, this truth was not unknown. Love was the third in the Trinity of Hesiod. And in Parmenides we read how strife has entered into the deepest places, " but in the centre Love stands calm." But in the teaching of Egypt, the Creator's love, so conspicuous in the sublime hymn already quoted, is the motive power of the universe. "I am the Inundation," says the Creator in the Ritual—the fulness of the torrent of life. And again, "I am the Fount of Joy," the inexhaustible source of happiness to the soul. Most striking too is the allusion which occurs in another hymn to Amen, where it speaks of the crown of illumination, or "Atf" crown of the monarchs, fashioned after the form of the zodiacal light which sometimes crowns the supreme heaven before the summer dawn. That crown we learn from the Ritual was placed upon the head of the Illuminate on his accomplishing the " Passage of the Sun," and the

hymn proclaims that " North and South of
that crown is love." That Love it was, wherein
the catechumen of the Egyptian Wisdom was
instructed from the Secret Scroll, and into the
mysteries of which he was initiated and illuminated by the Master of the Secret House.

CHAPTER VIII

THE SECRET SCROLL

"THIS Book is the Greatest of Mysteries. Do not let the eye of anyone look upon it—that were abomination. The *Book of the Master of the Secret House* is its name." So runs the emphatic declaration contained in the great papyrus, of which we have made such frequent mention; and the whole contents are in harmony with it. For throughout there is scarcely a paragraph the expression of which is not studiously obscure and difficult of interpretation. Yet recondite as are both subject and form, we find in it a clue, in some degree at least, to penetrate the mystical teaching of the Egyptian priesthood, that is to say, the doctrines which they taught not merely as to the nature of the Creator and his original relation to the creature, but also as to the means whereby the creature is admitted to participate in the mysteries of the Creator.

The papyrus in question, which was found in the coffin of a priest named Auf Ankh, is now preserved at Turin. And a facsimile of it was published by Lepsius in A.D. 1842. That distinguished Egyptologist thought good to call it the *Book of the Dead;* a title which usage has rendered almost too familiar to disturb, but which, in itself, is by no means happy, for it gives the idea of regarding the holy departed as dead, whereas the whole conception of the doctrine was the instruction in Life and Light. A much better description is that given by Champollion, who called it the *Funereal Ritual;* and though Dr. Budge vehemently controverts that title, his objections are urged with more warmth than force. But neither one term nor the other can, it is clear, compete in authority with that which the papyrus claims for itself, namely, the *Book* or *Scroll of the Master of the Secret House.*

The whole history of the sacred writings, among which this papyrus is perhaps the most important yet discovered, is by no means free from difficulty. They are made up of a great number of chapters, composed at various pe-

riods extending over several centuries, and
they occur sometimes carved on the walls of
the tombs, but more often written on papyrus
and hidden in the grave-clothes of the mummy.
Frequently only one chapter is employed, but
often also a considerable number, though no
papyrus has yet been discovered containing in
one the whole series of chapters. These sacred writings are usually divided by Egyptologists into four Collections, according to the
different periods to which they belong. The
first is that of the ancient empire, written in
hieroglyphics, to which the important inscription on the coffin of Amamu belongs. Then
comes the Theban recension, also in hieroglyphics, of which the papyri have been with
great labour collated and published by M. Naville ; followed during the succeeding (twenti-
eth) Dynasty by another written in hieratic or
priestly characters. And last of all we have
the recension of the (twenty-sixth) Saite Dynasty, to which the *Book of the Master* is due.

During the later ages, at least, there can be
little doubt that papyri were prepared for sale
with a blank left for the name of the mummy,
to be filled up before placing in the coffin.
But it does not follow that this was the cus-

tom in earlier ages, and the rarity of inscription on the tombs of that period tends to
contradict the probability.   Neither is it likely
that every chapter of the Ritual was open to
every purchaser.   On the contrary, it is by no
means improbable that, as the whole country
of Egypt represented various stages in the
path of the deceased, so the chapters employed in the various localities may have
varied also either in their order or in a portion of their wording.   And this latter suppo-
sition would account for the different readings
which we find introduced, especially in the *Book
of the Master;* implying not (as we with the characteristic carelessness of modern times suppose) an ignorance or indifference on the part
of the priests, but a collection of texts, to be
duly chosen, one or other, according to circumstances.   Moreover, from several allusions in
the writings, we find that the efficacy attached
to them arose from the deceased having been
permitted to become acquainted with them
during lifetime, so that the papyrus attested
the instruction in Wisdom of which the departed was possessed at death.   Now the object with which that instruction was conferred
was the union of the departed with Osiris, the

Creator, in virtue of which union we find the title of the Osiris prefixed in the papyri to the name of the departed, somewhat as we ourselves prefix the title of Saint to the names of those who shine like the light, and as the stars for ever and ever. And this again agrees with the direction given, for instance, in the *Book of the Master*, that the recitation is to commence on the day of the funeral, and accounts for the frequent commencement of the chapters with the words, "Saith the Osiris Auf Ankh"; implying that the whole Ritual was recited by the departed through the mouth of the priest.

The chief difficulty in understanding that book of mystery arises not merely from the great variety of the imagery, but much more from the complexity of its application. For the figures which are drawn from all kinds of familiar objects are rarely or never employed singly, so as to present a definite image whereby the signification might perhaps be detected; but parts of two or three are always used together, so as to present no meaning except to the instructed. Thus, for example, we find the holy departed addressed as "Osiris the Bull of the West," meaning the Strong One of heaven; the union with Osiris being assumed as begun, and the image being taken partly from the generative power of the bull and partly from the setting sun, which goes down into the west to illuminate the unseen world. Occasionally, also, the image of the doctrine signified is itself conveyed by another image. Thus Professor Renouf has shown how the partial eclipse of the sun, which is caused by the intervention of a planet, was represented by the Egyptians under the form of a tortoise crawling across the disc, and that image of the tortoise is applied in the papyri to the partial obscuration of Osiris' Godhead by his temporary death.

Among the different images, however, there is one class which in this papyrus occurs with a frequency unsurpassed except by those of light, namely, those which relate to some form of building. To this class belong the festivals of the " Northern Passage " and of the " Southern Passage," that of the " Hidden Lintel," that of " Osiris who dwells in the Roofed House " and in the " Pool of the Great House." So in the kalendar of Esne we read of the festivals of the Sockets, and again of the Opening of the Doors, which is closely connected in

the Ritual with the Raising of Osiris from the
Open Tomb.   The whole progress of the departed seems, in fact, to take place in some
kind of house.   The Ritual is full of references to his going out and coming in, to
"going in after coming out," to passing gates
and gateways, and doors and staircases.   And
though no doubt the secret places there mentioned have also a mystical significance, and
refer to those secret places of the universe
wherein, according to Egyptian belief, man,
when set free from the flesh, was initiated into
the mysteries of creation, yet inasmuch as
that doctrine was to be learned while still on
earth, so it was necessary that there should be
a house on earth wherein those places should
be illustrated.   And where shall we look for
such a building if not in that great house
wherein, according to Egyptian tradition, the
Secret Wisdom was imparted to the postulant ;
that house, the places of which claimed for
their Master the Master of the Secret Scroll ;
that house whereof every feature and every
proportion speak of the measurement of the
universe ?

Again, it was during the time of the Saite
Dynasty that the order of the chapters is said

to have been fixed for the first time. What canon, then, or standard of order did the revisers employ? It certainly was not the relative antiquity of the chapters, for the only one which claims to remount to the First Dynasty stands one hundred and thirtieth in the papyrus; while that which is attributed in it to the Fourth Dynasty, and which is entitled the "Entrance on Light in one chapter," as though it had once been the single chapter in use, comes sixty-fourth. But while the written records were liable to variability and error, no change could affect, no lapse of time could impair, the record erected in stone three thousand years before by the astronomer-architect Khufu. And thus as early as the Twelfth Dynasty, the inscription on the coffin of Amamu, buried in the sacred city of Abydos, shows that the secret places determine the order of the Ritual. "*Thou hast not gone dying,*" we read, "*thou hast gone living to Osiris. Now thou hast found the words of order, the Mystery of the Secret Places.*" For the doctrine contained in those mystic writings was nothing else than an account of the Path pursued by the Just when, the bonds of the flesh being loosed, he passed through stage after

stage of spiritual growth,—the Entrance on
Light, the Instruction in Wisdom, the Second
Birth of the Soul, the Initiation in the Well of
Life, the Ordeal of Fire, and the Justification
in Judgment; until, illumined in the secret
Truth and adorned with the jewels of Immortality, he became indissolubly united with Him
whose name, says the Egyptian Ritual, is
Light, Great Creator.   That secret doctrine
which the Ritual gives in writing the Secret
House materialises in its immutable masonry.
And so closely does the path embodied in that
masonry correspond with the Path of the departed as described in the sacred writings,
that the traveller who to-day penetrates those
mysterious recesses may follow almost step by
step the mystical progress of the holy departed
through the grave and gate of death to the
final resurrection of the Open Tomb.

CHAPTER IX

THE SECRET HOUSE

IT is difficult to conceive a greater contrast than is presented by the two forms in which the record of Egyptian doctrine was preserved. The papyri are fragile, numerous, varying in length and order. The monument in stone is unique, solid almost to indestructibility, incapable of variation, and standing unchanged and unchanging, regardless of the assaults, whether of time or of man. That extraordinary pile, the most majestic and most mysterious ever erected by the hand of man, stands close to the verge of the immense desert which stretches its arid wastes across the whole breadth of the African continent to the shore of the western ocean, just at the spot where the busy life of the earliest civilisation on record was bordered by the vast and barren solitude. Of all the other structures which

made the marvels of the ancient world, scarcely
a vestige is left.   Where are the hanging gardens, the boast of the monarch of Babylon?
Where is the far-famed Pharos of Alexandria?
Centuries have passed since earthquake laid
low the Colossus which bestrode the harbour
of Rhodes ; and a madman's hand reduced to
ashes the temple of Artemis, the pride of Ephesus.   But the Grand Pyramid of Ghizeh still
remains, undestroyed and indestructible, ages
after the lesser marvels have passed away, as
it stood ages before ever they came into being.
More than sixty centuries have gone by since
that building, which never since has needed the
care of man, first concealed from view its hidden places, those secret chambers of which no
other building on the globe, not even among
the later pyramids, contains the like.   Upwards of two million times has the sun risen
and set upon its mighty walls, since first the
pure and unbroken surface of polished casing-
stones flashed back the rays like a veil of dazzling lustre and vindicated its ancient title of
" The Light."

In external appearance the building erected
by Khufu differs only in a single feature from
the later pyramids.   Like them it is quadran-

gular in form and oriented towards the four cardinal points of the compass. Like the later pyramids also, within very slight limits of variation, its elevation (as is well known) is such that the perpendicular height of its apex bears the same proportion to the circuit of the base as the radius of a circle bears to its circumference. Like them also, it is constructed exteriorly in courses of huge stones, forming a series of steps, each from two to three feet in height, and level all round the course; these steps being now exposed to view, but originally concealed from top to bottom by perfectly fitting casing-stones, which offered no foothold for ascent and gave to Memphis its sacred title of the City of the White Wall. But whereas in the later pyramids the building is carried fully up to the apex (or point to which all the ascending lines converge), in that of Khufu the structure falls short of that point by about twenty courses, the pyramid being truncated and the summit forming a platform about twenty feet square; so that what the Egyptians called the " Benben," or pyramidal crown, is not to be found there. Seen from below, the ascending courses resemble a series of terraces or cliffs, rising majestically to the cloudless heaven.   But from this platform they present rather the appearance of four streams of stone descending from a common fount, like the four streams of the celestial Nile given in the vignette of chapter cx.   And the four together encircle the whole building in a cascade of rock, thus illustrating the " Beating Circle of the Waters," which we find inscribed in the same vignette; an illustration, it is to be observed, which could not have been detected by an Egyptian of old (while the casing-stones were still unremoved) unless he had been taught the concealed construction of the building.

From the fact that this peculiar feature is confined to the Great Pyramid, or at least for no other apparent reason, modern writers have assumed it to have been originally shaped like the rest, and have attributed the present height to havoc supposed to have been made by the Turks.   But though those barbarous destroyers were indeed capable of stripping off the casing-stones, many of which still lie in confusion around the foot, while others have been plundered for the buildings in Cairo ; yet to destroy a solid mass of masonry, firmly cemented together, over thirty feet high, with a base of four thousand square inches, and that at an elevation of upwards of four hundred feet from the ground, was a task which would require a very different class of engineer to accomplish. Besides which, we have a direct chain of evidence from three different sources to the contrary, extending back for nearly two thousand years, that is to say, to the time before the destruction had begun. About two hundred and fifty years ago, Professor Greaves, the Oxford astronomer, who visited the pyramid and has left a most interesting volume upon it, gives a drawing of the building which shows the summit shaped just as at present. Four hundred years before his time, Abdallatif, a historian of the twelfth century, tells us that at the top the Great Pyramid ended in a platform. And fifty years before the Christian era, Diodorus describes the building as "tapering up as far as the summit, which makes each of its sides six cubits."

Equally conclusive is the evidence borne by the building itself, the summit of which betrays no symptom either of incompletion or destruction, but presents a flat surface structurally enroofing the Secret House. On the centre of the platform and inseparably affixed to it are some huge blocks arranged in the figure of a rough cross. And on the highest of these stones are sculptured a number of holes, forming a square figure, consisting of seven ranks of seven holes each, exactly similar (except in the number of holes) to the " Hotep," or Table of Offerings, belonging to the time of Thothmes III., which is now to be seen in the Museum at Boulaq.[1] In a word, every detail goes to show that the founder never designed to erect

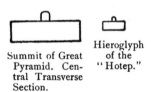

the Benben—the image of the Trinity invisible in the supreme height, —but raised in its stead a "Hotep," or sacrificial Table of Offering. And

Summit of Great Pyramid. Central Transverse Section.

Hieroglyph of the " Hotep."

agreeably with this, we find in the chapter already quoted that mention is made of the " Field of the Hotep," and of the Waters in the Field of the Hotep ; reminding us of the stone cataracts which descend from the summit.

To an observer immediately at the foot, the single entrance to the pyramid, opening at the seventeenth course, is hidden from view. But on mounting to the fifteenth step we perceive, two courses yet above us, a low gateway, surmounted by a double arch, opening downward

[1] See Note K, page 202.

to the dark interior ; just as the catechumen in
the fifteenth chapter approaches the " double
arched gate of the horizon," when he invokes
" Haroeris, the great guide of the world, the
guide of the souls in their secret places, the

Gateway of the Double Arch.

Light dwelling in the Horizon." From this
point the first veil of secrecy begins. For so
effectually was the opening concealed from the
uninstructed eye by a revolving stone, that its
position once forgotten was almost impossible
to recover ; and for two hundred years after
passing under the barbarous Omar, the build-

ing remained impenetrable, until Caliph Al
Mamoon, in the ninth century of our era,
forced an opening at random through the solid
masonry, and hit accidentally upon the entrance passage. Entering by the low gateway
thus built in the northern side at a considerable height above the ground, we see before
us the grave-like passage, gaping downwards
to the depths of darkness and pointing out-
wards to the pole-star—that boundary point of
mortal vision at which, as at the entrance of
the grave, the finite mystery of earth passes
into the mystery of the infinite heaven. As
we cross the gate on the seventeenth course,
we recognise the point where, in the seventeenth chapter, the catechumen is admitted as
a postulant and exclaims : " I go from the Gate
of Taser (the Ascent). What is the Gate of
Taser ? It is the Gate where the god Shu (the
Light) lifts the disc of heaven. The Gate of
the North is the Gate of the Great God," he
continues, speaking evidently of the same gate ;
exactly as in the pyramid the only entrance is
the Gate of the Ascent in the seventeenth
course of the northern face.

Bidding now with him farewell to the light
of earthly day, and treading the descending

passage, we pass, some little way down, a very
fine and beautifully ruled double line, scored
perpendicularly on the slanting wall so as to
point downwards to the foundation, and separating the upper from the lower section of the
passage ; corresponding to the point in the
Ritual where the departed, hitherto bereft of
every faculty except that of motion, begins to
have his faculties gradually restored to him.
Continuing the long descent, we arrive at an
aperture in the western wall, and passing
through the opening thus disclosed, mount
gently into a kind of grotto at the bottom of a
Well, or square perpendicular shaft, with footholds cut in the precipitous sides.   Into that
Chamber of the Deep Waters the postulant
descends on the western side, as the sun at the
close of day goes down into the western waters,
and bursts forth in splendour on the hidden
world.

Returning from the bottom of the well to
the passage, and pursuing our course still
farther downwards, we come, after a short
level continuation, to the subterranean chamber, or the Place of Fiery Ordeal, a chamber
hewn out of the solid rock, and having an
inaccessible floor covered with huge blocks

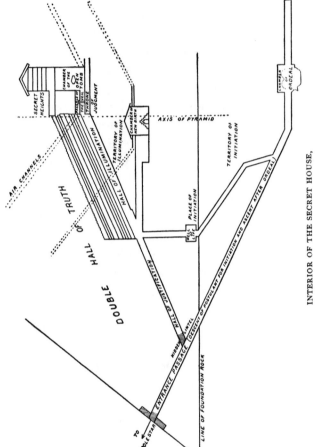

INTERIOR OF THE SECRET HOUSE,
CALLED BY THE EGYPTIANS OF OLD "THE LIGHT."[1]

[1] Throughout all the following chapters constant reference should be made to this diagram.

of varying height, resembling a pool of petrified flame, or the masses of the mountain
chains formed by the action of the earth's
central fire ; beyond which terrible chamber
a small passage leads to nothingness. Resuming our exploration of the edifice and coming
forth from the Place of Ordeal or subterranean
chamber, we remount the entrance passage
until, at a little distance below the scored line,
we come to a granite gate, or portcullis, built
in the roof. This important gate, which originally was totally hidden by masonry and was
only discovered by the falling of a stone when
Al Mamoon was forcing his entrance into the
pyramid, stands at the threshold of the Double
Hall of Ascent concealed within. Not only
was the whole gate carefully hidden, but the
lower portion of the passage within was
blocked with enormous stones, still unremoved,
and perhaps irremovable. So even now the
lintel is still hidden, and admission is only
effected through a hole forced by violence
in the wall of the passage above the blocks ;
while a precisely similar difficulty attends the
crossing of the Lintel of Justice in the Ritual
before entering the Double Hall of Truth.
Creeping with difficulty through the hole, we

find ourselves in a small, low corridor, the
floor-line of which (about 1561 inches in total
length) slightly projects beyond the gateway
at the upper end ; the whole corridor being
inclined upwards at an elevation slightly less
than that of the depression of the entrance
passage, and corresponding to the lower portion of the Hall of Truth where the Initiate
justifies himself before the judges of the unseen
world, "the Gods of the Horizon and the Gods
of the Orbit." Then, stooping beneath the
low gateway, by which it is terminated (but
not obstructed) at the top, the "Gateway
of the Festival," we stand upon a kind of
landing-place, from which the whole system
of the interior passage opens out. On every
side is "the crossing of the pure roads of
life" of which the coffin of Amamu speaks.
Straight in front runs a level passage leading
direct to the Queen's Chamber, the place of
"Isis, the divine mother, the queen of the
pyramid," as an ancient papyrus calls her ;
corresponding to the place where the soul
receives its second birth. Within that chamber,
on the eastern wall, is sculptured a staircase
of five ascents, representing the five degrees
ascended each month by the moon, wherein,

according to Egyptian teaching, Osiris, the
divine son of Isis, each month renewed his
birth. On the western side is the opening to
the mouth of the well ; and down the ladder
of the shaft (as we see in the papyrus of Ani)
the regenerate soul, on coming forth from the
Chamber of Second Birth, descends to become
re-united with the postulant awaiting it in the
Well of Life. And upwards towards the south,
above the roof of the passage leading to the
Queen's Chamber, runs the upper ascending
corridor, called by some writers the Grand
Gallery. This remarkable chamber consists
of a corridor, about one hundred and fifty-
seven feet long and twenty feet high, built
entirely on a slope, floor, walls, and roof,
except a small portion at the southern or
upper end. On either side of the sloping floor
are twenty-eight ramps, with corresponding
depressions ; the floor-line at the upper end
being closed abruptly, just above the Queen's
Chamber, by an immense stone forming a dais,
or Throne of Judgment. From the lower
entrance of the chamber at the northern end
to the foot of the throne, the direct ascent
is about 1816 inches, the height of the throne
is 36 inches, and the length of the seat about

61 inches, so that when the darkness is lit
up by torches it forms the most conspicuous
and dominating feature of that marvellous
chamber.   At the back of the throne the gallery is brought to an abrupt termination by
the southern wall closing down within a few
feet of the seat, and leaving as an exit farther
south a narrow and grave-like tunnel.   In the
sloping roof of the gallery, running upwards
from north to south at a somewhat greater
inclination than the floor, are thirty-six over-
lappings, like the waves of a river of light, and
corresponding to the number of decades of days
in the orbit of the Egyptian year.   On the
side wall of the dais at the upper end of the
gallery are also seven overlappings, one above
another, arching over to the summit as if
representing the orbits of the planets, and
having the effect of rays of light petrified in
the masonry around the throne.   And in the
position corresponding to the orbit of our
own globe runs a deep groove, or orbit, along
its entire length, offering a close connection
between the " Orbit " and the " Passage of the
Sun, in the Double Hall of Truth," in the
Ritual.   Above the throne rises the habitation of the " seven great spirits in the service

of their Lord, the Creator," who, the sacred books tell us, " protect the coffin of Osiris " ; while from its loftiest point a passage, inaccessible from below,—the " Opening of Hathor," to use the language of the Ritual,—leads to the secret heights. In that Hall of Splendour dominated by the throne of Light the Justified receives his Illumination and Investiture.

Now comes the most mysterious portion of the building. Stripped of its noble proportions and reduced to an altitude so low that a man must creep on hand and knee to pass, the passage pierces the southern wall of the upper gallery, and runs straight on, first into the ante-chamber, or " Place of Preparation," and then into the splendid hall, called the King's Chamber, in the most secluded portion of the building. In each of these halls is one, and only one, object. In the ante-chamber is a kind of veil of masonry, which no one can pass without bowing the head. In the King's Chamber is a sarcophagus, not closed, but open ; while the air-channels, wherewith this deeply buried room is amply ventilated, proclaim that it is not a chamber of the dead, but of the living, corresponding to the place of resurrection where,

in the final chapter of the Ritual, Osiris is
awakened from his slumbers. In this portion of the building the structure changes its
material for granite, forming, as it were, a
house by itself within the pyramid ; an inner
house yet, within the house of Osiris, entered
by the low and grave-like passage leading from
behind the throne.   This is the House of Glory
described on the coffin of Amamu already
quoted, the house to which the Illuminate
approaches, after passing the tribunal of Osiris.
Here is the " Gate of the Pure Spirits," which
they alone can enter who are washed in the
waters of life and radiant with the splendours
of the Orbit.   And here, too, it would seem,
takes place the solemn address, described in
the Sai-an-Sinsin, "of the Gods in the House
of Osiris," followed by the response of the
" Gods in the House of Glory " ; the joyous
song of the holy departed who stand victorious
before the judgment-seat, echoed triumphantly
by the inner chorus of their beloved who
have gone before them into the fulness of
light.   Over the chamber of the Open Tomb,
are the hidden heights, the secret spaces, to
which the Opening of Hathor, the Queen of
Imperishable Beauty, leads ; and the whole is

dominated and crowned by a gigantic triangle
of granite, immutably expressing the divine
Trinity of Egypt.

Such is the complex and hitherto wholly unexplained system of gateways and passages,
shafts, channels, and chambers ; some leading
upwards, some leading downwards, some level ;
some rough in the last degree, others exquisitely polished ; some magnificent in their proportions, some so low that a man must creep,
so narrow that he can with difficulty pass, to
be found within the Pyramid of Light.   It is
absolutely unique ; no other building, it may be
safely averred (not even among the later pyramids), having contained any structure bearing
the least resemblance to the higher chambers.
What then was the design, the secret and jealously guarded design, with which this wondrous
edifice was constructed ?   That its various features are meaningless, or the mere result of caprice, is a suggestion to which the forethought
and lavishness of calculation displayed in every
detail unmistakably give the lie.   Nor again
can we maintain that they are necessary for
the purposes of an ordinary tomb.   For, in the
first place, they are not to be found in the other
pyramids which were used for that purpose ;

and secondly, if there be any intention which
the architect has openly manifested, it is to
create such a series of obstructions that no human body could be buried there. What the
concealed significance may be of that secret
masonry; for what purpose the complex plan
was designed; at what epoch the huge structure
was erected, are questions which have perplexed
many minds in many lands, and have resulted
in a discord more akin to Babel than to the
grandeur of its silent majesty. It was built by
the Jews in the days of their captivity, just to
give them something to do, says, or rather said,
one school of theorists. It was built by Chemmis, but attributed by Egyptians in hatred of
him to the shepherd Philition, is the account
given by Herodotus. It was built by Ibn Salluk, say the Arabs, just before the flood, to
preserve the royal treasures from the predicted
inundation. It was built by Melchisedec—or
somebody,—vehemently asserts the Scottish
Professor of Astronomy, who seems always to
write in a whirlwind of miscellaneous indignation. It was indisputably intended by the
founder for his tomb, one party stoutly maintains,—a tomb in which he left especial instructions that he should not be buried, and in

which nobody could possibly have been buried, replies another. It was an observatory, maintains a third,—where every place for observation was carefully closed up, retorts a fourth. It is the "prophetic floor-roll of human history," screams Professor Smyth,—with all the dates gone wrong, softly sneers Mr. Flinders Petrie.

Only when we compare that Secret House with the Secret Book of its Master do we understand the meaning of its secret places— darkness illuminating darkness and mystery revealing mystery. And only then also do we perceive how, in those places, we possess the key to the "Words of Order" of the Secret Book. Thus, then, the determination of the Egyptian theosophy is removed from the indefinite domain of archæological speculation, and referred to the comparison of two existing and well defined records. Here is a papyrus claiming to be the secret scroll peculiar to the Master of the Secret House ; there is a secret house in which, according to Egyptian tradition, the secret Wisdom to which that scroll relates was communicated to the postulant. That scroll commences with the Entrance on Light ; and the Light was the name by which that house was known. The scroll is full of

references to secret passages and chambers ;
and secret chambers and passages make up
the whole interior of that secret house. Prominent among all those chambers mentioned in
the scroll is the Double Hall of Truth ; and
prominent among the chambers of the house
is the Double Hall of sculptured Splendour.
In the scroll, the final chapter tells of the Resurrection of the Body, and in the house the
final chamber is the chamber of the Open
Tomb. And while each record is in accordance with the other in expressing the Truth
in Light, the images, conveying the doctrinal
truth expressed in the Ritual, are in accord with
the relations of scientific truth expressed in
the building.

Such a method of recording the creed of a
priesthood is so alien to our modern ideas and
customs as at first sight to seem scarcely intelligible. But it is entirely in accordance with
that intense conservatism which, as Professor
Wiedemann has well insisted in his valuable
treatise, characterised the Egyptians from the
earliest times, and which still renders the fellah
of to-day so close a representative of his predecessor six thousand years ago. And it is difficult to conceive a device which could be more

enduring, or more effective for keeping the doctrines of that religion at once secret and immutable, than by embodying them in the hidden masonry of this stupendous building. Again, since the religion of the country was the foundation upon which the whole political system was erected, we have in the concealed chambers of this Great House or Pir Aa, from which the Egyptian monarchs derived their familiar title of Pharaoh, a key to the politico-religious constitution of the country—a key which none could imitate, none could alter, none destroy; which no man could comprehend, unless initiated, nor any forget or mistake, who had once received illumination.

Nor is it unworthy of notice that in the masonry of the different parts of that structure we may detect the forms of many of the mystic

Entrance Passage with Gateway.   Sceptre of Anup.

symbols, whereby the priests so expressed the divine conceptions as to be intelligible to those alone who had been initiated in the Secret House. Thus if we represent the Entrance Passage together with the masonry of the Gateway we have the form of the Sceptre of Anup, the Guide of the Soul. Again, if we

represent the descent traversed by the Initiate from the Head of the Well to the opening into the Chamber of the Fiery Ordeal, we have

Opening from Well to Chamber of Divine Fire.

Sceptre of Ptah, Spirit of Divine Fire.

the form of the Sceptre of Ptah, the Spirit of Divine Fire. Similarly if we represent the course traced by the overlappings of the rays in the roof of the Upper Hall of Truth we have a representation of the Celestial Nile as depicted in

Roof of Upper Hall.   Hieroglyph Symbol of the Nile.

the vignettes of the Ritual, and the hieroglyph of its earthly counterpart. And once more if we draw the great throne in the Double Hall of Truth with the central line of the light running down to depths of the rock on which it is built, we

Symbol of Divinity.

obtain the hieroglyph denoting Divinity.   And
if we add to this the lower portion of the building or, territory of Initiation, there
results the hieroglyph for the territory of the Holy Dead.

Nobly indeed does the stupen-
dous monument respond to its Territory of the
sacred title of the Light.   That Holy Dead.
secret house is the house of a tomb;   but
it is not a closed, but an open tomb.   It is a
tomb not of a man, but of a god; not of the
dead, but of the risen.   It is the tomb of the
divine Osiris, whose birth on earth, descent
into the under-world, resurrection and judgment of the dead, were the most prominent
features in the creed of Egypt, and in union
with whom the holy departed passed in safety
the divine tribunal, and was made glorious by
the Unseen Light.

CHAPTER X

THE ENTRANCE ON LIGHT

L IGHT is the first principle of created life. There is no life without growth; there is no growth without light. Colour, perfume, savour, every varied object of sense, vanishes if light be absent. Each beam is a separate celestial gift, direct from the hand of the Creator; as in the bas-relief on the tomb at Thebes, discovered by Mr. Villiers Stuart, where the diverging rays form a pyramid of light, and to each ray is attached a hand of blessing.

Universal, too, as is the necessity for light in living nature, equally extended is its manifestation in the form of motion. Wherever life exists in man or beast or bird or fish there also is that power which is denied to inanimate matter—the power to originate motion. To live and move and have our being are three

states inseparably connected with one another.
Mathematician and poet alike acknowledge the
universality of motion in living form.   " Motion, fount of beauty," exclaims Pindar, in one
of his loftiest odes.   " All nature is in motion,"
says Professor Price, in his lucid treatise on
infinitesimals. So, too, the unfailing harmonies of the heavenly bodies express themselves
in the periods of their orbits. And through
the correlations of those luminous circuits, as
through a veil of glory, the correlations of interior truth were shadowed forth by the Egyptian Mystery-Teachers of the Heaven.   Depth
below depth, space beyond space, height above
height, from the company of planets around
our sun, to where the " clusters of countless
stars are but a faint nebulous gleam," light is
everywhere the Omnipotent Creator, the laws
of light the expression of infallible truth.
    Yet how to seize with material grasp the
intellectual relations of the most ethereal
element known to man ?   How imprison in
permanent form the flashes of the fiery spark,
as it darts with inconceivable speed from space
to farthest space ? How render palpable to
the direct touch the distant courses of those
flying orbs ? In a word, how shall we build

up the mystery of the depths, and find material expression for the manifestation of light? Light itself gives us a reply. For if, as in the bas-relief at Thebes, the diverging flood of rays be represented as pouring down equally on either side, then we shall have the quadrangular form of the pyramid, its sides so oriented as to face the four cardinal points, as in the pyramid of Khufu, the " Light" of Egypt.

But earth and sun are both in motion. The earth perpetually encircles the parent orb. The sun, carrying with him the whole planetary system, proceeds, if Herschel be correct, ever onward with a somewhat slower motion, traversing in a period of four years (the grand cycle of the Egyptian astronomers) a space about equal in length to the annual path of the earth. Now we have seen already (chap. v.) that the length of the Nile in its course through Upper Egypt (from Philæ to the Great Pyramid) is just a millionth part of that orbit ; and that the positions of the great temples illustrate the principal relations by which that orbit is determined. But if, in accordance with the same principle of measurement, we take a thousandth part of that distance again (or

the thousand millionth part of the orbit),
we shall have (within a yard or two) the base-
circuit of the Great Pyramid, so that we have
a remarkable connection between the building,
the river, and the course of the earth, which
illustrates many allusions in the sacred writings.
And since the form of that circuit is square, the
base-line of the building will be one-fourth of
it, that is to say, it will be the thousand millionth part of the distance traversed by the
sun through space in a single year.   Again
if we take for altitude a line having the
same proportion to the base-circuit as the
radius of any given circle bears to its circumference, then that altitude will be the thousand
millionth part of the radius of our planet's
orbit, that is, of the earth's distance from the
sun.   And this is the well-known relation
between altitude and base to be found in the
Great Pyramid.[1]   Nor was that dominating relation a solitary instance, but it constitutes the
most marked and almost the only characteristic
which the later pyramids possess in common
with that of Khufu, thus constituting a sign
whereby the masonry of the lesser habitations

[1] Special attention to this relation between radius and circumference was paid by Mr. Flinders Petrie, who fully confirms it.

tacitly asserted their kinship with the Great House. That sign, too, was in itself significant of the light. For since the sun gives forth his rays in a direct line, while the illumined body travels in a circle around it, the re- lations thus embodied between radius and orbit image forth the relation between Illum- inator and Illuminate.

How then shall we avail ourselves of this mighty measure, this rule of light and standard of motion? A closer observation of the same wonderful edifice suggests a means. For on examining the base-circuit of the building we find it to be composed of casing-stones with a bevelled horizontal edge, so exquisitely finished that, according to Mr. Flinders Petrie, it is equal to the "finest work of the optician." Now on the occasion of the visit of the Empress Eugenie to Egypt in 1869, one of these casing-stones was measured *in situ* by Mr. W. Dixon, and found to contain just 25.025 British inches, that is to say, as Sir J. Herschel has pointed out, just the ten-millionth part of the polar axis of the earth. That this length was a standard measure among the builders of the early dynasties is shown by the discovery of Mr. Flinders Petrie, who found at Ghizeh, in

the neighbourhood of the pyramids, two specimens of twenty-five inches[1] (within a small
decimal) belonging to the time of Khufu.
And as the Egyptians were certainly familiar
with the decimal system, expressing units, tens,
hundreds, thousands, and millions by distinct
hieroglyphs, this stone in the base-circuit of
the Secret House supplies a simple and unalterable unit of length, based upon an invariable standard of universal measurement. Were
this relation, however, an isolated instance,
some question might not unnaturally arise as
to an accidental connection ; but the intention
of the architect is strongly confirmed by a kindred discovery, due also to Mr. Flinders Petrie.
For that acute observer has pointed out that
the length of the raised pavement around the
building was a simple measure (one-twentieth)
of a geographical mile. And since a geographical mile is a measure of the earth's circumference at the equator, a knowledge of it implies

[1] Professor Petrie maintains this twenty-five-inch cubit to be
"evidently an Egyptian edition of the royal twenty-five-inch cubit of
Persia." But why a Persian cubit should be employed at Ghizeh, or
what we know of Persia some thousands of years before the time of
Darius, he does not tell us.   It is difficult to see why he might not
with equal reason pronounce the Capitol of Romulus to be "evidently an Italian edition of the Capitol at Washington."

as well a knowledge of the length of the polar axis.

Striking, too, as is this relation, the connection of the stone with the base-circuit yields another result entirely in harmony with universal measures. For, taking as the measured length of that base a line of 9140 inches (being the average of the results obtained by the principal surveys executed since the great Napoleon first opened the dull eyes of Europe to the inexhaustible treasures of ancient Egypt), we find that the length of the casing-stone is contained just 365.25 times in it, thus giving the number of days in the sacred year ; while these simple details go far to show the nature of the wisdom which must have been professed by the officer of the Pharaohs who bore the title of the " Prophet of the Pyramid."

While these general relations between earth and sun suffice to determine the general aspect of the building, a closer comparison with the action of light discloses a yet more peculiar principle in its construction. For since our atmosphere may be conceived as divided into successive layers of air, each ray as it travels will be slightly deflected or refracted as it passes from a finer to a denser medium, the refraction being greatest when the body is on the horizon, and imperceptible when it is near the zenith. Conversely, if on any given day the position of the sun be observed at equal intervals, from dawn to noon and from noon to sunset, the apparent place of the sun will, owing to refraction, be slightly different from its true position at any observation ; and a diagram representing their mutual relations will offer the appearance of a house having many stories, slightly truncated at the summit, since near the zenith the true and apparent positions are identical (and the only motion is that of transit). And that is precisely the appearance presented by the Great Pyramid when the casing-stones are removed.[1]

To measure the motions of the earth, however, is the commencement, but only the commencement, of the universal scale. That which we need for the mystery of the depths is nothing less than the span of measurable space. In other words, we require to define the extreme limits, on either hand, within which no fount of original light is found except our own sun, since the distances of the stars are beyond accurate measurement. But the distance of

[1] See Note L, page 203.

the limiting point of measurable space, or rather the radius of the limiting horizon (since the distance will be the same in every direction), is about twenty billions of miles, or twenty-five hundred million times the length of the earth's polar axis. That axis, therefore, is contained in the radius of measurable space, two hundred and fifty times as often as itself contains the edge of the casing-stone. Now, if that casing-stone be divided into twenty-five equal parts, each of such parts will, as Sir J. Herschel has shown, be of a length differing from our inch by its thousandth part—in fact, less than the breadth of the finest hair. This unit, therefore, which we may call the polar inch, measures not only the axis of the earth but of the depths of solar or measurable space, being contained in the former two hundred and fifty million times, and in the latter two hundred and fifty thousand billion times. But in that ancient chapter of the Ritual (lxiv.) which claims to have been revealed in the days of the Fourth Dynasty, we read that the Creator, when revealing himself to the new-born soul as the measurer of space, employs this very ratio as standard. " I who know the Depths is my name," so

runs the text of this sublime chapter ; " I make
the shining cycles of the years, and billions
are my measurement."

That the inch, whether in our own or any
other form, was not an open and recognised
Egyptian measure there can be little doubt.
But the mention of these cycles of the shining
years suggests a principle of singular beauty,
involving the use of that polar unit as the secret key to the architectural standards of ancient Egypt. Among the many valuable
results due to the industry of Mr. Flinders
Petrie, is a collection of cubits of various
lengths, employed by the architects of the earliest dynasties. These architectural units are
very numerous and, unless referred to cosmic
principles, quite miscellaneous, having no apparent co-ordination, either among themselves
or with anything else. When, however, taking
as our unit the polar inch, we compare them with
the measure of light as expressed in the celestial periods (remembering always that the
radii of the " shining circles of years " are
both consonant with the construction of the
pyramid, and illustrate the analogy of illumination), we find a most remarkable correspondence in measure after measure, not

absolute indeed, but differing only by decimals of an inch.

For example, if we consider the cycle of the equinox as a circle of about 25,800 years, the radius is about 4,122 years; and taking a century to an inch, the half radius gives us the well-known cubit of 20.6 inches. But this measure is the more common form of the Egyptian cubit, the standard employed for the sacred "Tat," or Nilometer, which measured the waters of life, the symbol regarded as the highest expression of sanctity, and the final ornament placed upon the holy dead. Again, since the orbit of the earth is not strictly a circle, but an ellipse with the sun in one focus, there will always be one point in the orbit which will be in " perihelion," that is to say, nearer the sun than any other. And this point is not stationary, but makes a circuit of the earth's orbit in about one hundred and fourteen thousand years, whereof the half circuit gives us (at an inch to ten thousand years) the fifty-seven-inch cubit of the Eleventh Dynasty. Various other examples might also be added, while the same principle will be found to throw light on many of the serpentine forms [1] men-

[1] A single example must suffice. Thus, the famous Uræus, or sym-

tioned in the *Book of the Master*. It would
seem, therefore, that if we take as a standard a
scale representing the axis of the earth, the
sole immutable measure of space, and mark off
upon it a series of such units proportional to
the immutable periods of the heavenly bodies,
we shall have a table of the cubits employed
by the architects of those early times. And
thus when the film is brushed away, which the

bol of the snake, connected in some not very definite manner with solar
phenomena, has always been intimately associated with the royalty of
Egypt. But it appears to have escaped attention, that in the Ritual
are to be found several serpentine forms of various lengths, and, what
is most striking in itself but easily explained by the results already
attained, that when those several lengths are expressed in inches, they
prove to be proportional to the measures of the various serpentine
curves traced by the motions of the earth and moon. Thus, in chapter cxxx., we read of a snake "seventy cubits in his coil." But taking the well-known cubit of 20.6 inches, and repeating it seventy times,
we obtain 1442 inches, which is proportional (within the seven-hun-
dredth part) to the number of minutes of time (24 x 60 = 1440) in the
daily rotation of the equator or coil of the snake ; so that it expresses
our own division of the heavens into twenty-four hour-circles, each
divided again into sixty equal parts, or minutes of time, both which
measures were familiar to the Egyptians. And this central circle, of
which the unvarying rotation has, for countless ages, measured the
motion of the earth in reference to the celestial sphere, appears to be
"the great Uræus," of which elsewhere we read as gleaming and
guiding millions of years. Other examples of a more complex character might be adduced ; but these may be sufficient to show that in
the inch we possess a clue to the secret significance of numerous symbols, and that, for that very reason, it was not openly set forth as the
standard, but its place was supplied by the cubit, which betrays no
meaning except to one already so far initiated.

dust of ages has cast over these relics of antique science, their aspect remains no longer
lifeless and repulsive ; but we recognise in
them the glowing insignia of universal truth,
the gems from the azure depths sparkling with
the lustre of intrinsic light.

Turning now to the Secret House itself, to
the master of which the secret papyrus belonged,
we find a similar principle prevailing throughout the interior of the building, the lengths of
its various passages and chambers when expressed in polar inches (or twenty-five-millionth
parts of the polar axis) being apparently proportional to the radii of the celestial periods which
correspond respectively to the stages in the progress of the departed.   And so strongly marked
is the prevalence of this principle, that while a
mere knowledge of the measures, however exact, suggests nothing of the spiritual meaning,
the insight which we have already obtained of
the co-ordination of the building with the Ritual
enables us to determine the dimensions of many
of the parts.   For example : if we consider the
cycle of equinox, then its radius of 4122 years
will, at an inch to a year, give us the length of
the entrance passage which points to the pole-
star. Again, with regard to the double chamber,

corresponding with the Double Hall of Truth in the Ritual. For if we take seven cycles of eclipse, corresponding with the seven Halls of Judgment in Truth of which we read in the Ritual, then, since each of such cycles contains two hundred and twenty-three lunar months, we shall have, at an inch to a month, the total length of the floor-line of the lower ascending corridor (7x223 inches), or Chamber of Judgment. Similarly also with regard to the upper portion of the same double chamber, which is dominated by the immense stone or throne at the higher end, corresponding in the Ritual with the throne, or " Stone of God," in the Double Hall of Truth. For if we take the radius of the cycle of " perihelion," wherein the point of earth's nearest approach to the solar throne travels slowly around the orbit, we shall have, at an inch to a century, the direct ascent to the foot of the throne ; thus imaging the direct ascent of the Illuminate in the Hall of Truth to the throne, or " Stone of God," whereon, in the Ritual, Osiris sits to bestow upon him the " Atf "-crown of celestial light. And thus throughout the teaching of Egypt the visible light was but the shadow of the invisible Light ; and in the wisdom of that ancient country the measures of Truth were the years of the Most High.

With this brief survey of the celestial periods, and their analogues embodied in the masonry, we take up once more the *Book of the Master* of that Secret House—the earthly counterpart of the house not made with hands, eternal in the heavens—which the divine Horus built for his father Osiris, the "House of the Great God," to which, as the papyrus of Amen-Hotep tells us, Thoth, the Eternal Wisdom, conducts the Illuminate. And as we gaze around in silent contemplation, from every corner of the universe the profound words of the Ritual come echoing back to us: "Billions are my measurement. I who know the Depths is my name."

CHAPTER XI

THE INSTRUCTION IN WISDOM

A S the created light is the primary force manifested in the system of creation, so also is the Uncreate, or Self-begotten, Light (Kheper-Ra) the prime mover and creator whether of the visible or of the unseen universe. "Light Great Creator is his Name," we read in one of the chapters added to the Egyptian ritual at the Saite recension. And again in another ancient papyrus : "The God of the Universe is in the light above the firmament; and His symbols are upon the earth." Now it was with that divine Light, immortal, invisible, intolerable to mortal eye, the Light which none may look upon in the flesh and live, that in the ancient creed of Egypt, as in that of Christendom, the holy dead was to be at last united, person with person, in an indissoluble bond. No language less universal than that of faith can enable us to express that sublime belief. For in no other creed do we find that man never loses his individuality, which yet becomes united personally with the Deity in so intimate union, that in the Ritual the Osiris-soul can with difficulty be distinguished from the Osiris-Godhead. "The sun is worshipping thy face," says Osiris, in the Ritual, to the soul new born into the divine existence ; that is to say, the very splendour of creation, the source of light and life to the visible world, bows down in worship before him who has become a participator in the divinity of its creator. "He is I, I am he," the soul responds, almost in the actual words of the Gospel.

Long and manifold was the process whereby, in the teaching of Egypt, the human nature became united with the divine—an union effected, through the god-man Osiris, not as in the gross and distorted myths of the classic nations, by the conversion of the Godhead into flesh, but by the interior taking of the manhood into God. Without and within the transformation was complete. The soul, instantly illumined by the fulness of the Godhead, became forthwith capable of corresponding with

the divine Energy. The senses, restored to
incorruption, were gradually fashioned into
instruments capable of expressing the soul's
assimilation to that condition of infinite power,
for which the bounds of space and time exist
not, but past and future alike stand open in an
endless present,—that transcendent freedom,
wherein Act is coincident with Will, and Will
commensurate with Thought.

In order, then, that the senses may be so
quickened and irradiated as to perceive the
action of the creative mind in the exterior
universe, that progress must be made by the
departed in person which, while still unreleased
from subjection to the senses, the student of
science makes dimly through the intellect. For
whoever would understand the framework of
the heavens, the structure of man's sacred
dwelling-place, must commence by tracing out
the horizon of the point of Equinox, which
equally divides the light from the darkness, the
horizon marked by the star which indicates the
pole, and must apprehend how the axis of
the earth is for man the prime measure of
space and the standard rule of the Depths. If
he would learn the secret of living form, the
ocean will be his teacher, as he passes from

shore to profoundest depths and fathoms the
secret places of the teeming waters.   The
measure of the celestial orbits will be revealed
to him by the moon, as from that companion
orb he watches the rotation and the revolution
of our planet.   To understand not merely the
motion but the evolution of our globe, he
must dare the place of the earth's central fire,
undismayed by the cavernous gloom of the
lurid abysses.   And there, gazing backwards
for uncounted ages, he will trace, amid convulsions and cataclysms inconceivable, the
" Lord of Law" and the " Words of Order, "
as the huge mountain chains rise higher and
higher from the chaos to prepare the surface
of the globe for the dwelling-place of man.
Before him next stretches the shadow of the
earth, that dim and vast expanse where the
majesty of the open heaven is enshrouded in
night ; and he perceives how the conjunctions
of eclipse are due to the same power as the
orbits of illumination, and that the hour of
darkness is measured by the giver of light.
That shadow traversed, a yet more awful
vision, the terrible splendour of the solar fount
in all its fulness, bursts upon his sight ; and as
he mounts the seven-fold ascent of the planet-

ary spheres, he gazes undazzled on the
stupendous jets and sprays of flame that dart
thousands and myriads of miles on high.
Then, far beyond in the infinite depths of space,
his eyes, now radiant as "the eyes of Hathor,"
seek out the well-loved Sothis, the harbinger
of the dawn, the portal of the illimitable
heavens, "that land of a million fortresses."
And in anticipation of each successive stage of
this amazing progress, this reconquest of the
senses to the dominion of the reason, we may
watch the course of the postulant accepted by
the "Master of the Secret," as he is inducted,
chamber by chamber, into the hidden places
of the Egyptian Ritual.

Yet though a man understand the material
forces of the universe, though he know all the
phenomena of the heavens, and the composition of the most distant suns ; nay, though he
wield with so masterly a grasp the wand of
science as to evolve at will an organic world
from the atoms of the abysmal depths, all this,
in the mind of Egypt, was not sufficient, even
for initiation into the inner mysteries of divine
realities.   No mere expansion of the intellect,
however pure and lofty ; not even the scientific definition of absolute truth, could suffice

to open the secret things of God, any more
than the most exact acquaintance with the
features and the proportions of the Secret
House would disclose their interior signification, without the teaching of the hidden
wisdom. And hence, at the commencement
of the Ritual, in the heading of the first
chapter, before a word of doctrine has been
revealed, we are told how it proceeds from
Thoth, "The Mind and Will of God," as the
inscription of Hermopolis entitles him.

Now there are three modes in which such
knowledge may be communicated to those
prepared to receive it—namely, by simple instruction, by distant vision, or by personal
participation. Each of these modes is, it is
evident, an advance upon that which precedes,
a preparation for that which follows it. No
man can become a participator in the divine
nature who has not been illuminated by its
contemplation. No man can contemplate the
Deity who has not been instructed in truth;
nor can any receive that initiation until he be
dead to the flesh. As, therefore, in his induction in the Secret House the catechumen could
ascend but a few steps in the light of common
day, and passed, when the disc of the starry

heaven was opened by the Master of the Secret, into the profound darkness of the descending passage; so, too, when the great preparation of death had been accomplished, when soul and spirit had been released from the dominion of the senses, when, by the sacred purification of embalmment, the corruptible body had put on incorruption, then "on the day of the funeral," we read, the unseen Master commenced to instruct the catechumen in the stages which must be undergone preparatory to his initiation. For, to the Egyptian of old, to have become acquainted with the Secret House was to have mastered the Secret of the Tomb. For him the grave had no darkness, death held no terror; for he knew beforehand the starry path, wherein each step brought him nearer to the Creator-Light.

Taking in our hands now the *Book of the Master*, let us resume our position at the foot of the exterior ascent, beneath the entrance marked by the star, along with the catechumen; and with him let us forecast the time when, bereft of speech, of will, of life, he will go forth, senseless and soulless, to the mouth of the tomb and commence "the Entrance on Light" (chap. i.) while "borne to the land of

the holy dead." The very first words are a
welcome, addressed by Thoth, the Eternal
Wisdom, *not to Osiris himself, but to the departed, who bears, we must remember, the title
of " Osiris."* " ' Hail, Osiris, strong one of
heaven,' says the Divine Wisdom, King of
Eternity,"—so runs the opening chapter when
divested of the enshrouding imagery. " I am
the great God near the divine vessel, I have
fought for thee, I am he among the divine
beings who causes the Osiris to be justified
before his enemies, the day of weighing the
words of thy accusers. O Osiris ! "—so the
Teacher continues to the departed, with striking significance when we reflect that according
to Catholic teaching also, the Divine Wisdom is
the Second Person of the Blessed Trinity, the
Child of Mary—" O Osiris ! I am One among
the Divine Persons, the Child of the holy
Mother." And again : " O ye that cause
the soul to enter perfect into the house of
Osiris, let the soul of the departed enter the
house, justified with you ! May he see as ye
see. Hail, openers of the roads. Hail, guides
of the paths, guides of the soul established in
the house of Osiris. Open ye the roads, make
ye straight the paths of the departed trium-

phant with ye." "If this scroll be known on earth," so the chapter concludes, "write it upon his bandages. It is that by which he cometh forth, in full splendour [1] according to his desire, and goeth to his house." Then reciting chapter by chapter as we mount step by step, we become informed, in the course of that brief but steep ascent (ii.–xv.), of the preparation which awaits him when the last glimpse of earth is hidden from his sight. Thus we learn how, after death, the departed comes forth into the light of immortality, even as the sun, when he sets, bursts forth in radiance on the world which is hidden from our view. Then, since the departed cannot yet bear the judgment of interior justice, he is warned beforehand that when he has commenced the descent he must "pass the road above the earth," the ascending passage concealed by the hidden portcullis, behind the secret portal of which, we descry in the vignette illustrating the chapter, the face of the Unseen Teacher,— that countenance on which the holy dead, when Initiation has begun, shall presently be strengthened to gaze in distant but unveiled vision. Before that lintel can be passed and

[1] See Note M, page 204.

the road above the earth be traversed, many
trials, he now learns, are waiting for him.
There are tasks of justice to be fulfilled, if he
omitted those good works on earth, the
memorials of which may be his sponsors
("Ushabti"). Apep, too, the dark serpent that
devours the hidden Light, as the winding darkness of the autumnal equinox enshrouds the
light of the year, lies in wait to crush him in
its multitudinous folds, while he treads the
path where light and darkness balance.   Still
mounting upward, and at each step approaching nearer to the gate of the grave, the catechumen is instructed how, when that serpent
shall be passed, his foes shall be repelled and
his senses restored in the fulness of eternal
beauty.   Passing in silence over that which
shall happen to him in the well enclosed within
the western wall, the territory of "the lord of
the west," since that knowledge cannot yet be
imparted, the divine Teacher directs him,
when the mystery of new life is accomplished,
to the fiery ordeal, and, after entering and
coming forth from the dread chamber, to approach once more the Lintel of Justice.   For
then, and then only, can he set foot upon the
threshold of justification, when "the stains

have been burnt from his heart" by the raging
fire.

On the fifteenth course, now high above the
horizon of the earth, our eyes already face the
outer entrance of the secret places, revealing
the path of the horizon of heaven, the double-
arched gateway whereon the symbol of the
horizon is inscribed ; and similarly in chapter
xv. the departed "comes towards the land of
eternity."   "May I proceed," he continues,
"as thou dost, without halt, like thy holiness,
Ra, thou who hast no master, great traverser
of waters, with whom millions of years are but
a moment."   Then, as he bends his head towards the entrance of the Secret House, and
gazes on the dark passage which points towards the pole-star, "I proceed to heaven," he
says ; "I kneel among the stars."   And at the
conclusion of the chapter he learns the words
to recite when his sun is setting, and he kneels
with his hands towards the land (of the unseen), "O height of Love, thou openest the
double Gate of the Horizon."

With these sublime words of thanksgiving,
the instruction of the catechumen comes to a
close ; sufficient knowledge having been imparted to direct his course until the ordeal be

passed, beyond which he can as yet look no farther into the mysteries. In the following chapter (xvi.), as we ascend the last course before quitting the outer light, the divine voice is for a season hushed, and the Ritual silently offers three pictures for our contemplation. On one of these the sole object presented is the sacred scarab, a symbol of the Eternal One, the self-created being who knows no beginning and no end. On the second is the figure of the departed standing before Amen, the hidden deity; the third contains simply a blank stele or tombstone.

In that moment of silence the departed is alone.

CHAPTER XII

THE INITIATION OF THE POSTULANT

THE friends are gone. The sun, which from his earliest years has greeted the awakening of the departed, is for ever hidden from his sight. The "Gate of the earth" is passed; and the Catechumen of Wisdom has become the Postulant of Immortality. Silence inconceivable to mortal ear reigns around him, darkness unimaginable to mortal eye lies before him. But under the direction of Anup, the guide of souls, he passes on beyond that Gate of Ascent, where the divine light lifts the disc of the tomb. "It is the region of his father Shu" (the Light), the Ritual continues: "he effaces his sins, he destroys his stains." Then as the departed advances through the darkness, and fearlessly commences the descending path, the inner Light, unseen by mortal eye, reveals itself in vision.   He beholds the lower world (xvii.), the territory of Initiation, the entry of the hidden places, concerning which the divine Wisdom has instructed him, the place "wherein he must enter and from whence he must come forth," the transformations which he must desire to make that he may be transformed into the likeness of God, the good works which he must do, the throne of the regenerate soul, and the blessed company of Osiris after the body has been laid to rest. In that same vision, too, he sees the entrance of the under-world, or Rusta, and learns that it is the northern door of the tomb of Osiris, as the sole entrance of the pyramid is the gate of the north.

With the eighteenth chapter begins the "Book of Performing the Days," that is, the period of preparation for Initiation and Ordeal, the due performance of which enables him to pass "the road above the earth, there to receive the crown of justification when his victory is assured." He utters a prayer to the divine Wisdom for justification against the enemy through the heavenly circles of the guardian spirits. As he pursues the descending passage of the heavenly horizon, the

reconstruction of the inner man, the new creation to life immortal, slowly commences (xxi.).
One by one his faculties are re-awakened to
spiritual life; his mouth is opened that he may
respond to the teaching of the divine voice,—
the germ or "egg" of the illuminative life.
His heart is given back, never again to rise
against him with unruly passion; and he knows
no more the icy numbness of the paralyzed
affections.   Gradually the new-formed body
gathers force and substance; that is to say,
not the natural body, which never bursts its
sacred swaddling bands till wakened in the
last chapter of the Ritual, but the spiritual or
astral body (called by the Egyptians the
"Sahu"), wherewith man, already raised in incorruption yet still awaiting the open manifestation of Osiris's resurrection, converses with
the "Starry Spirits," the intelligences of the
transcendant spheres.   With the new life commences the attack of his spiritual enemies now
rendered palpable to his sight (xxvii.–xxxii.),
the dread inhabitants of the unseen world, that
wage in man the great battle of contending
light and darkness.   Sloth, the tortoise, strives
to delay his steps; the asps put forth their
venom; crawling reptiles infest his path. From

every side the raging passions, the devouring
crocodiles which inhabit the waters of life,
rush furiously to the attack; but he repels all
those creatures of darkness by the astral brightness of his starry nature. "Back, Crocodile
of the South!" he cries; "I am Sothis"—the
star of the eternal dawn. "Back!" he exclaims again to the serpent; "thou art over-
whelmed by the waters of heaven. Depart
from the place where Ra gives renewal of
life." His foes defeated by the divine protection (xxxiii.–xli.), the body raised in incorruption acquires in every limb and every
feature the seal of God. His hair, from which
the light glows forth in streams, is as "the
hair of Nu," the sacred Nile glowing with the
streams of life; his countenance, shining as
the sun, is radiant as the face of Ra; his eyes,
glorious as the eyes of Hathor, gleam with immortal beauty; his fingers are as the Uræi,
the sacred serpents, the insignia of the royal
power; his feet burn with the fire of the
Creator-Spirit Ptah; his humanity is as the
humanity of Osiris, the incarnate God. "There
is not a member of him," says the Ritual,
"which is not divine."

Resplendently beautiful as is the astral body

assumed by the new being, he is not yet prepared for Initiation.   His self-dominion, the
head of his glory, may be taken from him ; he
may incur the second death of defilement from
the creatures of darkness (xliii.–li.).   But still
by the same guidance avoiding all these dangers, he comes forth as the day, through the
gate of the west, to the passage which conducts
him to the Well of Life, as the sun passes the
gate of the western ocean to the under-world.
And as he crosses that threshold he is fed
with the celestial food which they may not eat
who are partakers of that which is hateful to
Ra (li.–lxiii.).   Avoiding defilement through
the strength of that food, he receives the
breath of the Creator-Spirit Ptah, and drawing
near to the Well of Life, is granted a first
draught of its refreshing streams.   In the
depths of that Well, wherein, as the Sai-an-Sinsin tells us, approach is made to Osiris, shall
presently take place the regeneration of the
renewed man (or " Ka "), by reunion with the
new-born soul amid the living waters.   " I
give the waters of life to every mummy," says
the goddess Nut, who presides over the waters,
in the inscription on the vase of Osur-Ur (given
in *Records of the Past*), " to reunite it with

the soul, that it may henceforth be separated
from it no more forever.   The Resident of the
West has established thy person amid the sages
of the divine Lower Region.   He giveth stability to thy body, and causeth thy soul never
to distance itself from thee.   He keepeth remembrance of thy person, and saveth thy
body now and forever."

During this arduous preparation, while the
departed passes from earth in absolute weakness to wage the prolonged conflict of light
and darkness, the imperishable soul, restored
to her native element, is born a second time,
as Osiris was born of Isis, the Queen of the
Pyramid ; being at once her son, her maker, and
her spouse.   " I am Yesterday," says Osiris in
the sixty-fourth chapter, said to be almost coeval with the founder of the building ; that is,
" I am He who was before time began," since
however far back in time a day may be, yesterday was always before it.   " I am the Dawn,"
he continues, " the Light of the Second Birth,
the Mystery of the Soul, Maker of the gods, by
whom are fed the hidden ones of heaven."   So
in the inscription on the coffin of Ankhnes-Ra-
Neferab—that is, of her " whose life was the
Sacred Heart of Ra,"—we read concerning Isis,

that it is she "who opens for thee the secret
places by those mighty names of thine. Thy
name is Infant and Old Man, Germ and Growth,
Son of Heaven, who makes the road for thee
according to his word. Thy name is Everlasting, Self-Begotten, the Dawn, the Day, the
Evening, the Night, the Darkness. Thy name
is the Moon, the Heart of Silence, the Lord of
the Unseen World." And on another part of
the coffin of the same holy queen, the spirits
of Annu, called in the Ritual the "secret birthplace of the gods," are invoked as those "who
preside over the sacred birth." With the new
birth of the soul comes also the restoration of
power in its original divine image. For as in
the condition which is subject to decay, the
corruptible senses dominate and inform the
soul, so, according to the theosophy of Egypt,
in the condition of immortality does the illuminate spirit inform and dominate the regenerate senses. While we are subject to the flesh,
the external universe impresses itself continually upon the mind, dimming and imprisoning
the original "type" or image of the Deity,
which feebly struggles to express itself in the
masterpieces of poet or artist. But when the
soul is born into new life, it regains that cre-

ative image, and is endowed with the power of co-operating with the divine Energy. For, as we learn from an exquisite chapter in the Ritual, it is the fragrance of innocence, which perfumes the freshness of the lily and the breath of the creative beauty.

In that secret chamber the regenerate soul comes glorious as the day, and "opening the door,". once so carefully concealed, comes forth in full radiance to the fields of Aahlu, the territory of illumination, to take its seat upon the lower throne above the head of the Well, between the Chamber of the Orbit and the Chamber of the Shadow. "The gates of heaven open to me," he says; "the gates of earth open to me." That solemn enthronisation being witnessed by the postulant in the depths below, he remembers that the time of ordeal draws near, and after praying, as instructed beforehand, that his sins may be rubbed out, he celebrates the "festival of the soul passing to his body." But not immediately may that passage be accomplished. Raised, though he be, in incorruption, glowing, as he is, in every member with the immortal light, he cannot yet bear unveiled the overwhelming glory of the soul. Therefore, in the teaching of Egypt, around the radiant being, which in its regenerate life could assimilate itself to the glory of the Godhead, was formed the "Khaibit," or luminous atmosphere, consisting of a series of ethereal envelopes, at once shading and diffusing its flaming lustre, as the earth's atmosphere shades and diffuses the solar rays. And at each successive transformation (lxxvii.–lxxxvii.) it descended nearer to the moral conditions of humanity. From the form of the golden hawk, the semblance of the absolute divine substance of the one eternal self-existent being, it passes to the "Lord of Time," the image of the Creator, since with creation time began. Presently it assumes the form of a lily, the vignette in the Ritual representing the head of Osiris enshrined in that flower; the Godhead manifested in the flesh coming forth from immaculate purity. "I am the pure lily," we read, "coming forth from the lily of light. I am the source of illumination and the channel of the breath of immortal beauty [the nostril of Hathor]. I bring the messages [of heaven]; Horus [the Eternal Son] accomplishes them." Later, the soul passes into the form of the Uræus, "the soul of the earth," the serpentine curve traced, year by year, upon the earth along the path immediately irradiated by the vertical sun, as the senses are irradiated by the supreme illumination of the soul.

And finally it assumes the semblance of a crocodile ; becoming subject, that is, to the passions of humanity. For the human passions, being part of the nature wherein man was originally created, are not intrinsically evil, but only become evil when insubordinate to the soul. And thus the crocodile, which attacked the departed before new birth, is rendered divine in the regenerate form. Therefore it was that the crocodile was held in high reverence by the Egyptians, for it spoke to them of the time when man should regain the mastery of his passions, and when the last barrier between himself and his glorious soul should be removed forever.

Immeasurable as is the distance which thus separates the two beings which make up the perfect manhood, there is no hesitation or delay on the part of the soul. That radiant creature in its glory has not forgotten the frail companion in union with whom it dwelt during the days of its humiliation. Restored to its native purity, welcomed by the Almighty to a participation in his own Energy, throned

on its seat of absolute dominion, yet such is
the ardour with which that soul returns the
love of man that, like the Creator himself, it
cannot rest satisfied with its own inexhaustible
bliss, but hastens to come down from its seat
of power, that it may raise and glorify expectant humanity.   And thus the vignette shows
us the winged creature flying towards the postulant.   Meanwhile the latter, from below
watching its flight, prays in an ecstasy for the
reunion.   "O bringer!" he cries, "O runner in
his hall!"—the Hall of Truth, where the
throne of the soul is erected.   "Great God!
let my soul go where it desires.   O conductors
of the bark of millions of years, led through the
gateway clearing the path of heaven and earth,
accompany ye the souls to the mummies!"

The prayer is granted (xci.–xciii.).   Leaving
its throne on high,[1] and passing through its
various transformations, the soul descends the
ladder of the Well, as in the papyrus of Ani.
Then the divine protection is obtained, and,
amid the living waters in the pool of the Per-

---

[1] An inspection of the lower portion of the Upper Hall of Truth
just by the head of the Well (where the postulant is waiting) will disclose the Throne of the Soul formed in the masonry by the abrupt
termination of the lower part of the floor-line, and exactly corresponding to the Throne of Judgment at the head of the same ascent.

sea, the tree of immortality (as the Ritual elsewhere calls it), the earnest desire of the
postulant is fulfilled, and he is re-united with
his living soul. " My soul is from the beginning," he says, "from the commencement of
time. The eye of Horus [the divine son]
made for me my soul, preparing its substance.
The darkness is before them ; the arms of
Osiris hold them. Open the path to my soul
and my shadow [Khaibit] and my spirit, to see
the great God within his sepulchre the day of
making up the souls." If that knowledge is
possessed, the Ritual adds, he enters on Light ;
he is not detained in the lower world.

That priceless gift conceded, the postulant,
though he cannot yet participate in the divine
splendour until his ordeal be passed, yet can
he behold it openly from afar and enter on his
initiation into the sacred mysteries. Offering
a prayer to the divine Teacher, and "holding
in his hand the sacred mysteries," he turns his
opened eyes successively in three directions
(xcv.–cvi.). First he gazes toward " the opening where Thoth is " ; and he beholds the Secret Wisdom which gives to truth its splendour,
the countenance of the divine Teacher, whose
voice instructed the catechumen, and whose

power protected the postulant. Then, as his eyes
grow clearer, he offers a prayer to Anup, the
starry guide who has led him thus far towards
his heart's desire ; and, turning, he discerns the
bark of Ra, the vessel of God, foretold to him before his entry on the path by the divine Teacher,
—the vessel which shall bear him safely across
the deep waters.   And in the
vignettes of the Ritual, we see
the vessel bearing upon it at
one time a fivefold, at another

The Fivefold Throne.

a sevenfold staircase, the fivefold dominion of
the regenerate senses, and the sevenfold elevation of the illuminate intellect.   Yet one more
vision opens out to the Initiate.   As he raises
his eyes to the extreme end of the Chamber
of the Splendour, far removed from the head of
the Well, yet forming part of the same divine
structure, he discerns the "opening where
Hathor is," the azure depths of ethereal loveliness leading to the Secret Heights above.
For a moment he gazes in silent rapture on
the far-off opening of the unimaginable vision,
and then calls to his aid "the Opener of the
Great Sanctuary": "Oh, assistant! — oh,
assistant!" he exclaims, "I am among the
servants of Immortal Beauty!"

CHAPTER XIII

THE ILLUMINATION IN TRUTH

FORTIFIED by the remembrance of that enduring vision—the far-off glimpse of the divine Wisdom, Holiness, and Beauty which is granted to him who has received the waters of life and is initiated into the divine mysteries,—the departed turns from the scenes of future Illumination, and descends towards the place of impending trial (cvii.–cxvi.). Around him stand revealed the " Gods of the Western Gate," the spirits who came unseen to his assistance at the hour when the sun of earthly life went down into the west. From above flows down the torrent of the " Celestial Nile," and mingles with the stream which waters the fields of Aahlu, the home of the regenerate. And high aloft, far as his quickened eyes can pierce, are assembled the bright companies of starry beings from every quarter, to assist at his victory, his judgment, and his coronation, as he enters and comes forth from the subterranean Chamber of the Fiery Ordeal.

That ordeal undergone, the character both of the doctrine and of the scene in which it was imparted appears to undergo a transformation. Not that the air of mystery is in any way lessened, rather it deepens, if possible, as we penetrate into the more secret parts. But, the period of weakness and of expectancy once passed, a sense of power and triumph grows more and more distinctly perceptible as we enter

Well of Life and Chamber of Fiery Ordeal.

the secret places of absolute "Truth" (cxvii.–cxxv.). Turning back with the Initiate from the "Meskwa," or place of ordeal, we retrace our steps upwards, under the direction of the celestial guide, who conducts us to the "Gate on the Hill," the lintel hidden in the roof far up along the passage of the star. In remounting the ascent, the Initiate once more "enters and comes forth" from the gateway of the well, that he may again receive strength for the coming judgment. And as he approaches the hidden portcullis, which now he is called upon to pass, and behind which sits in person the Eternal Wisdom, he recites for himself the unforgotten words wherein the divine Teacher warned him of the hour drawing near of entering into judgment and of issuing from thence. Arrived at the hidden portcullis carefully concealed within the roof, that arduous "Gateway reserved for the Gods," the divine Osiris-souls, the gateway which none can enter except "after coming out" from the place of ordeal, obstruction meets him at every step. Alike in the Ritual and in the building, each portion of that most mysterious gateway, the secret of whose masonry still remains undisclosed, refuses entrance to the upward path except to the adept. "'I will not let thee go over me,' says the sill, 'unless you tell me my name.' 'The Weight in the Right Place is thy name,'" is the profound reply of the adept. For, as the raising of the portcullis depends upon the true adjustment of the weight, so also is justice the virtue without which the path on high remains forever closed. "'I will not let thee pass me,' says the Left Lintel,"—so continues this strange dialogue,—"'unless you tell me

my name.' ' Return of the True is thy name.'
' I will not let thee pass me,' says the Right
Lintel, 'unless you tell me my name.' ' Return of Judged Hearts is thy name.' " For
without truth and without self-judgment no
step can be taken of progress in the upward
path. With that doctrine we may compare
the " Golden Words" of Pythagoras, himself a
pupil of the priests of Egypt :

> " Do innocence; take heed before thou act ;
> Nor let soft sleep upon thy eyelids fall,
> Ere the day's actions thou hast three times scanned,
> What have I done, where erred, what left unwrought?
> Go through the whole account, and if the sum
> Be evil, chide thee ; but if good, rejoice.
> This do, this meditate, this ever love,
> And it shall guide thee into virtue's path."

But to him who has learned of Wisdom, however long, however arduous the search, the
entrance into truth cannot finally be denied.
The Hidden Lintel is crossed ; and the memory
of that passage is forever kept sacred by the
grateful departed.   " I have come through the
Hidden Lintel," he cries, triumphantly, later
on ; " I have come like the sun through the
gate of the festival." The lintel crossed, the
person of the divine Teacher is disclosed,

having before him the true balance of light
and darkness. The "secret faces at the gate"
unveil themselves ; and the adept stands within the Double Hall of Truth—of truth in
death and truth in life, of truth in justice and
truth in mercy, of truth in darkness and truth
in splendour. Then, as he surmounts each

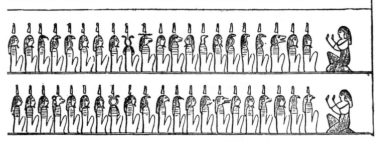

The Judges of the Dead.

obstacle besetting the entrance to the path
which leads on high, and achieves the triumph
over death, he beholds the long array of the
Judges of the Dead, the celestial powers who
take account of the mortal actions of mankind,
each supreme in his own province of the holy
land, each bearing on his head the Plume of
Truth.   And to each in turn the adept, whose
stains have been washed from his heart in the
furnace of the ordeal, pleads his innocence of

the sin of which that power is the special avenger.   Very terrible are the images under which
those heart-searching spirits are presented—
terrible as the moral effects of our own transgression, when viewed by the inner light of
truth.   The " Eyes of Fire," the passion which
shrivels the intellect ; the " Face of Smoke,"
the pride that clouds the judgment; the
" Crackler of Bones," the sin which corrodes
the entire manhood, these and such as these
are the fearful insignia of the infernal powers.
Most terrible of all is the spirit " whose mouth
is twisted when he speaks, because his face is
behind him," the spirit of conscience, which
keeps its dread eyes inexorably on our past,
and speaks to us with mouth contorted in the
agony of self-condemnation ; like the cry of
the penitent, which echoes as bitterly now as
when uttered three thousand years ago, " My
sin is ever before me."

Undeterred by that august tribunal, which,
as we learn at the threshold, none can endure
but he who has truly judged himself, the departed, protected by the divine guardian, ascends the Passage of the Shadow where the
light is eclipsed, and achieves through truth
his victory over death (cxxvii.–cxxx.).   As he

draws near the low but unobstructed gateway,
the glow of the splendour begins to appear,
and he sees before him the sacred orbit of the
circling earth, defined by the four burning
points of Solstice and Equinox, like a basin of
fire surrounded by four jets of flame. In front
of those cardinal points of the heaven, are
seated the four divine spirits, having the resemblance of an ape, the form nearest akin to
humanity.   To those four universal guardians
and heralds of truth, the justified prays that he
may be purified yet further from his trangres-
sions.   "O ye," he says, "who send forth truth
to the universal Lord, nurtured without fraud,
who abominate wickedness, extract all the evil
from me! Obliterate my faults and annihilate
my sins."   "Thou mayest go," is the gracious
reply of the four heavenly teachers; "we obliterate all thy faults, we annihilate all thy sins."
In this manner, as the Ritual declares, his separation from his sins is effected "after he has
seen the faces of the Gods." From henceforth
death has no more power over him, and in rapture he returns thanksgiving to the supreme
judges, the Gods of the Orbit, towards whom
he now advances, and to Osiris on his throne.
As he stands at the entrance of the upper

chamber, where the slight projection of the
lower floor bears witness to the passage from
death to life, the divine voice, which has been
silent till its first lesson is exhausted, recommences his illumination, and he is "instructed"
to stand at the bark of Ra—no longer in the
lower portion of the vessel, but free of every
part.   Obedient to the divine command, he
passes the "Gate of the Gateway," and celebrates the birthday of Osiris, the Opening of
the Eternal Year.   Then as he advances a step
and stands within the hall upon the slight projection, he beholds the whole building before
him, the vast universe of space, in its immeasurable grandeur now free to his immaculate
spirit.   And as at the lintel of justice all was
barred, so here every part lies open.   "The
heaven opens," we read,[1] *i. e.*, the chamber of
the splendour with its sevenfold rays around
the solar throne ; "the earth opens," the chamber of the shadow ; "the north opens," to the
chamber of the pole-star ; "the south opens,"
to the inner heights ; "the west opens," to the
entrance of the Well ; "the east opens," to the
Chamber of New Birth, with its fivefold eastern

---

[1] Here again special attention is invited to the Interior of the
Secret House.

ascent ; "the northern and southern chapels open," to the ante-chamber and the Grand Chamber of Resurrection. Here, too, is the "crossing of the pure roads of life," of which the coffin of Amamu speaks. Behind are "the roads of darkness," which the departed, in the Ritual, once prayed so earnestly that he might pass. In front lie the fields of Aahlu, the blessed country where the justified executes the works which he is privileged to do for Osiris.

A burst of triumph greets the justified when, having accomplished the passage of the sun, he enters the Chamber of the Orbit, the Hall of Illumination. "The deceased," we read, "passes through the Gate of the Gateway. Prepare ye his Hall when he comes. Justify his words against the accusers. There is given to him the food of the gods of the Gate. There has been made for him the crown which belongs to him as the dweller in the Secret Place." In another place the justified himself exclaims : "I have opened the gate of heaven and earth" (at the junction of the Halls of the Orbit and of the Shadow). "The soul of Osiris rests there. I cross through the halls. No defect or evil is found in me." And once more the deceased prays that he may pass this hall. " Place me before thee, O Lord of Eternity. Hail, Dweller of the West, good Being, Lord of Abydos. Let me pass the roads of darkness ; let me follow thy servant in the gate."

A similar note of exultation marks the passage in the Sai-an-Sinsin, where we read of the great tribunal and the House of Light. " Thou comest into the House of God with much purity," exclaim the mourners, addressing the departed. " The gods have abundantly purified thee in the great tribunal. Thou art not shut out of heaven ; thy body is renewed in the presence of Osiris. Thou hast not been shut out from the House of Glory. Thou seest the Path of Beauty, completing every transformation which thou desirest." And the ancient coffin of Amamu bore on the outside this inscription, full of desire and hope : " An act of homage to Anup, who passes the deceased over the distant paths, the fairest of the holy land "—that is, the land of the holy dead. " Thine eyes," say our own sacred writings, " shall see the king in his beauty ; they shall behold the land that is very far off."

The gateway passed, the divine voice resumes its instruction, and teaches the justified

of "going to the heaven where Osiris is"; of
being "received into the Sacred Heart of Ra,"
the fount of life ; of "the adoration which he
must render"; of the vessel of eternity in which
the holy souls forever move; of the rejoicings
of heaven in the manifestations of the Godhead to man, and of the names and places
wherein those manifestations are vouchsafed.
And now the justified stands within the full
glory of the Orbit and looks forth, not with
the vision of mortal seer, but as the deathless
spirits who encircle the throne. While he
stands gazing, splendour after splendour, revelation after revelation, bursts upon his sight.
Down from the radiant throne of the burning
sun, along the limitless floor of space, along
the sevenfold wall of the planetary heights,
along the overarching roof of the celestial
vault, streams, rivers, floods of light come
sweeping down on him whose eyes are opened ;
each orb, each satellite, each distant luminary
mingling its unveiled lustre in a glory beyond thought, like the torrent of the summer
rays, like the inundation of the overwhelming
Nile.   But the Illuminate breathes freely the
air of opened heaven. His senses, forever
vivified, pierce through the utmost bounds of

space; his quickened intellect grasps each
starry law and harmony; his purified spirit,
undazzled by the blinding radiance, discerns
the hidden love that occupies the throne.   No
longer as a stranger, or at a distance, but as a
prince admitted to the highest honours of the
court, the justified takes his place in the very
line of direct approach, while around and above
him the measureless expanse is filled with rank
beyond rank of spirit-ministers.   " He has
passed his billions," we read ; "the circle of
flaming ministers is around him.   His blessings follow him.   'Come,' says Truth ; and
he approaches her Lord."

CHAPTER XIV

THE MASTER OF THE SECRET

A T that gracious word of Truth, the abysses of mystery reveal their most secret depths. First, the Chamber of the Shadow is lit by the irradiating brightness; and the Illuminate discerns the nature of sin viewed in the light of truth (cxliv.–cl.). The seven halls of mortal sin, each measured by its cycle of eclipse, lie open to him who has looked upon the face of God; and each name of mystery betrays the form of darkness. "Babbling" Malice, that delights in overthrow; "Fire-faced" Anger, leaping on a sudden to the front; Envy, the "Eater of Dirt"; Hatred, silent and "vigilant"; Lust, the consumer, the overthrower in a moment, "that lives off reptiles"; Pride, with its "face of stone"; Sloth, that hardens irretrievably the heart, the "final stopper of the rejected";—all these betray their nature to him over whom death has power no longer.   And he discerns (as in the vignette of the Ritual) the seven avenging spirits, each armed with the two swords of physical and spiritual destruction.

Mounting then the steep ascent, he beholds the mystery of judgment disclose itself in successive stages as the gates of Aahlu,—those gates of the divine being whose "Heart is Beauty"—unfold before him.   At each of the first ten portals flows a celestial stream of

Osiris on Throne of Judgment.

sparkling waters, which shed their undying lustre over the person of the Illuminate.   Ascending still towards the throne of Osiris, at the nineteenth portal he is clothed with robes of power ; and at "the gate of the Burning Crown" he stands beneath the sevenfold arch of the planetary spheres.   Immediately beyond is the "Stone of God," where he receives from the divine occupant a "Crown of Illumination," the "Atf"-crown of Egypt fashioned after the zodiacal light of highest heaven. And behind the throne is seen " the Gate of Peace, the end of the course," with its seven crowns of joy.

" I have finished the course," he cries (cxlv.), " I am the Lord of the Resurrection, the Avenger of his Father, the heir to his Father the Holy One.   I am come.   I execute for my Father the throwing down of all his foes.   I come full splendour with all the truth of the word.   The Master of the Devotion in the dwelling of my Father.   I come full splendour into the temple to offer the incense.   I distribute the sacred garments.   I receive at my rising the diadem and crown myself with it on my throne in the dwelling of my Father, and the princes of heaven."   And again in the following chapter: " O Masters of the Altars, I have made the ways, I am Horus the son of Osiris.   My Mother, Isis, protects me.   I come.   I bring the serene life to my Father, Osiris.   I come full splendour to the gates of the recess, and I know the mysteries that are in it.   I come full splendour to the gate of the Master of the height.   O Lords of Eternity, I have performed my course, I am Horus the son of Osiris, the Heir of the Holy One."

The Master of the Secret   183

But not as yet can the Illuminate attain the infinite serenity which lies beyond that gate. Death and judgment are not the only secrets to be disclosed when the eye of faith becomes the eye of sight. The place of the divine birth, the chamber in "the fields of Aahlu," must be visited before the Illuminate become the Master of the Secret. And as he passes portal after portal of the fields he recites the titles of her whose habitation he now approaches: the "Mistress of Holy Awe," the "Mistress of Heaven," the "Regent of the Earth," the "Help of the Meek-hearted," the "Mistress of Prayer," the "Light of the Secret River." Then having learned the majesty of its queen, he scans the sevenfold arch, the mystery of the transcendent heaven, to hold converse with the seven supreme Intelligences who overarch the splendour of creation.

And now the "writing which confers perfection" is delivered to him (cxlviii.), the scroll which none but the king and the chief priest may look upon; and from it he learns the prayer "for the food and drink of the dwellers in the house." Yet once again, in the strength of that divine refreshment, must the depths be sounded and the secret places be traversed, before the Illuminate can pass as Master through the gate of Peace (cli.–clxiii.). One secret of death still remains, most terrible and inscrutable of all. While we are yet imperfect, we can gain some knowledge of the effect of moral death upon ourselves, and even form a faint adumbration of its nature when viewed in the light of absolute truth. But the mystery of its divine permission who can penetrate? If the Omnipotent be all good, why did he ever allow of evil? If he be all merciful, why does he permit his creatures to suffer? How can our actions be justly "balanced" when the forces which produced them were not of our creation? Why are we to be made parties to the battle of light and darkness when no choice was given whether we would exist or not? Why are the souls of just men secretly snared and overthrown? Whence comes the "foul flux" which is purged from man, and which causes all living creatures to shudder? Such questions as these we ask, and ask in vain. Yet if that darkest shadow, that horror which forms the depth of human agony,—the enshrouding of the eternal justice in the blackness of utter eclipse,—is still liable to arise and overpower the soul, how can man

ever repose in safety, and what revelation or
degree of glory will suffice to bring him peace?
But that it, too, is destined to pass away in
light, when the secrets are revealed and illumination is transformed into union, who can
doubt? So at least we read in the creed of
ancient Egypt, where, when the other mysteries of death and of judgment have been
disclosed to the Illuminate; when he has entered into the secrets of the new birth, and
conversed with the supreme Intelligences who
"watch before the tomb of Osiris"; when
time exists for him no more, and he understands the design of the eternal House from
foundation to consummation, he makes a final
circuit of its secret places. Clothed in power
and crowned with light he traverses the abodes
or scenes of his former weakness, there to discern, by his own enlightened perception, how
it is "Osiris who satisfies the balance of him
who rules the heavens"; to exert in its supernal freedom his creative will, now the lord, not
the slave, of the senses; and to rejoice in the
just suffering which wrought out his Illumination and Mastery.

Finally, when that grand progress through
the habitations of humanity has been com-

pleted, the Master returns in majesty to the celestial company assembled in their ranks before the solar throne. Mounting beneath the sevenfold arch, he treads the stone of God itself, and passes through the gate of Peace, with its seven crowns and titles of victory. Then, outstripping in his flight the power of mortal thought, he passes beyond the shining orbit of the earth, beyond the vast expanse of solar glory, across the awful chasms of the unfathomable depths to far-off Sothis, the land of eternal dawn, to the ante-chamber of the infinite morning. He " has his star established to him in Sothis," says the Ritual. And here the Illuminate, now become a Master, is instructed in the last mysteries which precede universal glory, the mysteries of the divine sorrow, the " tears of Isis," whence comes the source of the celestial Nile, the fount of illumination to man. Here he passes within the triple veil, and is invested with the imperishable jewels of supernal lustre.

Then comes the final mystery when the tomb is opened and the body is raised in immortality. " Hail thou, my Father of Light," we read in the chapter (cliv.) which tells us how the body of the holy one shall not see

corruption. "I come having this my flesh
freed from decay; I am whole as my Father,
the self-begotten God, whose image is in the
incorruptible body. Do thou establish me.
Do thou perfect me as the Master of the
Grave. This," so the chapter proceeds, "is
the mystery of the change, in the body, of the
life that comes from the destruction of life."
And as we read we cannot but recall the words
of the apostle : "Behold, I show you a mystery. We shall not all sleep, but we shall all
be changed, for the dead shall be raised incorruptible and we shall be changed." So too
in the final chapter of this book we hear the
resurrection proclaimed as with a trumpet
blast, as in the innermost chamber of the
House we find the Open Tomb. "I have
opened the doors," exclaims the Osiris-soul,
now glorious in the house of Light and united
indissolubly with the Creator,—"I have opened
the doors. . . . Well is the great one who
is in the coffin. For all the dead shall have
passages made to him through their embalming," when their body in the flesh shall be
raised in incorruption. Again and again is
celebrated the mystery of the open tomb.
As the eclipsing planet which moves nearest to

the sun crawls like a tortoise across the face of
that orb, defacing it for a moment by its own
darkness and then is swallowed in the radiance,
so also death, that dark spot which crawls across
the vision of the eternal splendour, is swallowed
in the resurrection of Osiris Ra, the Uncreated
Light.   Four times is that gospel of ancient
Egypt proclaimed in the final chapter, which
bears no title in the *Book of the Master*, but
which elsewhere is called the chapter of the
opening of the heaven.   "The tortoise dies ;
Ra lives !" Death is swallowed up in Light;
God lives for evermore.   "O Amen, Amen,"
so continues that chapter of mystery, "Amen,
who art in heaven, give thy face to the body
of thy Son.   Make him well in Hades.   It is
finished."

Thus ends the strange and solemn dirge of
ancient Egypt.   Once perceived, the intimate
connection between the secret doctrine of
Egypt's most venerated books and the secret
significance of her most venerable monument
seems impossible to dissever ; and each form
illustrates and interpenetrates the other.   As
we pursue the dark utterances and recognise
the mystic allusions of the book, we seem to
stand amid the profound darkness enwrapping

the whole interior of the building.   All around
are assembled the spirits and the powers that
make the mystery of the unseen world : the
" Secret Faces at the Gate," the " divine beings
of the Horizon and of the Orbit."   And dimly
before our eyes, age after age, the sacred procession of the Egyptian dead moves silently
along as they pass through the " Gate of the
Hill " to the tribunal of Osiris.   In vain do we attempt to trace their footsteps till we enter with
them into the hidden places, and penetrate the
recesses of the Secret House.   But no sooner
do we stand within the mysterious light than
the teaching of the sacred books seems lit up
as with a tongue of flame.   The luminous veil
itself melts slowly away, disclosing the Path of
Illumination and the splendours of the unseen ;
the spirits of the just grow lustrous with the
rays that proceed from the tribunal.   For
though none may look upon these things unveiled till the guardian of the starry Gate has
opened for him the portal of the Light, yet
for him who has been mystically initiated in
the deep waters, and illuminated by the Spirit of
sevenfold beauty, the invisible things become
manifest by the visible creation, and a light
which is not of earth reveals in its divine unity

the full secret of the Hidden Places : the Entrance to the Path of Heaven, the Well of Life, the Initiation into New Birth, the Ordeal of Fire, the Lintel of Justice, the Judgment in Death, the Illumination in Truth, the Throne of Radiance, until within the veil the passage of the grave is passed and we reach the grand chamber of the Open Tomb.

Thus only, according to that primæval creed, could man fulfil his marvellous destiny ; and thus only can that destiny accomplish his heart's desire. If it be true, as some have held, that

> Veil after veil shall lift,—but there must be
> Veil after veil behind ;

that man, throughout all eternity, shall never know, even as he is known, then is his creation vain, and his resurrection a mockery. No skill in the secrets of the material universe, no dominion over the forces of life and death, no power to pierce the veil which hangs before the unseen world and to hold communion with the spiritual Intelligences, will satisfy his secret aspirations. For the soul of man—so the very craving for infallible Truth, the rudimentary

instinct of the heart, proclaims—can know no
rest, nor can his spirit ever be satisfied, so
long as the thinnest film remain to interrupt
the unclouded vision of the Hidden Love;
until he stand face to face and eye to eye with
" Him who knows the Depths."

NOTES

NOTE A

The motion of the moon seems also to have been expressed architecturally in a different and very curious form. Since that body moves in an orbit which differs from that of our planet by about five degrees, and crosses the ecliptic twice in the course of each lunar month, five degrees will be the limiting distance which it will attain each time ; so that the motion of the moon relatively to the earth may be represented as a series of five ascents and descents, each of one degree, as in the following diagram. And this appears to have been the form of the ancient pyramid of Meydoon, which is situated not far from the spot where

The Fivefold Throne.

the plane of the lunar orbit intersects the course of the Nile. And a similar figure is sculptured also on the eastern wall of the Queen's Chamber in the Grand Pyramid.

A more practical application of the moon's motion is found in the lunar kalendar of Egypt. For the interval between the dates when the moon successively comes to the full (always in relation to a given place, such as Memphis) consists of about twenty-nine and one-half solar days. Suppose now we take as an unit of time thirty solar days, then each lunar month would fall short of that period by half a day ; and from this we obtain the key to a most singular correlation between the lunar motions and the Egyptian months (consisting always of thirty solar days) pointed out by Dr. Brugsch in the Table of Edfu ; which kalendar was made public in the days of the Ptolemies, but never apparently while a native monarch reigned. On the first day was celebrated the " Conception of the moon," when that orb, unseen amid the lustre of the day, was on the meridian at noon. On the second day took place its Birth or first appearance in the heavens ; and so forth throughout the circuit, each day being dedicated to some festival connected with that orb ; and the fifteenth day being held in especial reverence, since on it the moon would come to the full, crossing the meridian at or near midnight. And thus in the lunar representations on the walls of the temple of Denderah we have fourteen steps leading up to the fifteenth or highest, whereon was enthroned Thoth, the Lord of the Moon. During the first month, therefore, the lunar intervals would of course correspond more or less precisely with the solar days. But whereas the two sets would grow progressively asunder, the lunar names remained affixed to the same solar days. Thus the first day of each solar month was called the " Conception of the moon," and the second, " New moon," although neither phenomenon might have taken place anywhere near the time,—a method of expression necessitating, it would seem, a double form of register, and simple enough to those who held the clue, but to a stranger hopelessly misleading.

NOTE B

With regard to the designation of the particular months, the practice appears to have differed in the sacred and civil kalendars. In the former, the different months are expressed merely as the First, Second, Third, or Fourth Month of the particular Season, the days being numbered like our own. But for popular use their names were as follows :

Season of Inundation (*Se*)	*Season of Winter* (*Pir*)	*Season of Heat* (*Semou*)
Thoth	Tybi	Pachons
Paophi	Mechi	Payni
Hathor	Pharmuti	Epiphi
Choiak	Phamenoth	Mesori

NOTE C

From this highly important cycle we may draw some conclusion as to the date of the foundation of the Egyptian kalendar ; the date, that is to say, when mere tradition came to an end, and systematic records organised upon astronomical principles began to be preserved. Since in the course of each cycle (of 1460 years) the heliacal risings, or orients, make the circuit of the civil year, and since there is also a corresponding series of settings performing a similar round, the two series would in each cycle make up a double interchange. When, therefore, Herodotus tells us in a well-known passage (*Euterp.*,

143) how, according to the Egyptian records, the stars
had changed their order four times since their reckoning
commenced—"the risings twice taking the place of the
settings, and the settings twice taking the place of the
risings,"—the meaning becomes perfectly clear if referred (as Rawlinson suggests) to the heliacal risings
and settings of Sothis, the determinator of the kalendar.
And the very circumstance that Herodotus himself in all
probability did not understand—and was not intended
to understand—the drift of the extract, strongly corrobo-
rates his statement that the passage was not his own but
was read to him from the Sacred Books. For it is little
less than inconceivable that a person, ignorant of astronomy, should so misrepresent a statement made to him by
astronomers, as to blunder by accident into the correct
exposition of a different and highly complex astronomical relation. We learn, therefore, that two such cycles
(four reversals) had been completed since the institution
of the scientific kalendar ; so that the cycle current in
the time of Herodotus would be the third. And as there
is evidence that that cycle was completed in A.D. 139, it
would have commenced in B.C. 1321 ; at which epoch
Sothis rose heliacally at Memphis about a week before
the solstice, and the Rising of the river was heralded by
the Orient of the star. Hence, therefore, we conclude
that the commencement of the first of such cycles and
the institution of the scientific kalendar took place
(2 x 1460 years previously, *i. e.*) at midsummer of B.C.
4241,—a few years before the reign of the astronomer-
architect Khufu, the most famous monarch of antiquity.

NOTE D

This property may perhaps be clear from the following considerations. Suppose C to be the centre of the earth, P the situation of the Great Pyramid, N the North Pole, and E the point where the meridian of the building cuts the equator, then E C P will be the latitude of the building, viz., 30°, whence it will be seen at once that the triangle C N P will be equilateral, since the angle at C is 60°, and the radii C N and C P will be equal to each other, assuming the earth to be a sphere.

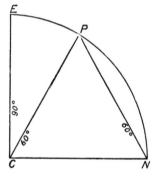

Hence therefore P N, the distance from the Pyramid to the North Pole, will be equal to P C, the distance to the centre of the earth.

NOTE E

Since, owing to the effect of precession, there is a gradual change in the right ascension and declination of every star, there is also a corresponding change in the day of heliacal rising. Thus, while the star whose orient at Philæ (in Egyptian, Pilak) marked the period of the solstice for the third cycle was, as we have seen, Sothis, or Sirius, that for the second cycle appears to have been Pollux, and that for the first Regulus, the principal star in the constellation of the Lion, which is identified by Professor Renouf with our own constellation of the same name. In making this and similar calculations, I have taken 50".2 for the yearly precessional motion, and half-a-minute of arc per century for the variation in the obliquity. The formulæ for finding the day of orient, or heliacal rising (when the right ascension and declination of the star have been determined for the required epoch), are given, I may observe, in Maddy's *Astronomy*.

Before quitting this subject, it is worth noticing how many classical names of stars and constellations, meaningless in the Greek and Latin, acquire a signification when referred to the Egyptian tongue. Thus Ur Oon (Great Being) gives us Orion; Kas Pehu (Lake of the Inundation), Cassiopeia; Ark Ter (Shrine of Meeting), Arkturus; and Kha Nub (Place of Gold), Canopus. Some names indeed are scarcely distinguishable from the Egyptian words, so slight is the change in pronunciation when compared with the immense difference in time and place, such as the star Khaph in the constellation Cassiopeia, signifying, in Egyptian, Power; Scheat (Schete) in Pegasus, Secret; and Nath (Nut) in Taurus meaning the heaven.

NOTE F

PLACE OF THE ORBIT. PAGE 63

In connection with this point, a singular illustration suggests itself with regard to the form (hitherto unexplained) of one of the most important symbols of Egyptian monarchy. At the present epoch, the earth reaches the apsides, or turning-points, of her orbit, that is to say, her greatest and least distances from the sun, a few days after passing, respectively, through the summer and winter solstices. But inasmuch as those points have a slow relative motion round the orbit, the period of the year at which they were attained six thousand years ago (or about the time of which we speak) took place about the times of equinox. Hence if we represent the orbit in its true elliptic form, a tangent at the extremity of the major axis will define both the

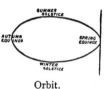

Orbit.

point of equinox, through which it passes, and the direction of the minor axis, or line of solstice, to which it will be parallel, thus indicating the relations of the universe. And the figure thus described exactly gives us the royal cartouche always encircling the names of the Egyptian kings;

Royal Cartouche.

which thus images forth the celestial foundation and universal jurisdiction of that monarchy so long as the earth preserves its divinely appointed course.

NOTE G

From the foregoing considerations, when bearing in mind the archaic date of the erection, and the celestial bearings of the temple at the epoch, we may clear up a peculiarity of some difficulty in the records, which M. Mariette, the famous authority on this temple, has pointed out but left without any solution. It is beyond dispute, says that eminent writer, that when the records speak of the north, they mean the east—a peculiarity, however, which he seems to regard as a mere Egyptian eccentricity, scarcely needing discussion. And he then proceeds to point out that "the North of the hieroglyphic records" is just 75 degrees to the westward of what he calls "true North," that is to say, the north as defined by our cardinal points, which of course shift slowly round the heavens as the axis describes the precessional circuit. But the time which has elapsed since Pepi fulfilled the command of Khufu by erecting that temple is between 5400 and 5500 years ; and 75 degrees, therefore, will be about the arc of precession which the celestial axis has traversed during that period. Hence, then, if the north of which the temple speaks is not the shifting north of our planet, but the changeless point of the heavens to which the axis of our planet pointed when the pole-star gave the signal for the erection of the temple of the universe, the expression is exact.

NOTE H

HIEROGLYPHIC INSCRIPTION RUNS ROUND THE BORDER.
PAGE 73

As no translation, so far as I am aware, of this inscription has yet been published, I beg to submit the following, which commences on the point marked as north on the planisphere and follows the order of the hieroglyphs:

Turning-point of the circles of Light.

Head of the circles of Annu (Denderah) ; Horus, Entrance of the Golden Heaven, Seat of Sacred Dances in the six Heights of Horus, Son of Osiris.

Palace chamber of Height of Holy Adoration ; Palace chamber of Height of Light.

Ahi, Lord of the Palace Chamber, Height of the Hour of living Osiris, Burning Height of priestess of Holy Moon.

Chief of the Southern Splendour.

Meeting-place, Region of Gods.   Head of nurse of Ra, Living Breath of the waters of passage of the double Hour.

Heavenly Flame of Burning Gold.

Golden Heaven of Isis.

Horizon of Light.

The Great One of the Lady Mother.

With regard to the deities represented on the planisphere, which are very numerous, their various characteristics are the same as are ordinarily portrayed in the sacred pictures.   And of the different figures here depicted the following may be more particularly mentioned. The Thigh and the Knife, both well-known Egyptian constellations, are found, respectively, in the vignettes of Chapters 15 and 50 ; the sacred Ankh or symbol of life, in Chapter 41 ; the Lotus, in Chapter 81 ; the Cow (Mehuret) with the Ankh, in Chapter 71, and again in Chapter 162 ; the Plough in Chapter 110 ; the Balance in Chapter 125 ; and the deity with the Uræus head in Chapter 145 ; all these with others being in the *Book of the Master*, which contains also a great number of allusions in the body of the text.   Another of the sacred writings to which we have also referred, the inscription on the coffin of Queen Ankhnes Ra Nefer Ab, possesses no vignettes, but contains several allusions which are illustrated by the planisphere, as, *e. g.*, the " Ram," the " Four Heads on the Neck," and the repeated allusions to the " Eight."

NOTE J

While there is nothing much to surprise us—when once we have brushed aside the schoolboy scholarship so predominant at our Universities, which cannot imagine any conception of antiquity originating except in Greece—in finding the sacred images employed in this mystical temple of incarnate Light repeated again and again in the mystical writings, we may well be astonished to find that this same planisphere illustrates also nearly all the images employed in one of the most familiar passages of the prophet Isaiah (chapter xi.)—that which relates to the Rod from the stem of Jesse. There is the "Rod" itself, fashioned like a "stem," with roots, and forming the "Tam" sceptre of Egypt ; and close by it is the Branch, in the hand of the woman. There are the "two girdles" —the sole vestments of the divine Horus—one round his neck, the other his loins. And there too are the Cow, the Bear, the Lion, the Lamb, the Asp, and the Little Child. And this resemblance is all the more striking when we remember that the temple to which the planisphere belongs was dedicated to the mother of God, and observe that the most conspicuous figure depicted upon it is that which is also displayed so prominently on the walls of the building,—the sacred mother holding in her arms the divine infant, the second Person of the Egyptian Trinity.

NOTE K

TABLE OF OFFERINGS. PAGE 110

In his interesting work *Noemi*, Mr. Baring Gould speaks of an archaic relic near Sarlat in the Dordogne,

which is evidently a Table of Offerings. He describes
it as a dolmen, or sepulchral chamber, roofed by a flat
stone having a number of holes scooped in the centre ;
and he mentions that the market women lay their fish
upon it for luck ; a most singular survival of the ancient
custom, since fish, as may be seen in the vignettes of the
Book of the Master, formed a principal portion of the
offerings. Indeed the burial customs of the most widely
scattered nations receive singular illustration when compared with the religion of the dwellers on the Nile, the
seat of the earliest records and the cradle of civilisation.

NOTE L

That this resemblance is not due to accident appears
the more clear when we consider the number of courses
of which the exterior of the building consists. For suppose that from dawn to noon on midsummer day (the
opening of the sacred year of Egypt) observations be
taken at every two minutes,—that being the time occupied by the moon, the great measurer of the heavens, in
performing an unit (one circular minute) of her orbit
relatively to the sun. Then since on that day the period
between dawn and noon at Memphis is about seven and
one-half hours (reckoning dawn to take place forty minutes before sunrise), the number of such observations will
be a little over two hundred and twenty ; and the corresponding number of courses, therefore, will be about two
hundred, a few being wanting at the top, since there is no
refraction at the zenith. And this result exactly corresponds both with the number of courses and the truncated
form of the Great Pyramid. Now at the commencement of each lunar month, when the moon, unseen in

the full lustre of day, comes to the meridian at about the same time as the sun, the entrance of Osiris into the moon was celebrated. And thus each course of that mysterious pyramid marks the unseen motion of the Queen of Heaven, as step by step she mounts the height, on the day when beneath the overshadowing rays the divine light entered unseen within her womb.

NOTE M

FULL SPLENDOUR. PAGE 151

Ra Neb : " Full Splendour." This expression is usually translated " Every day "; but Ra undoubtedly means " Noonday lustre," and Neb used as an adjective signifies " All."

THE IBIS WESTERN
MYSTERY TRADITION SERIES

The heritage of all Western spirituality, both open and esoteric, and all the systems, theories, and practices that relate to it, are drawn from a single source: the Judaeo-Christian spiritual tradition. This tradition has yet deeper roots in the distinctive religious faiths of the great civilizations of Egypt, Greece, and Mesopotamia.

At the heart of all of these great traditions lies their ultimate goal: the spiritual regeneration of humanity. There is more than one Way to its attainment, and it is the totality of the many paths that lead us back to our primal source that constitutes the Western Mystery Tradition. They are encapsulated in the countless texts that enshrine and reflect the work of the inspired men and women who have dedicated their lives to preserving, interpreting, and transmitting this tradition.

Many of these texts have become a part of the canon of Western literature, but there are many others which have been unjustly neglected, hidden in times of persecution, or have simply gone unrecognized. Some record exalted inner experiences, some are guides to esoteric practice, while others are speculative studies of esoteric knowledge and spiritual wisdom. All of them have one feature in common: an inherent power to enrich us spiritually.

It is from rare printed versions of these unknown or forgotten texts, and from studies of them that the Ibis series of classics of the Western Mystery Tradition is drawn. All titles in the series have new introductions, written by acknowledged authorities in the field, and many of them also contain additional notes or appendices.

Subjects and titles in the series include:

Pre-Christian:

Adams, *House of the Hidden Places and The Book of the Master*

Budge, trans., *The Book of the Mysteries of the Heavens and the Earth*

Rolt, trans., *Dionysius the Areopagite, On the Divine Names and The Mystical Theology*

Medieval thought and the Kabbalah:

Akiba, *Sepher Yetzirah*, Knut Stenring, trans.

Renaissance Hermeticism, Alchemy and the Rosicrucians:

Craven, *Count Michael Maier*

Smith, *John Dee*

Enlightenment and Romanticism

Eckartshausen, *The Cloud upon the Sanctuary*

Modern Esoteric Thought and Spirituality

Garstin, *Theurgy*

Greene, *The Blazing Star and the Jewish Kabbala*

Hartmann, *Geomancy*

Hartmann, *With the Adepts: An Adventure among the Rosicrucians*

Levi, *Magical Ritual of the Sanctum Regnum*

Levi, *Paradoxes of the Highest Science*

Wright, *Prayer*